What Women Want

What Women Want

The Life You Crave and How God Satisfies

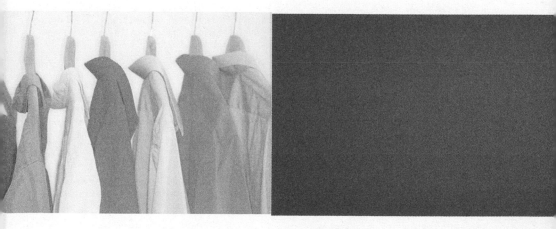

Lisa T. Bergren & Rebecca Price

WATERBROOK
PRESS

WHAT WOMEN WANT
PUBLISHED BY WATERBROOK PRESS
12265 Oracle Boulevard, Suite 200
Colorado Springs, Colorado 80921

This book is solely for inspirational, educational, and motivational purposes and is not intended to replace the medical, psychological, or emotional well-being advice of a trained medical professional. Readers are advised to consult a physician, psychologist, counselor, or other qualified health-care professional regarding medical or psychological problems, or before starting any exercise, nutrition, counseling, or well-being program. The authors and publisher specifically disclaim liability, loss, or risk, personal or otherwise, incurred as a consequence, directly or indirectly, of the use or application of any of the contents of this book.

All Scripture quotations, unless otherwise indicated, are taken from the Holy Bible, New International Version®. NIV®. Copyright © 1973, 1978, 1984 by International Bible Society. Used by permission of Zondervan Publishing House. All rights reserved. Scripture quotations marked (AMP) are taken from The Amplified® Bible. Copyright © 1954, 1958, 1962, 1964, 1965, 1987 by The Lockman Foundation. Used by permission. (www.Lockman.org). Scripture quotations marked (ESV) are taken from The Holy Bible, English Standard Version, copyright © 2001 by Crossway Bibles, a division of Good News Publishers. Used by permission. All rights reserved. Scripture quotations marked (KJV) are taken from the King James Version. Scripture quotations marked (MSG) are taken from The Message by Eugene H. Peterson. Copyright © 1993, 1994, 1995, 1996, 2000, 2001, 2002. Used by permission of NavPress Publishing Group. All rights reserved. Scripture quotations marked (NASB) are taken from the New American Standard Bible®. © Copyright The Lockman Foundation 1960, 1962, 1963, 1968, 1971, 1972, 1973, 1975, 1977, 1995. Used by permission. (www.Lockman.org). Scripture quotations marked (NKJV) are taken from the New King James Version®. Copyright © 1982 by Thomas Nelson Inc. Used by permission. All rights reserved. Scripture quotations marked (NLT) are taken from the Holy Bible, New Living Translation, copyright © 1996, 2004. Used by permission of Tyndale House Publishers Inc., Wheaton, Illinois 60189. All rights reserved. Scripture quotations marked (Phillips) are taken from The New Testament in Modern English, Revised Edition ©1972 by J. B. Phillips. Copyright renewed © 1986, 1988 by Vera M. Phillips. Scripture quotations marked (TLB) are taken from The Living Bible, copyright © 1971. Used by permission of Tyndale House Publishers Inc., Wheaton, Illinois 60189. All rights reserved.

Italics in Scripture quotations reflect the authors' added emphasis.

Some details in anecdotes and stories have been changed to protect the identities of the persons involved. All names, unless specified with first and last names, of responses from interviews and surveys have been changed to protect the identities of the persons involved.

ISBN 978-1-4000-7245-3

Published in the United States by WaterBrook Multnomah, an imprint of the Crown Publishing Group, a division of Random House Inc., New York.

Library of Congress Cataloging-in-Publication Data
Bergren, Lisa Tawn.
    What women want : the life you crave and how God satisfies / Lisa T. Bergren and Rebecca Price. — 1st ed.
        p. cm.
    Includes bibliographical references.
    ISBN 978-1-4000-7245-3
    1. Christian women—Religious life. 2. Satisfaction—Religious aspects—Christianity. 3. Contentment—Religious aspects—Christianity. I. Price, Rebecca. II. Title.
    BV4527.B454 2007
    248.8'43—dc22
                                        2007011295

Printed in the United States of America
2009

10 9 8 7 6 5 4 3

For Courtney, Lindsey, Olivia, and Emma:
May you each discover how God alone satisfies your deepest longings.

Lisa and Rebecca

Contents

PART 2 ◉ How God Satisfies

Welcome

A Letter Just to You from the Authors

Dear Friend,

Isn't it good to have sisters of the heart? Someone to share trivial happenings with as well as the heartrending, soul-shattering moments? We hope we can be sisters to you as you delve into this book. Know that we're praying for you as you dig in and find out what you really want and how God wants you to grow.

We thought it would be good for you to know a few key things about us and our book before you dive in. Although we're in very different phases and stages of life, we've seen firsthand the power of a sister of the heart, because we've been dear friends and in business together for almost fifteen years. That power of our friendship isn't in our similarities. At the time of this publication, Lisa will be leaving her thirties and hitting the big 4-0; Rebecca will have celebrated her fifty-fifth Princess Rebecca Week (complete with tiara). Lisa is married and raising three young children, while Rebecca is a lifelong single who invests herself heavily in friends and her extended family. Different as we may be, there are common causes that unite us: we've shared giggles over idiotic, funny moments, and laughter even in the midst of our crises. We've wept together, over the phone and face down on

Rebecca's carpet in prayer. We've challenged each other in areas where we know we can do and be better. And we've seen the power of what a friend can do, how sisters can help one another—encouraging and comforting when needed most, coaching and prodding where we can grow, and loving one another through it all.

In our own friendship, we've often talked about where we are; sometimes the exchange has been just girl talk, other times more serious. Often we've wondered: *Is it just us or do all women feel this way about certain longings and aspirations and the realities in chasing after those? Why are we always in a state of unrest, desiring something more? How do we find life and soul satisfaction this side of heaven? Who are the women who seem totally satisfied, and how can we be more like them?*

Our questions to each other turned to questions we asked other Christian women who crossed our paths: older, younger, married, single, divorced, stay-at-home moms, working mothers, new Christians, and saints rich in faith. Before we knew it, our questions turned into a national survey—not a scientific survey but one from the heart, one getting at women's real hopes and dreams, doubts, and fears. We began polling female business contacts and then e-mailing sample groupings of women across the country. *What do you want? What are you missing? What's going on in your life? Talk to us!* That survey led to this book.

We heard from women of all ages, from New Jersey to Florida, Washington to the Dakotas, and California to Canada. We even got some responses from Germany, Guam, and South Africa; and from all walks of life—single and married, parents, childless—all women who hunger for many of the same things we do.

We all seem to want...

- ⊙ inspiration and insight that lead toward a solid, growing relationship with God.
- ⊙ to know love, peace, and balance in life.
- ⊙ to find the way to true joy, and be able to remain there.
- ⊙ emotional, spiritual, and physical health.
- ⊙ deep friendships.
- ⊙ to have meaning and purpose.

We realized that every one of us is going to have unique hot-button topics— the things we most want to work on right now—even though hundreds of women chose the top eleven you see in this book. So for more than a year we followed up on some of the greatest wants with e-mail questions, in conversation, and through formal interviews. We talked to some of today's leading and most respected thinkers for Christian women. Stories poured from women's hearts and minds.

We formed the book's concept, discussed the issues at length, and coauthored it for all of us as sisters. Just as our mothers and their mothers passed along woman-to-woman know-how, such as recipes or advice before marriage, we're passing along to you the ideas and thoughts in these pages as a guide to getting more out of life, to getting on track, to getting to work on areas that God is nudging each of us to attend.

Our most fervent hope is that you find encouragement to begin your work here, that the chapters you read on your hot-button topics will be catalysts toward true growth in those areas.

As you get ready to read through this guide, keep in mind a few things:

⊙ Though both our hearts as authors are interwoven into each sentence of this entire book, Lisa took the lead in writing part 1, the main narrative sections (and hers is the "I" voice you hear), while Rebecca took the lead in writing part 2, the discussion and Bible studies.

⊙ The unvarnished, honest comments from women in our surveys appear as subtext sprinkled throughout the chapters, though all names have been changed to protect their privacy.

⊙ The insights in chapter 9 (since the roles and situations of mothers and wives rated high on our surveys) are aimed mostly toward women who are married or have children in proximity. If you're not married or a parent, we're convinced you'll still find the insights helpful; in particular, see the section called "Intimacy Is Not Just About Sex."

⊙ This book is designed to be your personal guide as well as a great tool for women to use in groups. For additional icebreaker, leadership, retreat, and group-formation ideas, see our resources at WhatWomenWant Book.com.

So are you ready to face your own transparent, gut-level thoughts on what you want, where you are, and where you want to be? Are you ready to hear the unvarnished thoughts of other women on these things too?

Details are just a page away. So get ready. Because, as we learned…

We're not done growing.

We want to heal where we hurt.

We want to shine where we're tarnished.

We want to connect, share, laugh, and squeeze the very marrow out of life.

We're willing to push to become all we're meant to be.

And we can think of no better way to realize these wants than in the company of you, our sister of the heart. Come, let's explore our lives together! This is what women do best!

Lija & Rebecca

Your Five-Minute Survey

Identify What You Want

There's an expectation behind every desire and longing for what you want out of life, isn't there? So what are yours for this book? Before turning another page, take five minutes for this quick self-test. Based on the subtitle of this book, "The Life You Crave and How God Satisfies," what do you hope to get out of *What Women Want*? Growth? Progress? What do you expect to learn? Something specific, something tangible in your life? Write down your thoughts about your cravings and satisfaction (or lack thereof) here:

Consistency for growth - Spiritual growth, marital growth, personal growth
Self-Sense of Self, personal drive to accomplish goals → voice, body, confidence,
job, drive, energy, faith. I crave happiness, laughter from the soul,
to feel good about myself + what I do. I desire to feel satisfied in
all areas of my home, my marriage, myself, sexually, emotionally + spiritually

What's on your list of wants for the coming year? What are your priorities and hot-button topics, the things that you want to work on most? Look at the eleven topics listed below—topics addressed in this book—and rate them in importance to you. Start with your number one personal priority, and continue to number each topic through number eleven, your lowest priority. Then jot down initial thoughts or goals beside each, so that even if a topic is rated at number eleven, you still have an idea of how you might grow in that area. For example next to Friendships, you might write, *I want to make it a priority to go to lunch at least once a month with so-and-so, with the goal of developing a deeper trust, understanding, and camaraderie.*

__1__ Relationship with God. My initial thoughts or goals…

In order to achieve all of the other goals, I need to connect more with God. To listen, walk with, talk with + feel Him along each step.

__6__ Friendships. My initial thoughts or goals…

I need to trust my friendships + know I can rely on them. My goal is to connect more - phone, email, going out etc… with my close friends.

__8__ Emotional Health and Balance. My initial thoughts or goals…

My emotional health is very tied to Josh's these days. My goal is to be sympathetic but not allow my emotional well being to become so consumed + absorb his emotions.

__5__ Physical Health and Appearance. My initial thoughts or goals…

My body feels awful. My goal is to be more aware of what I eat + drink. My goal is to make time to work-out, even if only 10-20 minutes as close to daily, as possible.

__1__ Home Life and Intimacy. My initial thoughts or goals…

For the most part we are good here. My goal is to be more aware of my tone, be more patient + be more intimate to help him feel sexy, happy + loved.

__9__ Peace and Contentment. My initial thoughts or goals…

My goal is to continue working on my voice ~ to dedicate any extra moments to my instrument, which will ultimately bring job contentment.

__3__ Joy and Happiness. My initial thoughts or goals…

I feel as though I used to be much happier. My goal is to find moments of joy + laughter each day. To seek out the things that bring me joy.

<u>2</u> Financial Health. My initial thoughts or goals…

I am getting better, however, still have for to go My goal is to eliminate debt, stop frivolous spending + find ways to save for a successful + safe future.

<u>10</u> Love. My initial thoughts or goals…

My capacity to love is great. My goal is to learn to love myself more as well as find a greater understanding to those I don't understand. To share love + honestly feel love for those I may envy - turn my envy

<u>4</u> Meaning and Purpose. My initial thoughts or goals… *to love.*

My greatest goal is to find this for my voice, my desire for psychology, to help + greatest of all, help Josh find his meaning + purpose. He is so needing direction right now.

Done? Did writing out your initial goals change the way you numbered them as priorities? Jane from our survey admitted:

> What's interesting to me is that my number one craving this month is different from what I would have chosen last month or last year. My number one priority seems to change all the time.

Is Jane's assessment also true for you? Why or why not, and how so? Explore your feelings by writing them down here, but don't use a lot of time on this or overthink it. Give yourself a few minutes at the most to write what you're thinking and feeling at this moment.

I believe it will perpetually change, by the hour sometimes. I know #1 + 2 will remain pretty consistent, however the other priorities, as mentioned above, have already begun to shift in my mind. I was surprised by my thoughts on love. Perhaps envy is what is holding me back on so many levels - desiring what I don't have.

Now we're ready to begin to go after all the things we really want.

Part 1

The Life You Crave

You, Fabulous You

A Phenomenal Creation of God

> The heart that has tasted of God's love will always turn
> back to Him with longing and say, "Only Your love can
> meet my deepest needs."
>
> RUTH MYERS

Why are we women constantly seeking? Why are our hearts restless, never at peace? That is the question that Rebecca and I (Lisa) bandied about, the question that ultimately led to this book.

In short, we decided that we are restless because God created us to crave more—to seek after all we could be and to find his satisfaction in every aspect of life, at least as close as we can get, this side of heaven. Every one of us will be struggling with a slightly different version of where we'd like to grow this year. *What Women Want* is meant to help you begin the process. It may well be that one or two chapters, in particular, start beeping like a smoke alarm that needs its battery changed. Pay special attention to those areas; begin your investigation there, then use the "Additional Resources" at the back of this book to delve deeper. Honestly seek where God is leading you.

Survey Says

Resoundingly, women said, "I want more": stronger relationships at home and beyond, meaning and purpose, with peace and health—a life not just endured, but over-flowing with love and joy; most of all, a life with a deepening relationship with God. What is it that you most want?

As students along the road with you, we've relied heavily on the experts in each area addressed. And our experience in Christian publishing has connected us with great communicators and teachers, helping us put together what we hope will be an easy guide to help you take steps toward ultimate satisfaction. Our first goal for *What Women Want* is to help you define what you hunger for—really figure out what *you* want this year—and to discover some of the answers. We think you'll find in the process that only God can ultimately fill you.

Lois writes: I feel as though I am doing all the talking in my prayer time, because I often forget a conversation involves listening. God can't speak to me if I don't take the time to listen.

We do the same thing, Lois! Our second goal for this book is that after you begin to think about each priority in your life, you'll find great questions for reflection, discussion (if you're reading in a group), and deeper study and application.

YOU ARE PHENOMENAL

But before we get to our study, let's start at the beginning. Why do you think God bothers with you, or with Rebecca and me? Even when we have so much to learn, so many ways to grow? Because God thinks we're phenomenal. In the dictionary, *phenomenal* is defined as "of or constituting a phenomenon; extremely unusual; extraordinary; highly remarkable."

When was the last time you honestly thought of yourself as any of those descriptive words—as phenomenal? Write your thoughts here:

Probably truly, never. There were moments I felt positive - in college, I felt confident + beautiful, there are times when I sing, that I truly feel blessed about my talent, when I was dancing, I felt sexy + beautiful. Phenomenal - I don't think I've ever used that word to describe me - sounds great though

Phenomenal. It's a word that makes us flinch, isn't it?

Phenomenal? Me?

Yes, you. There is no one like you, and that is on purpose—God's purpose. Our God doesn't make mistakes. You're just what God ordered up.

Turn to a friend in your group, or look in the mirror, and say, "I am a phenomenal creation of God."

No, don't just read over this—do it. We're serious. If you're alone, go right now and say it ten times, slowly, in front of the mirror:

I am a phenomenal creation of God.
I am a phenomenal creation of God.
I am a phenomenal creation of God.
I am a phenomenal creation of God.
I am a phenomenal creation of God.
I am a phenomenal creation of God.
I am a phenomenal creation of God.
I am a phenomenal creation of God.
I am a phenomenal creation of God.
I am a phenomenal creation of God.

· Success
· debt free
· beautiful
· talented
· star
· You will succeed
· bright
· bring joy
· big heart

Now pause and think on this. Really think: What do you know to be true? What do you hear God whispering in your ear? Don't just read past this. Stop! Stop reading until you've honestly done this. Even if you have to grit your teeth, do it.

You're back?

Okay, now practice saying throughout the day, this week, this year, "I am phenomenal." Or you can use one of these favorites:

◉ Liz Curtis Higgs encourages women to say, "Ta-da!" in front of the mirror.

◉ Stasi Eldredge teaches women to think of themselves as "captivating."

If you're like us, you probably deny such outrageous words. You're not used to them, so you think it prideful to say such things. That's what we were taught in Sunday school, right?

Phenomenal?

Ta-da?

Captivating?

We duck and feign modesty, but inside we long to hear these very words. We long for someone to reassure us this is the truth. What keeps us from believing we are phenomenal?

Ann writes: Intellectually, I understand this. Emotionally, I can be spun off center when someone uses triggers from my childhood when I was not treated with respect. I'm sixty-five and still struggle with this.

Heidi writes: Scripture tells me I am special in God's sight, that he knows every hair on my head, knows what I need even before I ask. Yet there is a fear in me that I am not good enough, that I do not measure up to others, that my work lacks the originality and quality of others. I could blame my feelings on how I was raised—in a rural area, in a poor, uneducated family. I could blame it on a difficult marriage in which I was led to believe that I was inferior and not as smart. But I will not wallow there. In truth, I do believe that in God's sight I am special. Yet I can't let go of what people think. I have not separated myself enough from how the world views me. How do I get there?

Jill writes: Sometimes, thinking about past sins, I wonder how God can still love me, even though I know he's forgiven me. Satan really likes to mess with my head in that area. I try to tune the thoughts out and focus on where I am now.

Samantha writes: Maybe it's because my husband has been married to me for four and a half years and I get so much more attention from everyone else of the male species. Maybe it's because I just don't get how I can be special and precious.

Voices, voices, voices, speaking to us all. Which voice are you hearing? The world's? Your past's? God's? When I praise my three-year-old son, Jack, saying, "I love you, Jack. You are smart and wonderful and funny and sweet as can be" (while kissing him all over his face), he returns, "Talk it again, Mama, talk it again."

When did we forget how to appreciate words of praise and delight and love? When did we forget? When did we learn how to avoid them, ducking like we duck a curve ball rather than catching it in a big glove?

Pit Thoughts Versus His Thoughts

I can't forgive myself. I feel so guilty.
He forgives me. I need nothing more than that (1 John 1:9).

My life is so hard; he must hate me.
He loves me and I can learn more about his love, even through these hard times (Hebrews 12:11).

He doesn't know the real me.
He knew me in my mother's womb (Psalm 139:13).

I am unworthy.
Christ has made me righteous (Romans 3:22).

I do not deserve love.
I am loved and forgiven and worthy in Christ (1 John 4:9).

Instead of thinking (or better yet, saying) "talk it again!" we think to ourselves, *I'm too fat. I'm too thin. I'm flabby—are there any muscles under there? Bad-hair day. Bad-skin day. Are those age spots? wrinkles? I have no style.*

Sometimes it's the deeper, tougher thoughts we allow to rise: *I'm nothing. I'm not special. I can't do anything right. I can't do anything well. I'm worthless. No one cares about me. I'm not worth caring about. I'm a failure.*

Rebecca calls these Pit Thoughts.

We want you to recognize them, to train your mind to isolate and reject such thoughts. Pin them to an imaginary bulletin board, and then imagine blow-torching them into ashes. Or write those Pit Thoughts down on a piece of paper that you crumple and throw into the trash. Our common Enemy wants us to believe Pit Thoughts that take us away from the oasis truth of our adoring Creator to instead wander among the desert of his lies.

A Phenomenal Creation of God (PCOG) craves satisfaction and focuses on His Thoughts not Pit Thoughts. Throughout this book, in every chapter, you'll see examples of some Pit Thoughts versus His Thoughts—common negative thoughts we have and how to transform them into God's thoughts for us. Add your own Pit Thoughts to these lists and what you know are His Thoughts from Scripture and what you learn of him there.

You can do it! You can! You can grow in every area of your life. You can learn to embrace peace, laugh every day, and challenge your mind, heart, body, and soul. We're on this journey too, walking beside you. No one can opt out—no one has arrived until she enters into heaven's glory. Until then, there's growing to do.

SHINE JESUS

When Reese Witherspoon accepted her 2006 Oscar for playing June Carter Cash in the film *Walk the Line,* her respect for the woman was obvious. She quoted June's response when someone had asked June how she was doing: "I'm just trying to matter."[1] I heard an even better goal expressed at my aunt Ruth's memorial service last year. Her friend said in the eulogy, "The goal for any of us is to finish life used up, worn out, and spit out, crawling to the finish line. Ruth did that."

We, as Phenomenal Creations of God (PCOGs, unite!), want to embrace our lives, not just survive them. We want to make the most of each moment rather than let life simply happen to us. We want to celebrate big, love fiercely, and be loved in return. We want to be healthy—spiritually, physically, emotionally, mentally, financially.

Write your own want here: *I want to...*

Feel beautiful, be financially abundant, laugh, listen to God, walk with God, bring my husband joy, feel confidant, love deeper, laugh harder, work out, feel strong, be a better friend, trust more, read more

Write another want here: *I want to...*

know + feel God at every moment, be financially secure, give more, release more, enjoy life more, sing, perform, be on stage to give back all God has given me, have more time

We want to be women who shine Jesus through our eyes. Who do you know like that? List them here:

Sabina, Mom, Linette Parks, Judy Heine, Chris Heck, Milena, G'ma Kitty,

We are privileged to know many women who shine Jesus through their eyes. We have dear friends who inspire us, and in our surveys, we've brushed up against many more out in the world who are just as inspirational.

Picture one of those people. Picture someone you know who really *sees* the person in front of her. Someone who loves freely and lets others know they are extremely valuable. Someone you would like to emulate. Picture someone who hugs without censure, who cries when the heart overflows, and who laughs often.

You know who we're talking about. She is one of *the satisfied*. What makes her the way she is? You want to be one of the satisfied, right? Then let's go after our wants, longings, and yearnings together. What's to keep us from being satisfied too? We are phenomenal! We are God's own creation!

Just so you know, for all this rah-rah talk, there are plenty of days that we feel less than phenomenal. That's why Rebecca reminds herself of this verse over and over and quotes it as God's claim on her life: "Whom have I in heaven but you? I desire you more than anything on earth. My health may fail, and my spirit may grow weak, but God remains the strength of my heart; he is mine forever" (Psalm 73:25–26, NLT).

The point is, on those less-than-phenomenal days, our direction is to always focus on Christ. Through him, we will find the truly phenomenal. Allowing him to work in and through us, we become PCOGs of amazing importance.

Rebecca says, "When I think back to the long line of women who have been my spiritual mentors, it makes me cry. I've been blessed by women who have challenged me, discipled me, and loved me from the time I was a brand-new believer."

Every one of those women has been vital to Rebecca's faith walk. Think about those who have been vital in your life. Each of us has these people. We once heard Lee Strobel, author of *The Case for Christ,* speak about our being "links in the chain" for other believers.[2] We don't each have to be an entire span of chain for another—don't panic—but we *are* each a link. You are a link. I am a link. We have to ask ourselves, are we paper links for another? Or are we the strongest metal? We need one another!

Life is precious and goes so fast; let's not waste a moment. We want to become women who shine Jesus through our eyes, reveling in soul satisfaction. We are sisters in Christ, and we want to grow into all that God wants for us, more and more each day.

We are the sisterhood of the Phenomenal One. In him we already know Love at its finest, and Love knows us.

It can only get better from here.

For he satisfies the longing soul,
and the hungry soul he fills with good things.
Psalm 107:9, ESV

Holding Hands with the Invisible

Your Relationship with God

> We do not want to be beginners. But let us be convinced of the fact that we will never be anything else but beginners, all our life!
>
> THOMAS MERTON

aving a vibrant relationship with God was the top desire of most women who responded to our survey. Many women, like Nanci, said, "Everything else flows out of my relationship with God." As Christian women, we know this is the basis of who we are and who we want to be. We are children of God, in relationship with him, and we want to grow in this relationship. If you've never thought of this, we urge you to give it consideration. (For further direction on beginning a relationship with Christ for the first time, see the section called "Meeting the Invisible" at the back of this book.)

The longer we live, the more we know that we know the following is true:

We are not all we think we are.

And we are more than we think we are.

It all begins with God.

And it all returns to God.

"All the areas talked about in the middle chapters of *What Women Want* are like fingers on my hand," remarked my friend and associate in ministry, Missie Bonser. "But a relationship with my God—that is like the palm of my hand; it is the connector. If there were no palm, there would be no fingers. It all starts there."

Survey Says

Fifty-four percent of women ranked their relationship with God as number one on their list of wants, needs, and priorities. And most everyone said their desire didn't match the way their priorities played out each day. How do you make your desire to better know God a daily reality?

That's why we address beginning and rejuvenating our relationship with God at the front of our book. The last chapter will bring the book to a conclusion with deepening that relationship. If our hand doesn't have a palm, we can't grow fingers, right?

These are not just pretty words in a nice little Christian book, are they? Relationship with God can infuse all of life.

Alexa writes: My relationship with God is what provides foundation for everything else in my life. If that isn't right, my entire world is "cattywampus."

Sharon writes: I want to know God and understand him better. When I lose sight of God and who he is and what he desires for my life, things fall apart.

Jaleesa writes: I know relationship with God should be my number one answer, so why do I prioritize everything else above him? Even taking this survey helped me get refocused again today!

Jaleesa describes what happens to us as well. We are resigned to what Thomas Merton described at the start of this chapter—always beginning again. And as we do, we build on the experience and history of our relationship with God. But let's back up…what does it mean to be "in relationship with God"?

Lauralynn writes: Relationships, by nature, are a give-and-take thing. To be in relationship with God means to bring everything you have. It also means that you have access to all of what God is. The true *relationship* is learning about the other and taking the journey together.

God calls to us all the time, inviting us to begin the dialogue that defines our relationship with him—through prayer, through his Word, through other people, through our circumstances. We often simply refuse to hear. We cover our eyes and ears. We stubbornly ignore the truth like people have throughout the ages. In the book of Acts, Luke is quoting Isaiah (so this isn't new information to them, either!):

Go to this people and say,
"You will be ever hearing but never understanding;
    you will be ever seeing but never perceiving."
For this people's heart has become calloused;
    they hardly hear with their ears,
    and they have closed their eyes.
Otherwise they might see with their eyes,
    hear with their ears,
    understand with their hearts
    and turn, and I would heal them. (Acts 28:26–27)

Reread the "Otherwise…" sentence. There's hope! We can hear! We can see! So why are we continually disobedient and obstinate, even as confessing followers of Christ? Sometimes we falter because we're afraid, *ashamed of how we've missed the mark.*

> Mariah writes: Even after I became a Christian, I continued to sin in a very overt way. I had sex with many men and dabbled in drugs. I'm married and off drugs now, but what kind of person gets to know Jesus and then deliberately sins?

What kind of person deliberately sins? Umm…pretty much all of us. (We'll address that more fully later in the book.)

Sometimes we falter because we're *listening to the wrong voice.*

> Shelby writes: Satan's lies keep me from believing God at his word. I constantly have to battle against his lies and come back to God's truth.

Other times we falter because we think we can do this thing—life—on our own. We think we know enough, are strong enough, moral enough, and good enough. But deeper in our souls, we know we are never *enough* without God.

WE AREN'T ALL WE THINK; WE'RE MORE

Perhaps it's not a stubborn refusal to accept the words of Christ, but a sense of unworthiness that sends us scurrying to be enough without God. Time and again, shame ranks high as an obstacle for women in trying to get beyond their pasts and on to the future. Shame holds us back, claws at us, pulls us down. Dr. Gary Chapman writes that "the world is filled with people who walk with their heads down. Shame has enslaved them."[1]

It's an evocative image. Suddenly I can see us all trudging the streets of New York City, moving quickly, efficiently, but with our heads down.

Shame is a complex subject. But Liz Higgs once said to me over lunch, "Shame is the result of a search for perfection, and perfection is impossible." We believe that it all boils down to that striving for perfection—and the inevitable miss. The only way to get past the drive for perfection, the constant feeling that we are only what we achieve, is to accept a theology of grace. A theology of grace assumes that we are all imperfect and that only Christ's love makes up the difference. Christ's love always makes up the difference. As a creation of God, and covered in Christ's love, we are enough. (For more from Liz, and her thoughts on grace, see our interview with her at the end of this chapter.)

In the Alpha course, a series of studies that explains a life of faith specifically for nonchurched people, the gospel is described as "a check that God has written to you free and clear. But you must accept, endorse, and deposit the check if you want to make use of it."

You wouldn't cash or deposit a check you believed was written by someone without funds in her bank account, would you? Trust the Lover of your soul as One who has funds to cover a wealth of checks, One who pursues you with a transcendent love. This is the central truth to which we each must cling: Jesus came

Voices from Your Hall of Shame

We all hear them, those nagging, negative, put-down voices in our heads. Rebecca calls their litany the Pit Thoughts we must battle against (or succumb to). Check off any of these thoughts that run through your mind on occasion:

- ○ *I'm not good enough.*
- ⊗ *I missed the mark.*
- ⊗ *I didn't hit my goal.*
- ⊗ *My mistake shows I am unworthy.*
- ⊗ *I could have done better.*
- ⊗ *It will make me look bad.*
- XX ⊗ *Look how much better she is.*
- ○ *I am what I achieve.*

- ⊗ *She doesn't like me.*
- ⊗ *He doesn't approve of me.*
- ⊗ *I should have known better.*
- ○ *I blew it. I'm a failure.*
- ○ *It's all my fault.*
- X ⊗ *I'm not smart enough.*
- X ⊗ *It's all up to me.*
- ○ *I don't deserve it.*

to earth and would have died for me alone. I am worthy; Jesus loves me that much.

To trust this central truth, to get past the shame that holds us back from fully embracing God's unconditional love, we begin with repentance and accept forgiveness. Alan Wright, in his terrific book, *Shame Off You*, says,

> The cycle of shame can only be broken when repentance replaces bitterness. Shame can only be healed when honor replaces dishonor. To let go of shame, you must let go of your sinful reaction to it. Be angry, but do not sin. Hold no judgment. Harbor no resentment. Nourish no bitter root. Whether your repentance is primarily for the shame you've inflicted or the unforgiveness you've harbored, now is the time to change.... No one can repent for you.
>
> Repent. Then turn your eyes heavenward to the Source of grace and honor....
>
> Eons ago, seeing the devastating consequences of the shame that slithered into the Garden and into the fabric of humanity, Father God knew that healing would require an expensive gift of honor. He saw the shame of His betrothed, and instead of sending her more condemnation, He sent His most fragrant offering. He sent the beauty of His holiness. The thorns upon the Savior's brow would only accentuate the aroma of His grace. God sent a rose to His beloved—He sent the Rose of Sharon.
>
> Behold Christ's beauty.
>
> Breathe in the fragrance of His mercy.
>
> It is God's highest act of honor to His people—a Rose for a rose.[2]

Through repentance and forgiveness, we begin to know that we are both less than and more than we previously thought. Put in proper context, in connection and relationship with Christ, God will continue to mold us into everything he sees we can be.

Christ totally loves you, adores you. He even protects and leads you, if you allow it. He sees every smidgen of potential in you, you as a PCOG. He sees you as beautiful, knows you as gifted, and always views you as God created you—perfect. He sees you with your Jesus-layer on. You are covered in grace like another layer of skin, hiding all the times you've failed him, refused to listen to him, refused to even ask his advice. Once confessed, those failures are no longer remembered by him. Jesus sees you as whole. You're not a project he needs to work on, but more like a single flower ready to grow into maturity, then spreading like an antique climbing rose bush. You are a rose bush, not giving out just one beautiful blossom, but three or twenty or fifty, more luxuriant every year.

Hear it again! He sees you! You are not invisible to him, despite how you may feel.

Jerri writes: I feel invisible to just about everyone in my life. I feel as though no one really knows the true me.

In contrast, read these inspiring words from Aisha:

I've felt invisible at times. But I believe God allowed me that so I would rely on him instead of others to know my self-worth. I am incredibly important to Someone. I am beautiful to This Person. I have worth beyond my wildest expectation to the Lover of my soul—the embodiment of the Spirit within me. He has more love than I could ever imagine. He bought me. He paid a price for me. He gave his only Son for me.

Amen! A life lived as a disciple, a learner, is not something any one of us can pull off on our own. Many of us get caught up in the perceived rules of Christian living rather than living a life of grace, much like the Colossians whom Paul addressed in Colossians 2:20–3:4:

Since you died with Christ to the basic principles of this world, why, as though you still belonged to it, do you submit to its rules: "Do not handle! Do not taste! Do not touch!" These are all destined to perish with use, because they are based on human commands and teachings. Such regulations indeed have an appearance of wisdom, with their self-imposed worship, their false humility and their harsh treatment of the body, but they lack any value in restraining sensual indulgence.

Since, then, you have been raised with Christ, set your hearts on things above, where Christ is seated at the right hand of God. Set your minds on things above, not on earthly things. For you died, and your life is now hidden with Christ in God. When Christ, who is your life, appears, then you also will appear with him in glory.

Paul continued in Colossians 3:5–17:

> Put to death, therefore, whatever belongs to your earthly nature: sexual immorality, impurity, lust, evil desires and greed…anger, rage, malice, slander, and filthy language…. Do not lie to each other…[but] clothe yourselves with compassion, kindness, humility, gentleness and patience…. Forgive as the Lord forgave you. And over all these virtues put on love….
>
> Let the peace of Christ rule…. Let the word of Christ dwell in you richly…. And whatever you do, whether in word or deed, do it all in the name of the Lord Jesus, giving thanks to God the Father through him.

It's important to note the distinction between living rightly by the world's standards and living a righteous Christian life in relationship with God. Sometimes the two ways of living outwardly mirror each other. If you met a woman who avoided all the sins of the earthly nature that Paul lists, you would consider her a moral woman, wouldn't you?

But God clearly calls us to more. He wants the word of Christ to dwell in us richly. He wants us to do everything in the name of the Lord Jesus, and to continually give thanks. We cannot get to the "more" on our own. Richard Foster, author of the spiritual classic *Celebration of Discipline,* writes,

> The demand is for an inside job, and only God can work from the inside. We cannot attain or earn this righteousness of the kingdom of God; it is a grace that is given.
>
> In the book of Romans the apostle Paul goes to great lengths to show that righteousness is a gift of God. He uses the term thirty-five times in this epistle and each time insists that righteousness is unattained and unattainable through human effort. One of the clearest statements is Romans 5:17, "…those who receive the abundance of grace and the *free gift of*

righteousness [shall] reign in life through the one man Jesus Christ [italics added]." This teaching, of course, is found not only in Romans but throughout Scripture and stands as one of the cornerstones of the Christian faith.[3]

If it's all up to God, and we can't do anything to earn righteousness, why bother? We bother because God asks us to *allow him* to transform *us*. Doing everything in the name of the Lord Jesus and calling ourselves *Christian* is like sharing the same family name. It is a tall order, a big responsibility, to bear Christ's name. We can live up to the task only if we are fully in relationship with the Triune God, submitting to his discipline, allowing him to mold us into his likeness.

In many ways, our relationship with God through Christ might be like the best possible marriage. If you could get everything you wanted in a marital relationship, what would that look like?

We Need to Rethink How We're Building Our Relationship with God When...

- ◉ our busy lives overtake time with God.

- ◉ we have no prayer life to help us develop a relationship with him.

- ◉ we have no discipline to keep his commandments or follow where he leads.

- ◉ we do not believe who he says he is or that he can do what he says he can do.

- ◉ we do not believe that Christ abides within us.

- ◉ we do not believe that God finds us lovely, winsome, desirable.

"Adventure, mutual encouragement, praise, passion, peace, laughter, balance and support," is how one woman from our survey describes it. But this also depicts the relationship God wants for us. If we know him as well as he desires and pursue a deep relationship with him, we're going to have a marriage with him that bears the fruits of the finest relationship possible.

So how does one go about pursuing a relationship with the Divine? Is this what we're missing, what we're craving?

Some of you are considering this for the first time, just barely turning your faces to God, knowing you're needing something more, something outside yourselves. Others of you are reading this and realizing it's high time to rekindle your relationship with the Holy One, to take it to the next level.

Even writing that, I'm laughing at my own audacity: *Take it to the next level?* Okay, thankfully, it's not all up to us. It's not really all about us. It's about him. It's about our response to him. The Lord is constant, always waiting.

James wrote, "Draw near to God and He will draw near to you" (4:8, NASB). It is our choice. We're given freedom to take God's hand, speak to him, worship him, learn about him, listen to him—or totally ignore him. Many of us remain silent. It may have been months or years since we tried our hand at prayer or opened ourselves up to relationship with the Holy. It's odd, isn't it, to think about walking hand in hand with One who seems invisible? But God is not invisible. As we grow spiritually, we see his hand more clearly.

> Gayle writes: I know he's with me all the time and he sees what is going on with me, what I'm thinking and doing. I can talk to him at any time about anything. He cares about my life and my future, and I sense this in a way that comes only from knowing him personally through Christ.

We all want to get to this kind of assurance that Gayle describes—and stay there! But we don't. We get distracted and continually block the holy from our lives, focusing on what we believe is the "here and now." "Naked I came from my mother's womb, and naked I will depart," Job said (1:21), echoing a thought we all know but continually ignore. We cover ourselves with clothes we buy from the store, of course, but we clothe ourselves in other things as well: money, stature, a fine house, an admirable job. Yet life on earth is temporal, and the only thing that truly matters, when all is said and done, is what links us to the eternal. If we begin and end naked, our focus should be on the Creator who formed us and the Savior who greets us at the end. How will we live in between these two events, such that our relationship with God reflects his light?

Where do we begin? We begin by keeping it simple. Think of how we build any loving relationship. How do we form a bond, learn to love, and desire to please another person? We begin, first and foremost, by getting to know one another. This holds true for our relationship with God as well. Since God made us the way

Pit Thoughts Versus His Thoughts

He doesn't want me.
He rejoices over me like a shepherd who finds his lost sheep (Luke 15:6).

I've done some really bad things. He must have turned his back on me.
Nothing, absolutely nothing can ever separate me from God's love (Romans 8:38–39).

He has forgotten me.
He never will leave or forsake me. He is here (Hebrews 13:5).

It is all a lie.
Jesus is the Son of God…the way, the truth and the life (1 John 5:20; John 14:6).

Is this all there is?
There is so much now—and so much ahead of me! (John 10:10).

we are and knows our capabilities and our limitations, he knows us well. To complete the equation, we need to get to know God well. And when we begin to really know God, if we're honest, we inevitably embrace humility and submission.

DISCIPLESHIP 101: THE PURSUIT OF THE DIVINE

The tyranny of the urgent and the chaos of our day-to-day lives often supersede our acknowledgment of majesty. Our schedules often keep us from getting into any sort of meaningful conversation with God. When we do approach God in prayer, we still get in our own way.

Prayer to God as Father

(Lisa's version of the Lord's Prayer)

Dear Papa,
You are holy and beyond my imagining.
You knew me before I was born.
You'll greet me when I die.
You are in charge right now,
Here on earth, just like in heaven.
Please continue to provide for me—
Give me food and shelter
(and help me not to worry about the rest).
Please forgive me for my sins.
Help me to forgive others.
I know you can!
For you reign,
You are all-powerful,
You are glory defined,
For ages and ages and ages.
Amen.

Andrea writes: I want to learn how to pray, but every time I try, my words sound lame, like I'm trying to be an old pastor from *Little House on the Prairie,* using "thees" and "thous" and afraid I'm going to offend him. I know I'm getting in the way of myself. How do I get past that?

If humility and submission are the starting points in a life of discipleship, then prayer and meditation upon Scripture are the second and third steps. God doesn't ask us to do prayer eloquently. He invites us to call him "Abba" which means, literally, "Daddy." He gives us a no-fail format in the Lord's Prayer, in case we don't know where to start. This is a God who wants to be in communication with us, a God who wants to fully reveal himself through Scripture and prayer.

Maybe it's the sheer "otherness factor" that keeps us from approaching God in prayer. How do we get into relationship with Someone we can't see? Someone we can't hear speak like another human? Someone we can't smell? Or maybe we see him up in heaven, and he feels way too distant.

Jessie writes: I'm afraid of him—Jesus Christ is holy, perfect, and different. He is our judge, and he asks for it all. But he also was created to be like us, so God could fully know us, and so we could fully know him. Jesus adores us! God adores us! Surely someone who adores us cannot be alien to our lives.

If we intend to see Jesus as the Lover of our souls, we have to get to know him, right? Think about some of the questions you've asked people you're interested in knowing better. Where did you grow up? Do you have sisters or brothers? What are your parents like? What do you do? Why? What do you think about? What kind of music do you like? What do you read? How do you relax? Do you enjoy the outdoors? What do you like best about people? What drives you crazy?

We find answers to our questions about God in Scripture, of course. John Eldredge writes about the process this way:

I could tell you a few facts about God.... He is omniscient, omnipotent, and immutable. There—don't you feel closer to him? All our statements about God forget that he is a person, and as Tozer says, "In the deep of His mighty nature He thinks, wills, enjoys, feels, loves, desires and suffers as any other person may." How do we get to know a person? Through stories. All the wild and sad and courageous tales that we tell—they are what reveal us to others. We must return to the Scriptures for the story that it is and stop approaching it as if it is an encyclopedia, looking for "tips and techniques."[4]

Then there's the fact that we think it will be simple, and when we find out it takes effort to know God, we give it up. Jan Winebrenner uses the story of learning to ride a horse as the metaphor for her Christian life: "As weeks of riding passed and lessons piled upon lessons, reality hit me in the chest like a flailing hoof. This riding thing, the whole equestrian thing, the way I wanted to do it, was a full-time endeavor. It was not something I was going to be able to just 'pick up.' "[5] Winebrenner is saying that we can *dabble* in Christianity, or we can endeavor to become a *disciple*. As seen in her metaphor, we can learn to get up on the horse but quickly return to ground, or we can learn to gallop and hop fences. We alone determine how much we're going to put into it.

Every day, every hour, Jesus stands ready and waiting with one hand reaching out to us. He urges us to draw away for a few minutes, a few hours, or a few days in order to be with him, speak with him, and get to know the Father. He waits patiently while we chat on the phone with friends, our families, and co-workers. Will you take the time to be with God? Will you commit to begin or rejuvenate your relationship with the Holy?

You are forgiving and good, O Lord,
abounding in love to all who call to you.
Psalm 86:5

In the Beginning Was Grace

A Chat with *Liz Curtis Higgs*
About the Relationship with God That You Crave

After a lost decade of sex, drugs, and rock'n'roll, Liz Curtis Higgs found herself at the bottom of a pit, facing the sad truth about her sinful self—and the glorious truth about a Savior who loved her "as is." Talk about amazing!

Twenty-five years later Liz still celebrates God's gift of grace, both on the platform and in print. Through keynote messages, interviews, articles, and books, Liz encourages women to embrace the forgiveness of God, made possible because of the priceless sacrifice of his Son.

Here, the best-selling author of *Bad Girls of the Bible* and *Embrace Grace* discusses how we can leave the past behind "so we too might walk in newness of life" (Romans 6:4, NASB).

Rebecca: Liz, you're one of our favorite Christian women, committed to helping other women have a real relationship with God. As a self-described former "bad girl" who came to Christ as an adult, what advice do you have for people just starting their walk of faith?

Liz: Know this first, dear sisters, you're on the right path! We were created to have a relationship with God. He placed that desire, that longing, that need in our hearts from before the beginning of time. It's wired onto our hard drive. It's who we are meant to be. We're called to receive the love of God and love him in return—it's our primary purpose in life!

Rebecca: So what gets in the way?

Liz: We talk ourselves out of it, convinced we don't deserve a relationship with God. We look at perfect God and imperfect us and think, *How dare I walk into a church and bow my head in prayer?*

Rebecca: Even as a committed Christian, I have Sundays when I feel I have no right to be in church! How do we get past that?

Liz: I cling to this promise: "God demonstrates his own love for us in this: While we were still sinners, Christ died for us" [Romans 5:8]. God is not withholding his love until we clean up our lives. He loves us right now. He always has! Our sin would keep us separated from God except for the person of Jesus Christ. He's the One who opens the door.

Rebecca: What about the good girls? Or those who think they are good?

Liz: Hmm. I'm trying hard to think of any really, truly good girls [laughing].

Rebecca: Okay, "No one is good—except God alone" [Mark 10:18], but good girls need grace too!

Liz: Sure they do! I've learned over the years that good girls have all kinds of interior stuff going on. Their mistakes might be considered small compared to the flashy, splashy fiascos some of us have committed, but the fact is, sin is sin. God's Word makes it clear: if you sin in one thing, you sin in all [see James 2:10]. And good girls tend to be harder on themselves. They think, *I shouldn't have stumbled. I knew better.*

Rebecca: How do we get past that feeling of regret?

Liz: By accepting the truth: whether you've sinned a little or sinned a lot, God's grace is there for you. Not just the day you acknowledge him as your Savior, but every day, every hour, every minute! Sometimes I begin a conference presentation by saying, "Let me tell you the seven sins I'm aware of so far today…"

Rebecca: What?! A Christian speaker and author confessing sin?

Liz: Imagine that! I think it's important to confess our sins to one another, both to keep us humble and to hold the Enemy at bay. I never want women to think I've got it all together. Clearly, I do not!

Confession allows us to walk in a constant awareness of our need for grace, even as we're washed clean by the Word, giving God the glory at every turn.

Rebecca: You've said that your book *Embrace Grace* addresses a core issue for many of us—the dreaded, "I know God forgives me, but I can't forgive myself." How do you respond to women struggling with this?

Liz: When we say we can't forgive ourselves, what we're really saying is, "In my head, I acknowledge the existence of grace, but in my heart, I don't think I'm worthy of it." Or it may be an issue of unbelief. Perhaps at the deepest level, we don't really buy the concept of grace. It simply seems too good to be true. Whatever the case, we're (unconsciously) elevating our opinion over God's by saying, "Until I forgive myself, there is no real grace." God, however, says, "My grace is sufficient for you" [2 Corinthians 12:9]. Sufficient means the work is finished. His grace is all we need. And here's more good news: nowhere in the Bible are we commanded to forgive ourselves. What a relief, eh? God's forgiveness truly is enough.

Rebecca: So how do we embrace grace?

Liz: Here's the key: We embrace a God who has already embraced us. God hugs first! The thought of that takes my breath away. For the first twenty-seven years of my life, I was running, running, running, and all that time he was waiting, waiting, waiting, with his arms encircled around me, knowing the day would come when I would turn and see him. Even the ability to see God comes from him: "Ears that hear and eyes that see—the LORD has made them both" [Proverbs 20:12]. When we acknowledge that God is all powerful, and agree that his Word is true, we must accept as fact God's mercy described in both the Old and New Testaments. We can't explain it, we can't earn it, we can't add to it, we can't subtract from it. We often feel guilty because grace sounds too easy and we think we should have to work for it. We're a performance-based culture, so we want to deserve anything we receive. But grace is a gift, purchased by the One who know us best. It's all about God and not about us. It's about his goodness, his mercy, and his love.

Rebecca: And so we return to relationship. How do we truly know our God?

Liz: Ah, that's the mystery, both divinely complex and astonishingly simple. Some of us may feel that we know him because we can discern his voice. Usually that comes from planting his Word so deeply within our hearts and minds that the Holy Spirit can stir those truths inside us when needed.

Rebecca: But because we can't see, touch, or feel God, it makes it hard to know him in the same way we know people.

Liz: You're so right. We have to rely on faith. The wonderful thing is, like with grace, we don't have to strive at earning faith. It, too, is a gift.

Rebecca: If we want to start a relationship with God, or rejuvenate our relationship with him, what tools do we need?

Liz: It comes back to God's Word, every time. It's his love letter to us and the most logical place to begin. The dear people who were cheering me on, demonstrating God's embrace by hugging me on a regular basis, gave me three key messages. The first was, "God loves you exactly the way you are." The second was, "God wants a relationship with you." And the third was, "Let's study the Word together so you can meet the Author. Not a god created by humans to suit their needs, but the one, true God who created everyone." I was receptive to my friends' teaching because they loved me and because they assured me that God loved me. They made me feel safe.

Rebecca: And so it began with love.

Liz: Indeed. It always does. When we're sharing God's Word with people, it's so much more effective if we prepare the way with genuine affection, with caring about them and for them, before we start planting the seeds of truth in their hearts.

Rebecca: How do people hear the Word as a love letter? What if you've never really delved into Scripture before?

Liz: First, choose a translation that speaks to you. The New Living Translation or the paraphrase The Message make great entry points. The New American Standard Bible is considered the closest to the original text and is my favorite for memorization. Spend a few minutes online or in a bookstore and compare the same passage in several translations. You'll find the one that's right for you. Then study the Word daily and read it slowly. Savor each word, each phrase, each verse. (I'm as guilty as anyone of reading the Bible too quickly, wanting to check it off my to-do list.) Instead, take your time. Read a passage aloud. Then wait. And listen.

Rebecca: Any final words about God's wanting a relationship with us?

Liz: When we realize that God is not only interested in us, but also loves us completely, that he created us for his pleasure, and that he wants us to know him, even as we're known by him—honey, that is so appealing to us as women! Now is the time to respond to his love. Receive it. Embrace it. His lovingkindness is unending and immeasurable, a far greater love than any earthly man could ever give us. "This is love: not that we loved God, but that he loved us" [1 John 4:10]. Amazing!

Heart's Desire

Love in Your Life

> God loves you. Personally. Powerfully. Passionately. Others have
> promised and failed. But God has promised and succeeded.
> He loves you with an unfailing love. And his love—if you will
> let it—can fill you and leave you with a love worth giving.
>
> MAX LUCADO

I n the kids section of an old issue of *Time* magazine, five words were
listed as those most looked up at Merriam-Webster.com: *effect, affect,
blog, integrity,* and *love.* The last one gave me pause. *Love?* I wondered incredu-
lously. *People don't know what* love *means?*

As Rebecca and I began talking about this part of our survey, it struck us as
incredibly sad, that as a society, we don't model, preach, and teach love well enough
to spot it the second we see it. But it's a big word, isn't it, *love*?

Gabrielle writes: What does this mean? With a husband? With a friend?
With God? Sex? I pretty much want love on all fronts, but every month I
might be hungering for one of these over another. And then I sometimes
wonder what love really is.

Merriam-Webster's Collegiate Dictionary defines the noun *love* as "strong affection for another arising out of kinship and personal ties; attraction based on sexual desire: affection and tenderness felt by lovers; affection based on admiration, benevolence, or common interests; warm attachment, enthusiasm, or devotion; unselfish, loyal and benevolent concern for the good of another: the fatherly concern of God for humankind: brotherly concern for others; a person's adoration of God." The definition of *love* as a verb is "to hold dear: cherish: to feel a lover's passion, devotion, or tenderness for; caress; to thrive in; to feel affection or experience desire."

Survey Says

Many Christian women found love a term that needed qualifying. They wanted to know "what kind of love was meant regarding the importance of love in our lives" and indicated there were many different kinds. What's the first aspect of love (and then the next) that comes to mind for you?

How is it that our perspective of love is often skewed? We talk about loving our hair stylist, a new musician, and the sandwiches at the deli on Main Street. We say things like, "I love General Tso's spicy chicken." We bandy about the word without thinking, and yet it underscores the most vital aspects of our lives. *Love* is not a word we should toss around lightly. It deserves respect and consideration. *Webster's* defines the verb (versus the noun) *love* as "to thrive in"—as in, a rose loves the sunlight. In the same way, we hunger for love, and when we give and receive it, we thrive like a rose.

Here's what some of our survey respondents think about love.

Tara writes: As the source of all life, the more I seek to love with God's love, the more fulfilled I am and the more I have to give others in all areas of life. Everything else falls into place the more I love.

Molly writes: I need to feel loved and to show love in order to function.

Amber writes: I believe that love is the root of everything, even our relationship with the Lord. He created us out of love, and he continues to love us even through all our faults and sin. Without love there is nothing.

Love is the beginning and the end, for us. And God is the Alpha and Omega. That makes him the first, last, and only true Lover of our souls. He created us to know love—extravagant, outrageous love, beginning with him.

What happens when we don't feel love? We shrivel up and fade. What happens when we do? We grow and flourish.

In high school we probably all learned about how babies respond to touch and care—how those who were ignored and left in a bassinette all day, versus those who were held all the time, looked and acted differently. The babies who were properly cared for even gained more weight, and faster! Is that any surprise?

The need for love is essential, and it doesn't end with our infancy—love fuels us throughout life. My beloved aunt Ruth died last winter. She was stricken with a form of corticobasal ganglionic degeneration, a disease that has similarities to Alzheimer's. Four years before, we began to notice significant skips in memory during conversations with her. Then three years ago Ruth stopped smiling. The disease was deadly in its intent to take her memory as well as her ability to speak and communicate. In the end, her hands curled into each other, and she held her neck stiffly as if it pained her to hold up her head. Ruth's features were largely frozen. She spoke only to her husband, Joe, and to immediate family or caregivers.

Uncle Joe, a twelve-time Montana Coach of the Year (and in the National High School Coaches Hall of Fame) found himself in the play-offs of his life. For more than two years, he provided almost all of Ruth's care, from bathing and feeding to more intimate necessities. He took over writing birthday and thank-you cards and arranged for outings and doctor visits. Joe and Ruth had been restaurant eaters, going out almost every night of their married empty-nest years. But in Ruth's last year at home, Joe had to feed her, placing each bite in her mouth. He cared for her to the end, growing exhausted and sad. Trapped at home, Joe was unable to travel. (Getting out and playing a round of golf was a rare treat.) But Joe rarely complained. He kept his chin up and smiled at Ruth. He stayed with her. He patted her hand. He talked about things she loved. He read the books she enjoyed. He told her jokes. He kissed her lips.

In the end, when Ruth's care became physical around the clock, Joe had to put her in the local nursing home. Still, he spent most of his time with her, chatting up the nurses and other residents as he pushed her around in her wheelchair or as she napped. He ate with her every day. He moved her to a different room when one with a bit of a view became available. He installed an air conditioner in her room when it got too hot. He tacked pictures from grandchildren on the walls, and he watered the plants. He brought Ruth food from her favorite restaurants.

When the local paper ran a story on the plight of people stricken with a life-altering disease and their caregivers, they profiled Joe and Ruth. In response, a woman named Holly Miller wrote this to the editor:

> Thank you for honoring the hospice families on the cover of a recent Sunday paper. The strength and tenacity of the patients, as well as the love of their families, moved me deeply.
>
> One photo in particular caught my attention—a picture of a couple I'd seen many times at Perkins restaurant but never knew their names. It was always hard not to notice him wiping her expressionless face with a napkin or him carrying on a complete conversation by himself. His love for her was so obvious....
>
> Because of this story, I can now put a name to these acts of selfless devotion; these acts devoted to a life lived only in memories now. Mr. McKay, if I am ever fortunate enough to see you or your beautiful wife again, I will get up from my table and hug you myself. May God bless you both.[1]

Holly Miller saw what love looks like at its finest.

THE THREE LOVES

In a perfect world, we'd experience all three biblical definitions of love: the love of a brother, sister, or friend on a heart level; the passionate love of a spouse; and the godly, all-encompassing love of the Savior.

Do you want to know the good news? The best of these three is God's unfailing, uncompromising love for us. Even if we're hurting from a lack of friends or spouse, or love on either front, God's love covers us all. It has an undergirding, transforming power. It is available to each one of us.

> Corinna writes: God is the Friend of all friends. A friend loves you, encourages you, forgives you, listens to you and is there for you. God provides all of those things for me, and I can count on him always!

If you get one thing out of this book, hear this: God loves you. He loves you completely, from head to toe, inside and out. He wants to know you, and he wants you to know him. He is the ultimate love of your life, hands down. A hundred times over. Enough said? If not, read on. Let Scripture speak to you like the love letter you always longed for.

Rob Bell, in his inspiring NOOMA *Flame* DVD, talks about the way the Bible describes and defines love.[2] Bell believes that if we're missing any one of the loves, we're not fully experiencing the love that was meant for us. He expounds on the three Hebrew definitions of love: *raya,* the love of a friend, *ahava,* the love of the eternal, and *dod,* physical love. The problem, Bell maintains, is that we tend to focus on one or even two aspects, but not the other(s), which leads us on a hapless search to fill the gaping hole that the lost aspect leaves behind.

If we focus on only *raya,* we may attempt to fill our need for godly love through the love of friends, and that can never be as perfect and unfailing as the Savior's love. The love of friends may lead to frustration and disappointment. An overactive *dod* lover may become dissatisfied with fidelity and attempt multiple affairs, thinking what he or she seeks lies just around the corner with someone else. A focus only on the *ahava* aspect of love precludes God's power to speak his love through the people in our world. While many saints have found great satisfaction in the *ahava,* and it remains our highest calling, God still longs for us to experience the love expressed via friend and lover as well. Our charge, as Christians, is to pursue all three kinds of love.

SHE'S NOT MY FRIEND; SHE'S MY SISTER

The love of a friend can at times surpass the depth of a familial relationship. But just as sexual love can go awry, so can that of a friend's love. Contrast the two stories from survey respondents below:

> Mia writes: I have two special friends who stood by me through my divorce. They were the hands, feet, ears, and voice of God during that time for me. They stood by me, listened to me, made food for my family, took care of my children.... One of them was even my birthing coach since my husband had left us the month before our third child was born. What an incredible example of God's love!

> Deanna writes: I was betrayed by two best friends...one being my spouse and the other being a best friend and business partner—both professing Christians whom I loved very much. They became involved together and caused the divorce in my marriage while I was pregnant with my third child. Obviously it ended both relationships and was very difficult. She was a godmother to my daughter! And she ended up marrying my former husband! It was the greatest betrayal I've ever experienced.

God clearly asks us to venture into the realm of friendship to explore the depth of relationship he offers via the love of *raya*. In the New Testament, it's called *philos*. The gospel of Luke (see Luke 14:10) describes *philos* love for another as placing that person in a higher or honored position. Luke 15:8–9 speaks of how we feel one another's pain and celebrate one another's joys when we are in the midst of true *philos* love. But the reality is that we are all sinful. We do fail one another. We make bad decisions at times, decisions that hurt the ones we love.

Though it's a simple fact that friends will betray us, just reading about Deanna's story makes us nervous. We can't help thinking of those we love and those who love us. *She would never do that,* we think. We rely on the trust and respect factors implicit in all our relationships. The reality is that nine friends out of ten will fail us at least once in our lives. It may not be an out-out betrayal like Deanna suffered, but it will almost always be based upon a choice to preserve themselves, their needs, and their desires over ours. It's just human nature.

Still, we reach for friends. We want to be loved. We want to love. It's not enough to have our families. We want a circle of girlfriends we can count on, trust, and confide in.

> *The supreme happiness*
> *of life is the conviction*
> *that we are loved.*[3]
> VICTOR HUGO

In the best of friendships, we are emulating God's love when we love one another. Our highest command is to love even those who do not love us. This is confusing at first, a paradox. If another doesn't love us, isn't our immediate reaction to batten down the hatches and protect our hearts? But as Jesus's followers, we're asked to emulate his love to the world, and to strive to be as comprehensive in our love as God himself (see Matthew 5:48 and Romans 5:8). We are to love our friends, our families, our enemies, and even those who persecute us. That is, we are to love everyone.

The only time Christ commands us not to love at all is when we are considering sin. He wants us to hate sin and do everything we can to avoid it. Conversely, he wants us to do everything we can to pursue, ignite, and inspire love.

What does it mean to love our friends? As we get older in the faith, we understand the impact of calling our friends brothers and sisters. Galatians 6:10 suggests we consider our fellow believers as family. You may be like I was at first, chafing at such references, feeling as if the references were too familiar, too churchy, too close. (I need my personal space!) But there is a reason Paul considered others in the faith as close as kin. It is because we've been baptized into the same family. As I grow in my understanding of my faith and, in particular, love, I begin to see all people within the body of Christ as true brothers and sisters.

Read this inspiring Christian sister-story from Steffi:

My three, dear women friends prayed for me throughout my husband's illness. Distraught, I could not pray or connect to God. But they sat with me and prayed for us all. They saw that our needs were met. It felt so natural to have them by my side. When my husband died, paramedics took his body to the hospital in an ambulance. We followed behind and found ourselves standing outside the emergency-room door. A nurse asked if I wanted to go in. I said that he was gone; there was no reason. But my friend said she wanted to say good-bye to him, and so we all went in. I

Godly Attributes of a Friend's Love

Ask yourself, *Which of these attributes do I exhibit in each of my love relationships, and how well?*

- ⊗ encouragement
- ⊗ wise advice
- ⊗ guidance
- ⊗ empathy
- ⊗ sympathy
- ○ patience — *always needs work*
- ⊗ kindness

- ⊗ celebration
- ⊗ praise
- ⊗ compassion
- ⊗ loyalty
- ⊗ acts of service
- ○ other:

  _____

experienced an intense moment of receiving the gift of love from my husband and God in those moments of saying good-bye that carried me for well over a year, all through the lonely depths of grief. I will always thank God my friend spoke up and said what she did—that was Christ's love passed on to me. I would have missed that blessing without her presence and her strength in speaking up.

Not all blood relatives invite our love. Consider some family members you don't like much. They may be in your immediate clan or be distant relatives. Even though you don't like them, don't you feel a special affinity to them? They are family. They are of your same blood. If you had to choose saving either a stranger on the street and your not-so-likable cousin, wouldn't you still choose your cousin?

In the same way, we are called to find that connection in the family of God. We are sealed with the same Holy Spirit (see Ephesians 4:30); we are fellow citizens with God's people and members of God's household (see Ephesians 2:19). The Holy Spirit who pierces my heart and infiltrates my entire life is the same Holy Spirit who moves in you. We are already of Christ's clan!

To experience love born in kinship, and lived out in care, affection, and devotion allows us all to thrive and grow stronger. It enables us to venture further, take risks, challenge ourselves, and explore what it means to be Phenomenal Creations of God living in a fallen world.

XOXO: The Physical Longing of Love

The apostle Paul, a single guy who spent an inordinate amount of time in prisons and on the road, was called to speak to his people about the need for *eros,* a word that means "longing and desire."

In 1 Corinthians, Paul makes it clear that our bodies are not our own. As believers, we are the temple of the Holy Spirit, who is in us. However, as married believers, our bodies also belong to our spouses (see 7:3–6). Paul goes on to say that the only time we're supposed to abstain from sexual relations with our spouses is upon mutual consent in order to "devote yourselves to prayer."

Now, we know a lot of marrried women don't have an active sex life, but is prayer the culprit?

Maybe one in ten thousand cases!

According to Scripture, when we deprive our spouses of eros, or a sexual relationship, it gives Satan an edge. He will tempt us and use our lack of self-control to sway us to a path that leads to ruin. I appreciate what Bible teacher Beth Moore says,

We can easily understand how *eros* came to be associated with sexual love. Unless sexual love is redeemed by the presence of God, it becomes possessive. It seeks to conquer and control. Human sexuality can be a destructive force, but such was never God's intention. He created the physical attraction between a woman and a man. He did not intend selfish *eros*.[4]

Moore continues,

Beloved, Satan is out to destroy the church, which is best accomplished through destroying the family.... If you or your mate are depriving each other, Satan is not missing the opportunity to ultimately use it against you.[5]

We need to address these concerns as sisters. Sexual love is still often not something we're likely to suggest as a topic in Bible studies or our small groups. But it's obviously important to God—and to us! Rebecca and I are definitely not the "sex-perts," but hope to encourage you to discover what God is telling you right now. For further guidance, check out the other books we recommend in the "Additional Resources" section.

SO WHY AREN'T WE MAKING LOVE?

Men and women are faced with countless sexual images every day—racy headlines on newsstand magazines, tawdry stories of *The Star*, nearly pornographic ads on television and in socially acceptable catalogs like Victoria's Secret.

Sex moves us, motivates us, thrills us, and threatens us. It's visceral, particularly for men. Shouldn't we want to fall into our lover's arms and love him the way God designed us to love? Ongoing deprivation of sexual relations without appropriate reasons leaves our marriages open to Satan's attacks. Sure, there are times when physical limitations keep us from pursuing the dance. But we need to be aware of what's really going on with our spouse. Let's make sure that the impediment is not a mental or emotional barrier that needs to be broken through…because for women, sex is more about the mental and emotional connection than the physical. To get you thinking about those possible barriers, see the boxed questions below. If you can't get to the bottom of it quickly, consider speaking with a friend, pastor, or counselor.

Sometimes it's not us. Sometimes it's our spouse who never seems to be "in the mood" or has a medical condition interfering.

For Wives: What's Keeping Me from the Act of Love?

Ask yourself (or discuss with him),

- ◉ *Do I feel he loves me?*
- ◉ *Is there something I need to resolve with him?*
- ◉ *Do we need to have some fun?*
- ◉ *Do we need to do something different?*
- ◉ *How can I focus on him?*
- ◉ *Have I told him what I need?*
- ◉ *Am I stressed? Tired?*
- ◉ *Have I made it clear that I desire him?*
- ◉ *Do I feel good about myself?*
- ◉ *Do I feel desirable?*

Read this from Raina: My husband is diabetic and twenty years older than I am. I'm at my peak (almost 40), and he's winding down (almost 60); plus, the diabetes has made it impossible for him to sustain things in a manner to have intercourse. A few times, we tried medical methods to resolve this, but then it stopped working. This has taken a toll on our marriage, of course. My husband started becoming depressed, and there was a period when he wouldn't touch me or kiss me or anything. Needless to say, I became depressed and vulnerable to attack. A young, good-looking, non-Christian friend of mine, who always told me I was beautiful, started contacting me. We got "involved" for a month, because what I needed most was affection and love.

For Husbands: What's Keeping Him from the Act of Love?

Ask him:

- *Do you know how much I love you?*

- *Is there something between us we need to resolve?*

- *Would you be up for a night away from the kids, just us?*

- *Am I giving you what you need?*

- *Are you stressed?*

- *How can I help you?*

- *How can we improve our sex life?*

- *What can I do to entice you?*

- *What is the most stimulating thing I could do for you?*

- *How can we bring the fun back into our relationship?*

We have to figure it out, know what drives us to (or away from) our spouse, and make it a priority to put things right in order to facilitate a happy, healthy sex life. Raina's affair might have been circumvented if she could have told her husband how she felt—and if together they found ways to fulfill both their needs. Many couples let crisis loom until it's a tidal wave about to crash. Pay attention to the rising or ebbing tide of sexual desire in your relationship; it can't always be high tide. Exhaustion and stress are big obstacles and part of every chapter of our lives.

Adara writes: Sex life? Ha! Wake me up, give me energy! *Help!* My husband? Oh yeah, that man that I dearly love and never get a second alone with? He has the interest in a great sex life, but I'm just *too tired.*

Cori writes: *Agh!* My sex life is a bummer. I don't ever want sex. When my husband and I were first married, I had a stronger sex drive than he did! It was that way for four years. Then I got pregnant, and my sex drive dwindled. After our second child, my sex drive completely vanished. I love my husband and I would never want to be with anyone else. But for most of our twenty-three years of marriage, our sex life has been the pits. I think he's sexy; I just don't want to "do" it. I think there's something wrong with me. I've talked to a doctor, to no avail. Is there hope out there for me?

There's *always* hope, Cori! The point is not to ignore matters. Talk about them. Aim for a healthy sex life: Gratification. Pleasure. Completion. Fulfillment. Total access. (A note to mothers of young children: Explain to your husbands that if you were able to go to bed for two nights at 8:00 p.m. to read and get an excellent night of sleep so that on the third night you'd have the energy and interest in making love, I'd wager your hubby would step up to the plate with glee. Go to bed, read, take a long bath, get psyched up for a night of romance and have fun!) If your situation is as extreme as Cori's, stop and do an inventory, making sure all the other factors that impact sex are in order, that there's no barrier. Again, see other resources listed in the back of this book for more advice on this front.

A healthy sexual relationship affects us and our relationships in many ways. It's worth the trouble. When *eros* love thrives in a marriage, it strengthens the relationship for both the man and woman involved. It builds intimacy, connection, and bonds that keep the Enemy out and the warmth in.

THE LOVE OF ALL LOVES

And yet regardless of whether or not we have a healthy sex life or friends we can call sisters, we have the opportunity to know God's outrageous love. In Romans 5:8 we see that "God demonstrates his own love for us in this: While we were still sinners, Christ died for us."

I think of the sinner on the cross beside Jesus, fully cognizant of his own justified punishment (see Luke 23:41). In those final moments, all he has to recognize is that Jesus is both sinless and Savior. "Jesus, remember me when you come

Agape Is	Agape Is Not
patient	impatient
kind	unkind
truthful	full of deceit
protecting	hurtful
trusting	unfaithful
hopeful	despairing
persevering	tiring
unfailing	faltering
admiring	envious
cheering	boastful
humble	proud
polite	rude
self-sacrificing	self-seeking
forgiving	keeping record of wrongs

into your kingdom," he says. And Jesus immediately answers, "I tell you the truth, today you will be with me in paradise" (Luke 23:42–43).

Take a moment to think of yourself there, hanging on a cross beside Jesus, his weeping mother and friends below you. You are a sinner. You deserve death. But you look into his eyes, and he looks into yours, and you see no condemnation there. Only forgiveness. Only peace. *Only love.* And he promises you that this is not the end, that there is more ahead…paradise. *And you can be there simply by recognizing him for who he really is.*

Thankfully, most of us have accepted these truths, and we will not be facing a death-bed conversion of our own. The point is to move out from this foundation of outrageous, sacrificial love, and to grow and flourish like those babies we talked about at the beginning of this chapter. We want to make the most of this life, here, now. And we want to know and show God's love, agape love, in everything we do.

You think you crave love in your life? We think God craves love most of all.

If agape love is not the hallmark of our faith and the identifiable way that others are to know we are Christians, then we are failing big-time. What would our faith communities look like if we embodied the list of qualities defining agape on the previous page? If we loved as Jesus loves us, how could the world not be attracted to us, not want to join us?

Read through that list again about what agape is and is not. Close your eyes, and imagine a church filled with kind, truthful, protecting, trusting, hopeful, persevering, unfailing, admiring, cheering, humble, polite, self-sacrificing, and forgiving people. Imagine yourself as a part of such a community. Wouldn't our experience be like living in heaven? Is that not what we all truly crave—to love and be loved in these ways? Is this not one way God offers to satisfy us?

Monica writes: A dear lady in my small group is going through a rough time. Her family has been without a paycheck for the past six weeks, and they have been unable to make their house payments the last two months. During this time, she made a big pot of vegetable soup and took time to bring a couple of containers for me to share with my family (my mom had just had a stroke). She shared how this time of struggle has helped her to grow in her relationship with the Lord and her husband. It was a great reminder that God takes care of and provides for his own, even when the days are rough. Seeing her faith in the midst of her problems helped me to see my problem with proper perspective too!

Paula writes: Shortly after my divorce a good friend of mine at work saw through the charade I was putting on every day. She told me that she knew I was unhappy and invited me to go to church with her and her husband. She pushed the issue and didn't stop until I agreed to go. It was such a blessing! She didn't give up on me, even when I turned my back on her. She had enough faith in me that she never stopped pursuing me and the issues at hand. I started attending a singles group, met my new husband there, and overall, found renewal.

Pit Thoughts Versus His Thoughts

God doesn't love me.
God is Love (with a capital *L*!) and he loves me! (1 John 4:8, 16).

I don't even know how to begin to love.
I can love others because he loved me first (John 13:34–35).

I try to love, but I never get it in return.
I am to live a life of love as Christ lived; sometimes it will require a sacrifice on my part (Ephesians 5:2).

I'm too damaged to love.
God will heal and restore me (Jeremiah 30:17).

But I'm afraid I'll be hurt; I don't want to risk it.
There is no fear in love. Perfect love casts out fear (1 John 4:18).

We know churches fail, every day. They fail to reach out to us or to meet our needs, and they often disappoint us. But that's because churches are filled with humans! Church is not the answer; God is. Our only charge is to follow him as disciples and to love as he loved, hopefully transforming our congregations.

Loving in an agape fashion is a tall order—one that we all will spend our entire lives trying to emulate (and often failing). But the point is to try. When we fail, we try to figure out why and endeavor to change enough to get on God's course. Look for opportunities to reflect his love for you to others—reach out to the unlovable, the people that make you crazy, the people who require sacrifice to love, and see if you don't get more out of it than they do. The more we do this, the more we recognize how God loves us and accepts us from the inside out.

Raeleen writes: The more I seek to love with God's love, the more fulfilled
I am and the more I have to give others in all areas of life. Everything else
falls into place the more I love.

Most of us understand love as a noun. But the important thing is to understand love as a verb, to know love in action—both to act it out and to receive it. Then, like the rose bush with a gardener who whispers to her, weeds her soil, trims her dead branches, and nourishes, waters, and exposes her to rich summer sun, we thrive.

So that Christ may dwell in your hearts
through faith. And I pray that you, being
rooted and established in love, may have power,
together with all the saints, to grasp how wide
and long and high and deep is the love of Christ.
Ephesians 3:17–18

Why What We Perceive May Be Off-Base

A Chat with Shaunti Feldhahn About the Love You Crave

Shaunti Feldhahn always wondered about the ways women and men tend to love differently. What truth was there to the stereotype that women crave more romance and men more sex? Do women need the love of friends more than men? How is love in human relationships like the love in our God relationship?

So when this Atlanta-based speaker and nationally syndicated newspaper columnist went to work to find answers, her typical statistical and research analysis turned into groundbreaking national surveys and best-selling books: *For Women Only: What You Need to Know About the Inner Lives of Men,* and *For Men Only: A Straightforward Guide to the Inner Lives of Women,* the follow-up, *For Young Women Only,* and the new *For Parents Only.*

Men and women do view love differently, Shaunti discovered. But her discoveries surprised her—and aren't what you might think. In fact she blows away the myths and preconceptions that men and women have about each other, which she chats about in this exclusive interview conducted in-between her cross-country travels.

Lisa: In researching your books about the inner lives of men and women, what's the most surprising thing you learned about how we see love?

Shaunti: When in a romantic relationship, men do see love differently than women. Typically a man tends to think his wife feels loved because he has proclaimed his love by marrying her. A man sees his wife walk down the aisle and puts a ring, signifying love, on her finger, and that's love. He has proclaimed it to the world. The very act is meant to be a demonstration that speaks volumes. It doesn't occur to many men that the woman he loves needs to be shown that love over and over—because he's already told her she's loved, and he still has these feelings inside. It's sort of like in a guy's mind he's a radio station emitting signals, and the woman he loves is a receiving station. Just because you don't receive the signals doesn't mean they're not going out, right?

Lisa: But we want to be close to our radio station, touch it…

Shaunti: Right. We have to *see* it, and that's actually one of the most surprising things I learned. Eighty percent of the women I surveyed said they felt insecure about the love from their husbands. If a woman doesn't *feel* loved, to her it's the same as if she *isn't* loved, because the women say love has to be *perceived.*

Lisa: So that's the rub.

Shaunti: Yes, and it can lead to all kinds of things that disrupt relationships, like a woman who nags her husband to be more loving. This criticism cuts to the heart of a man's identity—he feels he's not being believed or trusted and respected, and men in the survey said they'd rather be respected and believed in than loved. In fact *perceiving a wife's trust, belief, and respect in him* is *love to a man.* So men and women have to work at love through language, behavior, and such.

Lisa: So give us some language and behavior we women should use with our husbands… Be as specific as possible. Help us!

Shaunti: We women are not wired the same as men—it's so easy to totally miss it when we do something that isn't respectful and sends them the wrong signal. We don't recognize what builds them up. If you say, "Honey, I love you," (which we women love hearing) to a man, it's not nearly as powerful as saying, "Honey, I'm so proud of you." When I have audiences practice saying these words to their husbands or boyfriends, you can see the guys' eyes light up. It *feels* good to them. Another thing is to choose not to question your husband's every decision. Even if you don't agree with his decision immediately, force yourself to stop and say, "You know, I'm not sure I agree with that totally, but you've got good judgment, and I'll go with you on that." Voicing that you *believe in him* reinforces his belief that you see him as having good judgment and trust him.

Lisa: Umm, okay. I may need some duct tape over my mouth so that I don't keep talking and contradict myself. What do you do if you think he's really off track?

Shaunti: Never begin a statement with, "Why did you…" Men hear that as, "Why did you do that, you dodo?" He'll take it that you don't think he knows what he's doing. Instead, practice saying, "I know you had a reason for that decision, but I'm really confused. Can you help me understand what that was?" You are purposefully demonstrating that you are saying you respect and trust him, and that you don't believe he's an idiot (even if you want to discuss something further). Such purposeful demonstration of respect is the female equivalent of his surprising you with two dozen red roses. It speaks volumes.

Lisa: Okay. Then what are some ways our husbands are trying to express their love that we may be missing?

Shaunti: This will sound foreign to most women, but one very common way is by working eighty hours a week. A man might be killing himself at a demanding job, when he'd much rather be at home with the family. But he's doing it because he sees providing financial security for his wife and family as one of his primary ways of saying, "I love you."

Lisa: Really? So he's not saying he'd rather be at work than home with the family?

Shaunti: Right, but many women misunderstand it as saying, "I don't care about you." We assume just that—that he'd rather be at work. There obviously has to be a balance, but it's important to understand how many of our men are laboring under that misconception and that it really is, first and foremost, a way of expressing love.

Lisa: So how would you encourage that man to come home?

Shaunti: I had to tackle this one myself! From what I've seen, it's helpful to explicitly tell your husband: (a) "I appreciate you and how you are busting your tail to provide for us"; (b) "I want you to be aware that I would much rather have more of you, my husband, than anything you could provide"; and (c) "I'm willing to even look at how we can cut back, as a family, if that's what it takes, for you to be happier and in a job that allows you to be home with the family more—I don't like to see you under this stress."

Lisa: And this works?

Shaunti: In many cases, yes, as long as the alternative-job option is also one he finds fulfilling. Make a note: this is a conversation you may have to have several times. Guys have a hard time believing we actually mean it when we say such things—that we'd be willing to have less stuff in order to have *him* more.

Lisa: What about friendships? Do women have a deeper need for loving friendships than men?

Shaunti: Friendships are wrapped up in a woman's heart. A woman can't replace the need for friends with other things. Friendships are absolutely essential and life giving, and every person, regardless of gender or marital status, needs loving companionship.

Lisa: What are some ways we women can best express love to our girlfriends?

Shaunti: In this season of my life, I'm on the road doing fifty events a year, gone almost every weekend. Fortunately, I'm working out a schedule where my family can travel with me more. But it still means I'm away from my friends. One of the best ways for a true friend to reach out to me is to actively pursue time together. I love it when a friend says something like, "Hey, I haven't seen you for three weeks. I'm showing up tomorrow at ten, and we're going to coffee." We need to be wise about boundaries and each other's time, but a true friend mirrors God's pursuing love.

Another thing a friend can do is trust—to risk by asking. I heard the best story about this from a pastor in Boston. He described how he was awakened in the middle of the night by friends out West whose house was in the danger zone for wildfires sweeping the area. Everything was at stake. They called the pastor at 3:00 a.m. and said, "Will you please pray?" Right then, the pastor and his wife got down on their knees and prayed. The friends called back at 6:30 a.m. to say that the winds had changed and everything was spared. They thanked the pastor and his wife for being such good friends that they knew they could call them, count on them.

The pastor said, "Actually, *you* are the good friends. Thank you for being willing to ask, to be willing to 'inconvenience' us when you needed prayer so desperately."

I am not a good asker—but I'm working at doing more of it. When we risk and ask our friends to help us, we show them we trust them as true friends, as people we can depend on.

Lisa: How does God show us love on a day-to-day basis?

Shaunti: If we're not experiencing the love of God, it is because we are not open to it or seeking it—there's some block there to be discovered. God's love is like the air—we may not always see it, but it is always present. We need it to survive. God is always there, and God is love, so by definition it means his love is always there. I found Blackaby's *Experiencing God* powerful in helping me tune my receiver to receive God's love.

Lisa: How might we see his love in action?

Shaunti: When I first came to be a Christian, the idea surprised me that God might show me his love through other people. If I needed comfort and suddenly a friend called to talk, I realized that it was God loving me through my friend! Suddenly I saw God's love in so many places I never thought to look for it. It had never occurred to me! We so often don't see or give God credit for how he reaches out to us every day. God still allows heartache and hurt, but that doesn't mean that the love isn't there. "I will always be with you until the close of the age": that's Jesus's promise. If you've asked Jesus into your heart, you will never be alone or unloved.

Lisa: How has your experience in becoming a mother broadened your own personal understanding of love like God's?

Shaunti: In a word—*completely.* Before children I thought I understood love and what unconditional love meant. But once I had kids, I finally got for the first time what that means, what God is feeling.

Lisa: And that is…?

Shaunti: There is *nothing* my kids can do that will make me not love them. I can get ticked at them, exasperated, sad about things they've done or choices they've made, but nothing can make me not love them. That's like God's ultimate love—the love every person needs, the love that can't be replaced by any other.

Soul Sisters

Your Friendships

> Our relationships with other women are among our significant emotional bonds. While men provide the sense of *other* (as husbands and friends), women are *mirrors* for our femaleness our whole life long. From our symbiotic friendships of preadolescence to our friendships in old age, we look to other women to help us understand and shape our lives.
>
> BRENDA HUNTER

A t one point in my marriage, my husband said he didn't feel the need for friends because he got what he needed from me. I was flattered but struggled to understand. "What was that?" I asked, "You don't need anybody but me?" I was a little shocked by his statement.

Katherine writes: Men need connection, but more in an army sort of way. Give them shared food, shared work, shared laughter, and they become brothers. Women need all those things, but have to go deeper.

Survey Says

Few Christian women rated friendship as their number one craving, but 75 percent ranked their need for friends as a Top 5 priority, often above things, such as joy or physical health. What are you truly seeking in friendship? What do friends bring you that family cannot?

Eventually I realized that most men don't have the same need as women to know and be known by others. Our need for deep, meaningful friendships is felt more urgently than it is for men. Women seem to hunger for a sense of belonging and ties on a deeper level than men do. We want other people around us who understand despair and joy, tenderness and fury, the same way we do. Women need to know that they can express all their emotions and still be loved, connected, supported, prayed over, and prayed for. This is not to say that men do not need or benefit from solid friendship, but often their needs are felt differently.

THE GOAL: CLASS V FRIENDSHIP

We all know women who seem surrounded by friends. But how many of us are willing to go the distance and put in the work to develop a higher quality of friendship? How many of us are willing to sacrifice for one another, as Christ gave himself to show his love?

Recently, while dropping off the kids at camp, the Bergren family car died. Taking refuge in a whitewater-rafting shop, I waited for my friend Sarah to come rescue us (adding two hours to her own trip). I began to study the rafting brochures and learned that in white water, Class I represents the easy day trips over nothing more than an occasional riffle. In Class II the water gets choppier. Bigger rocks and bigger waves mean Class III water, something older kids can handle but "still gives them a thrill." Class IV is sometimes dangerous, tossing rafters into the water. Class V is only for pros, because it is outright treacherous.

Whitewater Classes of Friendship

Class I. Acquaintances: flat water, but scenic and enjoyable.

Class II. A little history together: a few riffles get the heart pumping.

Class III. Moderate history: moderate waves with some highs and lows.

Class IV. Major history: big water with plenty of highs and lows.

Class V. Historic: together, you've made it through the best and worst water possible.

Which of your friends do you want with you through the Class V rapids of friendship?

Sonia writes: In the early years of my marriage, I expected my husband to be everything. To complete all the emptiness in me, I put too much pressure on him to be the perfect husband, and he started to pull away from me. It was then, because of my loneliness, that I joined a Bible study in order to meet new friends. Turns out that study helped me meet the Best Friend I could ever have, Jesus, as well as a ton of great women who have become incredibly close to my heart. I learned that my emptiness could never be filled by one person, or even a hundred. As a result, I let go of unreasonable expectations I had placed on my marriage, and it has never been better.

We often hear a particular scripture read at weddings. It's a familiar one that speaks of love, passion, and soul-deep connection: "Where you go I will go, and where you stay I will stay. Your people will be my people and your God my God" (Ruth 1:16). This passage from the Old Testament book of Ruth and is not presenting a woman speaking to a man. Ruth is speaking to her mother-in-law, Naomi. Theirs is a God-sent, soul-sister, Class V friendship (between a mother-in-law and her daughter-in-law, no less!), one we'd be blessed to have ourselves. Ruth and Naomi's friendship took years to build and grow, and when they went through rough waters, they were ready to move on and sail through them together.

SAY YES TO EVERYTHING

Depth, sincerity, and connection: this is a Class V friendship, what we all aspire to know. Most friendships take years to get to Class V. Sometimes girlfriends don't even get in the same raft together, however. They cruise along on the same river, side by side in rafts, keeping things very superficial. Other times we get in the same raft and get to a Class I friendship, enjoying one another's company but still keeping things pretty surface level. It's only when we take a risk that we begin to deepen in our friendship and progress from Class II to Class V—whether we're sharing dreams, joy, or pain. We women like to help and support one another; when we refuse to let anyone come close, there's little chance to develop the history and trust that creates a truly great friendship.

Moving to a new area makes it particularly tough. But the only way forward is to dive in. Rebecca coached my cousin, Leslie, on how to make it work. Rebecca learned, the hard way, through many moves to new cities, that if you don't get out there and risk, you never form any connections or even *begin* the work of forging new friendships. Her core advice? Say yes to everything. Invitations to Bible study, a movie, a neighborhood party, coffee…whatever it is, say yes.

Rebecca says, "This is particularly important for singles like me. Without a husband, without kids, there is no automatic way to connect with others." But I think the advice applies to married parents as well. We all need to be open, friendly, and seeking others if we're to have half a chance at making new friends.

Leslie writes: I followed Rebecca's advice when I first moved to Dallas, and it worked like a charm. Within a few months we were feeling very much at home, and I knew I had at least three women in my new world who had the potential to become very dear friends. I already love them, and they love me!

DON'T GIVE IN TO FIRST IMPRESSIONS

Sometimes we misread rafting signals from people we do not know well, a good reminder to not count women out just because we don't instantly connect. We may be passing by some of the best and most lasting friendships God will ever send our way.

Anne writes: I was introduced to a woman for the first time at a board meeting. Later that evening, when I finished my presentation, she was so incredibly critical! I was hurt, not to mention offended, by her negative words. I was so surprised since I had heard such nice things about her. Needless to say, she wasn't at the top of my Potential Friends list, if you know what I mean. I did not look forward to serving on the board with her. Not too long after that, I had to e-mail her a question. I dreaded her answer! Lo and behold, she responded almost immediately, and her response was not only pleasant, it was lighthearted and funny. We e-mailed back and forth for an hour, and I finally picked up the phone and called her. We've been close friends ever since!

We are exceedingly hard on one another as women. Remember to look at every possible friend as just that—*a possible friend*—resisting poor first impressions and digging a little deeper to make sure your initial perceptions are correct. The quiet woman who barely speaks in a group may be your most loyal, deep, and inspiring future friend when you get to be with her one-on-one. The boisterous girl in the center of the group might have your exact sense of humor.

Rebecca was my first real boss in my first real job. After I interviewed with her and the vice president, I knew the vice president was impressed with me, but I was pretty certain Rebecca didn't like me at all. I called my husband and told him,

"That Rebecca woman—she hates me." Talk about your wrong first impression! In fact, as soon as I left the office, Rebecca went to the vice president and told him to hire me. Never would I have dreamed that she would become one of the Class Vs in my life.

We all know that different friends fulfill different needs in our lives. I once got my best friend from high school together with my best friend from college and they—um—did not connect. I couldn't believe it! How could these two women I loved and who loved me not like each other? One of your friends may be the one you can be gut-level honest with and pray with. Another might inspire you to follow your dreams. Another may be a walking buddy you laugh with all the time.

Pit Thoughts Versus His Thoughts

I don't know if I'll ever find a good friend.
I can ask God to send me a good friend, while being kind to all (Proverbs 18:24).

I'm unworthy of good friends.
If God sees me as worthy, I can both have and be a friend to others (Colossians 3:13).

I'm lonely and forgotten.
God loves me like a mother cares for her babe (Isaiah 49:15).

I cannot trust anyone.
God will grant me the wisdom in knowing whom to trust (Proverbs 2:6).

I'm a loser at relationships; why even try?
I can try again, learning from my mistakes (Hebrews 12:3).

Fill your world of friendship with many dear friends who meet your needs in certain, definable ways. One of them may surprise you, becoming one of those deeper-level Class V friends down the road…if you give it time.

CHRIST IN COMMUNITY

When you're in a great friendship, mutual trust allows you to challenge one another. Our goal is to be in relationship with others who will encourage us to be everything that God intends us to be. Our dearest heart friends could ask us hard questions about our lives, and rather than get defensive, we would take their queries as a desire to see us in a place of peace or joy or deeper maturity. Why? Because we know that each of them loves us, celebrates who we are, wants to see us at peace and filled with joy. We know they are also willing to help us work through the obstacles that keep us from those things. Having a rich foundation with a friend, coupled with a deep trust, allows us to communicate on an uncommon level. We all want to develop gut-level honesty that rivals what we can experience with God and that echoes our relationship with him.

If you pop onto the Internet site www.friendship.com, you'll discover that eight thousand people log on each day. What are these people seeking? They're responding to their God-created need to connect with other people. God calls us into community—to know and be known. He wants us to invest in one another, risking honesty, gaining intimacy, and developing clarity of thought. We are designed to be a reflection of Christ to one another. We are made to encourage, to empathize, to help, and to spur one another on. If we were the perfect Christian community, no one would be lonely, without support, without connection, or without love. Let's face it; we're all muddling through our lives, trying to make good choices, trying to live as Christ wants us to—but it's hard. We need others who understand this wild-river ride we're on.

Mutual Christian service can draw women together in ways they've never experienced before. When Paul used peoples' names in his letters, most often it was when he wished to uphold treasured friends' shared mission with him. Christian service can take the form of working at the local soup kitchen, cleaning the church, running the Sunday school, serving on a council or elder board—wherever

What Do You Look For in a Friend?

Do the things you look for also describe you? It's important to offer what we wish to attract. Check off what's most important to you. *My ideal friend…*

- ☒ supports me.
- ☒ encourages me.
- ☒ is faithful in times of trouble.
- ☒ brings out the best in me.
- ☒ overlooks my failings, weaknesses.
- ☒ accepts me unconditionally.
- ☒ is honest with me—in trivial or big matters.
- ☒ understands me.
- ☒ intercedes/prays for me.
- ◯ rescues me when I need it.
- ◯ lets me flounder when that's what I need.
- ☒ encourages me to do my best.
- ☒ doesn't let me get away with anything.
- ☒ is sometimes "just there" with silent encouragement when I need her.
- ☒ grieves with me.
- ☒ laughs with me.

your gifts might reign. Rebecca and I find mutual joy and deepening friendship by working in Christian businesses together. My friendship with Sarah deepened in coleading a working-women's Bible study over the last two years. Missie and I share common vision and passion in ministry. Rebecca counts friendships across the country with women with whom she has led Bible studies or worked in ministry.

Is there a woman who feels called to the same things as you who could become a good heart friend for you? Keep your eyes open, and ask God to bring you together! And look for friends at your church before you look elsewhere. You already have one thing in common: a community in a box!

FRIENDS OUTSIDE THE FAITH

Should we be friends with people who don't share our beliefs? Yes. The Bible clearly asks us to develop relationships with those outside the body of Christ and to live our lives in a way that will motivate them to reach for what we have—the spark of light, love, joy, and peace.

Yet we cannot let friendships with those who do not know God drag us down, away from the holy. Being salt and light in a peppery world is a delicate balancing act. Some years we have more strength to follow this call than others. Pay attention to how God is leading you—be strong and sure in your foundation before you head out into friendships with nonbelievers. But by all means, head out! Helping a friend eventually understand Jesus as the Best Friend she could ever have is the best gift you can give her.

WHEN FRIENDSHIPS FALL APART

There are times when we have friends for just a season of our lives. One of two things happens—drift or breach—that causes the friendship to fall apart. Drift happens to all of us; circumstances change, we have kids (or don't), go to work (or don't), change jobs, move to another city or across town. Something happens—physically, mentally, emotionally—that makes it somehow harder to maintain the connection.

Ishiko writes: I became best friends with another woman who had a husband in the air force. Being in military marriages, we knew time was short—maybe that's what helped us become so close, so fast. She was like a sister to me! But then they moved to another base, and we've never been within two thousand miles of each other since. It's been three years, and our calls are getting farther and farther apart. I don't want to lose her!

Dear friends, heart friends, Class III or better friends come along only rarely. It's worth the effort to try and keep in touch and be involved in each other's lives.

Keeping Long-Distance Friendships Alive

Want to invest in relationships even from a distance? Try these tips:

- Commit to staying up-to-date with one another's lives via e-mail or phone.
- Share experiences: try an online Bible study together or read a book at the same time.
- Plan an annual trip to see each other. Trade locations, and share in the cost to cut airfare trauma.
- Share family pictures often: when you upload your photos online, invite your friend to view them.
- Set a time to share short-term goals—what you're each hoping will happen in the next few months—and then follow up.
- Commit to talking about more than what the kids are doing or how your job is going. Share how you're feeling and how God is working in your life, as well as the fun stuff!

Hopefully some day you might come back together and bridge whatever gap has kept you apart. At the very least, we want to be kind, God's light in the world, especially through our friendships.

Other times, something bad happens, ending a relationship. I'm a resolution girl, someone who doesn't like loose ends or unresolved problems. Want to address something, even something prickly? I'm your woman. Because of this, I rarely lose friends. But I'm currently mourning the apparent death of one of my best friendships, helpless in the face of her refusing to discuss the issues at hand. In hindsight, I think I hurt her; I was too forthright, too direct in telling her exactly what I thought.

This experience has left me dedicated to practicing a more subtle approach. I think of what Samuel Taylor Coleridge wrote, "Advice is like snow—the softer it falls, the longer it dwells upon, and the deeper it sinks into the mind."[1] Have you experienced a time when a friend's advice fell softly and sank deeply into your mind? Conversely, have you experienced a friend's advice that felt more like a bag of rocks heaped on your head?

I want to trust that my best girlfriends would tell me if they discerned that something was wrong, from a piece of lettuce stuck between my teeth to walking in sin, away from the Lord's clear leading. I want the kind of friendships where my friends can tell me anything because they love me. I want to trust my friends with everything—big and small—in order for our friendships to grow deeper. And I want to become a Coleridge-falling-snow-advice friend, because if a Class III friendship suffers a breach that cannot be bridged, there's no chance of its becoming a IV or a V.

THE BETRAYER

Women from our survey cite the primary reasons for friendships dying as an argument, constant comparison, jealousy, separation of common interests, a physical move, a change in family status, or a breach of loyalty, among others. Some of those things we can combat; others we cannot control.

Recovery from a blow to our hearts makes trust a tender topic. But we must not wallow in our pain; instead, we must allow our Savior to mend our hearts. Trust *can* be rebuilt, in time. Sometimes, it can even be stronger than before—with wisdom and boundaries. Other times, we find that we can never be with those people again, because they've not earned back our trust when we give them small chances at redemption. The important thing is to become wiser as we grow through hurt. We pick up on subtle signals we might not have seen or heard before, become more perceptive.

However, we cannot allow ourselves to become so hardened that we refuse to risk trusting again. If we never take risks in relationship, we remain safe, but static. We never have the opportunity to reap a potential harvest, using what we've learned. There is a time to let a friendship field lie fallow. Then God calls you to cast your seed again—and pray for rain.

> Susie writes: I've been involved in a codependent relationship with a woman twelve years older than I am. She was the mother I always wanted. This woman wanted to be with me all the time. She would always tell me that I was the daughter she always wanted. I was so overcome by her attention and affirmation that I totally alienated my husband and children. We would spend hours together, and if I invited anyone else to join us, she would ask me not to do that again, because it wasn't as "rewarding" when others were involved. She became extremely affectionate, and I was uncomfortable but feared her pulling away if I questioned it. She would only show affection when we were alone. I went into a deep depression and ended up in a psychiatric hospital because I was suicidal. After I found a Christian counselor and worked through many months of counseling, I was able to break free of this soul tie (emotional idolatry) with this woman.

Most friends will not expose us to the kind of emotional devastation that Susie experienced. But even our closest friends will disappoint us at times. In Matthew 26:35–56 and 69–75 we see Jesus's nearest and dearest deny him (even though they swore they would not), disappoint him by falling asleep (when all he asked was for somebody to stay awake with him), and desert him by running away. Even the most godly and devoted friends—Class V friends—someday may have bigger needs than yours, and they will choose their own needs instead of yours. They may even betray you. The question is, what will you do when that happens?

Reasons to Let a Friendship Go

If you've tried to address issues in a friendship and nothing has changed, it may be best to allow your friendship to fade. Perhaps it will be resurrected, but even if it isn't, you will have walked according to your understanding and your own conscience. Here are some things to count as red flags:

- She puts you down or makes fun of you.

- She attempts to trivialize your faith.

- She takes but doesn't give.

- She talks incessantly about herself and never asks you about you.

- She does not encourage you to pursue your dreams.

- She threatens you, subtly or overtly.

- She won't allow others to get close to you.

- She competes with you.

- She does not live a life of integrity or honesty.

- She demands too much of you.

- She exhibits character qualities you don't want to emulate, such as anger.

- She brings out the worst in you instead of the best.

- She won't listen when you attempt to talk about your needs in the friendship, or she listens but does not attempt to change.

- You see no hope of change in the relationship.

Janice writes: Betrayal put a serious strain on our relationship. I thought we'd never be friends again. I had to release the burden to God, and in his timing, he has brought us back together. I'm more careful, of course, but we appreciate each other's friendship.

Ivanna writes: I've chosen not to keep some back stabbers—even after forgiving them—in my close circle of friends, because I learned that our values differed tremendously. I accept that none of my friends are perfect, and once I know their shortcomings and weaknesses, I look to see our shared values, and that helps define our continued friendship. God helps me with forgiving and acceptance. Some wounds have been pretty deep, but through God's grace I've been able to forgive, overcome, and continue a close, intimate friendship after the incident.

When a friend disappoints you, you have to let it go and love her in spite of it, just as Jesus loved his friends (and us). Don't let the friendship die; just give your friend and your friendship a vacation if necessary. Return to it later, and attempt to view your friend through "Jesus glasses"—glasses tinted with his grace. See her as worthy of friendship despite her failings, just as we pray our friends will see us! Proverbs 18:24 says, "Friends come and friends go, but a true friend sticks by you like family" (MSG). Does your friend meet the mark? Can you give her another chance?

THE PERFECT FRIEND

Quick, think of your perfect friend! Most likely, she's a composite of several of your best friends.

There is a Perfect Friend, however. His name is Jesus Christ. He supports you, encourages you, assists you, cherishes you, and helps you sort out and resolve difficult situations. He never abandons you or becomes so angry he stops speaking to you. How do we get to know this Friend of friends other than through Scripture? We get to know him through the Holy Spirit, our advocate, intercessor, and counselor (see John 16:7). What does it mean to cultivate a friendship with the Holy Spirit? It requires respect, time, prayer, and a listening ear. Just as with our girlfriends, it takes time to develop friendship with our Friend of friends. Take time out to be quiet in order to cultivate a listening ear. The Holy Spirit speaks in a still, small voice. It's hard to hear a still, small voice in a room with others, or with the television blaring, telephone ringing, and dishwasher running. When you take the time to be by yourself, listening for him to speak to you, you can begin to hear him more readily. Find ways to develop your listening ear through Scripture, music, books, or teaching CDs.

Jill writes: I was working my way up the corporate ladder with two small children at home and a husband getting started in his own business. I was lonely and felt something was askew in my life. I assumed it was girlfriends

Our Friend of Friends

Jesus proves himself a Friend in the following ways:

- He never leaves us (Matthew 28:20).
- He loves us unconditionally (John 8:35–39).
- He demonstrates his love (John 15:13).
- He prays for us (John 17:9).
- He wants to be with us (John 17:24).
- He carries our burdens with us (Matthew 11:28–30)
- He accepts us (Romans 15:7).
- He forgives us (Ephesians 4:32).
- He gave himself up for us (Ephesians 5:2).
- He understands and helps us when we're tempted (Hebrews 2:18).
- He never, ever changes (Hebrews 13:8).

(or lack of them!). Due to my busy life, I had no time for a girlfriend other than a quick phone call here and there. When I was at the bottom of my loneliness, I cried out to God for his help and discovered that he is my Best Friend. He is the One I needed to make time for, and with that insight, I was able to see that seeking status in a professional position was not what he was calling me to do, so I left my job. Wonderful girlfriends enrich my life now, and I attribute it to his answering that prayer when I had no one else to turn to.

God delights in us when we embody love, joy, and forgiveness on a daily basis through our friendships. He satisfies our longings for dynamic Class V friendships when we look for friends who honor him. We'll most likely find them in community with others who challenge us to grow in our faith. Above all, let's seek the Friend who never leaves or disappoints us—and who always is available to us when there is no other.

The amazing grace of the Master, Jesus Christ,
the extravagant love of God, the intimate friendship
of the Holy Spirit, be with all of you.
2 Corinthians 13:14, MSG

The Eternal in Sharing a Story

A Chat with *Robin Jones Gunn*
About the Friendships You Crave

Ask Robin Jones Gunn about her passions in life, and relationships are usually at the top of her list. She is a wife, mom of two grown children, and the best-selling, award-winning author of more than sixty titles, which have sold more than three million copies worldwide. Those books include Christy Miller, Sierra Jensen, Glenbrooke, and the Sisterchicks series about women in deep friendships. She defines *Sisterchick* as "a friend who shares the deepest wonders of your heart, loves you like a sister, and provides a reality check when you're being a brat." Her ready laugh and easy manner make her an instant friend…and it's obvious why women the world over are drawn to her.

Lisa: You and I share a passion for writing that has bonded us as friends. How important is a shared passion to developing a friendship?

Robin: It certainly connects friends. Yet when it comes to my closest friends, oddly, opposites have greater attraction. My best friend of all time, Donna, would rather have a root canal than be asked to write or speak. She appreciates my love of words, while I appreciate her honest, open, caring approach to life and relationships. Donna went back to school after her three children left the nest, and now she's a semester away from having her nursing degree. When we get together, she gets all sparkle-eyed telling me about liver functions and blood pathogens.

Lisa: And you still connect?

Robin: Her passion for the human body makes me interested and amazed, and when I tell her delicately embellished stories of people, experiences, and places I love in this wide world, she sighs and says she feels a renewed passion for life. We're quite comfy on our teeter-totter of passions. Both of us have equal passion, just in different arenas. My closest writer friend, Anne, writes intense, epic novels based on places of conflict where she's traveled, and she looks for hope among those ravaged lands and lives. I could never write what Anne writes, and yet we deeply love and admire each other's writing. We crave times to be together so we can watch our writing ideas spark when we put our "iron sharpening iron" heads together. We are each other's greatest supporters and completely at home in our separate writing passions.

Lisa: Your popular series Sisterchicks has taken you around the world on research. But I know that while you think travel is fun, it's not your main reason for writing the series. Tell us the real reason—what was your inspiration?

Robin: First, let me agree with you. I love to travel, and being given a budget in order to research the last few Sisterchicks novels was a dream of a lifetime. But the travel to some beautiful settings like Venice and New Zealand was just a bonus. I wanted to take two midlife women who were stuck halfway through life, put them in an unfamiliar situation, and watch them discover that God is so much bigger and more amazing than they had ever imagined. In light of their out-of-the-ordinary experiences, these rejuvenated Sisterchicks return home ready to see their days become more God-filled than ever as they roll into the next season of life.

Lisa: What inspired you?

Robin: Inspiration came from a true Sisterchicks adventure Donna and I had fourteen years ago when she and I went to Finland. A publisher there had translated the Christy Miller books for teenage girls into Finnish, and I was invited to speak in the public high schools. Our experience was amazing, life changing really, and deeply affected who we are and what we value in life. We came home ready to trust God more than we ever had before; we were fully recharged to go about loving our husbands and our children more deeply than we ever knew we could.

For years after our adventure, whenever we gathered with friends, they would say, "Tell us again about the time the two of you went to Finland and how you went in the sauna." We'd roll out our story and laugh and get serious and laugh again. Many times I heard, "You should make that into a book." And so I did—with a few embellishments, of course. It's the first Sisterchicks book, *Sisterchicks on the Loose.*

Lisa: How can other women forge that sister-level kind of friendship?

Robin: Don't you think something eternal and bonding happens whenever we tell our stories? By that I mean our life stories, grace stories. I've seen it happen so many times. We can connect with other women on a surface level talking about all kinds of outward things like our hair or clothes or our children. But when we open up and tell our stories, we reveal to another eternal being who we are and where we've come from. In that truth-telling moment something deep and lasting happens. Our hearts get knit together. The eternal part of us starts interacting on the soul level.

Lisa: So what gets in the way of this happening?

Robin: We let fear make way too many decisions for us. We're afraid that if anyone really knew us, they wouldn't like us. So we hide, just like Eve. "I was afraid, so I hid." We try to cover up the nakedness of our souls so that we'll look good to others. The facade keeps us from interacting on that eternal, soul level, and as a result, true relationship doesn't happen. At the same time, going completely "heart naked" all at once with a brand-new friend can understandably send her running. Yikes! Too much information!

Lisa: [laughing] So how do we get there?

Robin: The most extravagant element of friendships here on earth is time. Lasting friendships need the luxury of being able to unfold petal by petal. What a gift it is to see another woman in the full bloom of her true self! It's at that soul level of a blossoming friendship that we truly begin to trust. And trust has a rhythm. Trust has a pace. It's a slow pace, but it's a steady pace. True trust endures much. Time + Truth + Trust = True Friendship.

Lisa: You're a Phenomenal Creature of God (PCOG, as I refer to all women). I love how you are so passionate about sharing your faith. How important is a shared faith in friendship? Can you be sister-chicks even if you're not both Christians?

Robin: I have only a few close sisterchicks in my life who are not yet believers. We enjoy each other's company, but when we get deeper into our lives and hit those soul spots where we step into the realm of all that is eternal, I watch them get swallowed up in the mystery. The conversations go rather "floaty" at that point, and we inevitably circle back to talking about more familiar, temporal topics like clothes, hair, makeup, and boys. The opportunity to go deeper does not come easily. But again, this is where the opulent gift of time makes space for truth and trust. On we go, watching the friendship open slowly.

Lisa: What's the most important thing one friend can do for another?

Robin: Be there—not always physically, because obviously that's not possible. But there are so many other ways we can show up in a friend's life and truly be there for her in the ups and downs. Isn't that what we all crave in a friendship—someone who cares, not just in word but in actions?

Lisa: They're the best! Now, your own little chicks have flown the coop, heading out toward college and adult life. How has an empty nest affected what you seek in your friendships?

Robin: I miss my daughter a lot, because we are super sisterchicks, and for years we had that luxury of endless time together. I'm sort of cir-cling in closer to the friendships that have been blossoming over the years. My two prayer pals, Cindy and Carrie, and I are closer than ever. We started praying together for our children more than ten years ago. Now that all our kids are out of the house, we still meet every week and pray for them and for our husbands. Each of us understands exactly what the others are feeling regarding our grown children. It's really beautiful, because one of us doesn't have to say much before the other two in our threefold cord begin to nod and we're all in sync. We know how to pray for one another, and we're there for one another all the time via short e-mails that might have only five or six words.

Lisa: Wow. How do you build that kind of friendship?

Robin: The luxury of such intimacy has taken a decade of consistent weekly times together. I do have more time now to spend with friends over leisurely lunches, and I think that's become my new hobby: dining at midday, European style, with long conversations that can't be rushed. Fabulous!

Lisa: Anything else you'd like to tell women who are craving friendship in their lives?

Robin: God told us in Proverbs that to have a friend we must be a friend. It's sort of the Golden Rule of "do unto others as you would have others do unto you." I receive e-mails every now and then from readers who say things like, "I wish I had a sisterchick like the characters in your books. I guess I'm just not good friend material, because I tried to get close to one woman a few years ago and she didn't return the interest; so I stopped trying."

Lisa: Good grief. What do you say to them?

Robin: The obvious counsel to a comment like that is, "Shake off the bad experience and try again." But I know how hard that is. I've experienced "unrequited friendship," and I immediately thought it was about me. I thought I was the one who was all wrong.

Lisa: And now?

Robin: Now I think it goes back to the gift of time. Give the friendship time. If it doesn't come together, then move on. Try pursuing a friendship with someone else. Take it slow. Maybe the two of you won't click at a heart level. That's okay. No shame in that. Try again. Really, I mean, did you get pregnant the very first time you tried? Did you fall in love and marry the first guy you had a crush on? Did you buy the first pair of shoes you tried on the last time you went shopping? If one friendship doesn't grow past the entry level of polite sweetness, don't go into that wicked deep, dark place in your psyche where you torment yourself for not being perfect. I'll tell you a little secret. You're not perfect.

Lisa: What?!?

Robin: No, not even you, Lisa. We're all human. Of course, the woman who's been hurt is afraid of being vulnerable and being hurt again. But please don't hide or let any roots of bitterness grow in your spirit. Bitter roots grow fast, and they choke out all the beautiful, slow-growing buds of friendship. There will be a bud or two that you will connect with, and those will be the ones that just need some time and truth and trust before they begin to blossom.

The Mind at Rest

Peace and Contentment in Your Life

> The woman who knows God intimately is able to face
> life's chaos with assurance, security, strength, and hope
> because her tranquility flows out of the glorious character
> of Almighty God.
>
> BECKY HARLING

P *eace.* Let the word roll around on your tongue. Hear it silently toll in your ears. Does it wash through you with the same note of elusive promise and hope like it does with us?

We hunger for the kind of peace that allows women to sit on their front porch, smiling at neighbors, inviting a child to come sit down for a chat, appreciating the view, obviously satisfied with her life. We hunger for the kind of peace that emanates from people who are healthy, balanced—people who seem to roll with the punches, take what comes, and make the most of it. We hunger for the kind of peace that means we are fully restored. We want to know that there is nothing holding us back from forgiveness, restoration, and salvation in the fullest sense of the words.

Much has been written about the quest for peace, and often it revolves around the need for margin and boundaries. When we get that in order, we become the satisfied woman on the porch, who has time for herself, friends, family, and God. That's doable, and we like doable—something we can control, something we can manage.

Survey Says

Even in the midst of these turbulent times, with terrorist attacks and war, most women in our survey equate peace with that settledness that comes when one's personal life is not in chaos, when there's time to slow down and savor life. Where—or how—do you find peace?

As Christian women, we're after something deeper. We're after the root cause of the *dis*-ease that makes us squirm and sweat and flit about like mad women on a giant whirligig.

To get to that place of margin and satisfaction, we want to know what balanced people we admire have learned. We want to learn from their perspective that God not only desires to see us whole, healthy, and well, but also that he has made a way for us to get there. We want to learn to see life and ourselves from God's perspective. (Okay, that's a tad harder.)

To get hold of God's perspective and find balance, we must shake off our shame, embrace God's forgiveness, and learn to love our lives and ourselves. We must see that we are phenomenal people living phenomenal lives. We can never earn the title of PCOG (Phenomenal Creation of God); we just *are*, because we are *his*. Whenever we fail, wherever we fail, we're still okay—Christ has covered every inch of the miles that we fall short.

When we know Christ's love and his constancy, we find joy, and in that joy, peace. The Bible puts it this way: "Rejoice in the Lord always. I will say it again: Rejoice! Let your gentleness be evident to all. The Lord is near. Do not be anxious about anything, but in everything, by prayer and petition, with thanksgiving, present your requests to God. And the peace of God, which transcends all understanding, will guard your hearts and your minds in Christ Jesus" (Philippians 4:4–7).

We want a big ol' piece of *this* kind of peace, and we hunger for contentment.

BARRIERS TO SATISFACTION

Kathy Boyles, women's ministry director at a large church, gives talks on the subject of peace to the local Mothers of Preschoolers (MOPS) group whenever possible. She calls it her "what if, when, if only" speech. "Women, especially young moms, are always saying things like, 'When my child is potty-trained...,' and, 'If only my baby slept through the night...,' or, 'When he goes to kindergarten...,'" she says. "The thing is, you never get to that perfect place in life where everything comes together. You have to live in the now or you'll regret it later."

It's the same for others. These barriers to satisfied thoughts happen to all of us. College students are waiting for graduation. Graduates are waiting for a job. Employees are waiting for retirement. Singles are waiting to get married. Married people are waiting to have children or waiting for their children to grow up. Empty-nest parents are waiting to have grandchildren. Life, it seems, is always just around the corner.

> Amanda writes: I know that we're supposed to find peace where we are. But I'm thinking that peace comes when your kids are in school and the house in quiet. Right now, I can't imagine having five minutes to myself without someone screaming, "Mommy!"

Rebecca and I tend to use other excuses as well, in particular the "when this is finished..." version. We're always thinking that if we can get through some phase of our business, some project, meet some goal, then it will be time to pull it all together, to live as women of peace. But that day never seems to arrive!

A recent marketing campaign by the MetLife Insurance Company is centered on the "if" in the center of life (L**IF**E). Life is indeed full of ifs, and the ifs can lead to wonderful imaginings and creative paths that direct us in a whole new way. If we don't wonder about the ifs, we tend to lead bland lives. Most novelists I know ask what-if questions to get them going on story lines. The trick is, <u>day to day, not to live more of your life in If Land than you do in the known.</u>

CONTROL AS FACADE: TEMPORARY AT BEST

We women often run our own lives and usually someone else's too. We are generally the central command of any home (and in most offices, whether recognized or not). We are most often the ones who decide on the family's diet, clothing choices, vacations, and social schedules. In my household, I am pretty much responsible for keeping my husband and three children on schedule—to doctor appointments, haircuts, youth group, school events, and practices. Tim will drive, but I'm the one who reminds him where he's taking the kids. Rebecca manages administrative staff. Her brother-in-law will go shop for her sister, but her sister

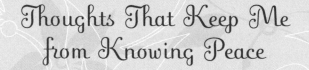

Thoughts That Keep Me from Knowing Peace

Make the phrases below complete sentences by finishing them with the first thing that pops into your head on the subject of lacking peace. Then star or circle the phrases you know are keeping you from knowing peace.

When I...
    have a better career + more money, I'll be happier.
    have more gigs, I'll quit UM
When he...
    is depressed, I am afraid to move myself in a successful direction.

What if...
    I lost my job

says, "It's *my* list!" Sound familiar? Women are used to directing and having people follow their directions.

We think we have it all together. We believe we are effectively steering our course—until something happens that wrests the wheel from our hands. Sailors the world over talk about the ships lost while attempting to round the treacherous Cape Horn at the southern tip of South America. Picture a strong and courageous female sea captain in this dangerous place at the helm in a winter storm. The wind is blowing wildly. The waves are crashing over the side of the ship, threatening to capsize it. The deck hands have all fled below deck. Hair whipping about, rain stinging her cheeks, the captain desperately tries to hold on.

Finally, she realizes she is weakening. Her strength cannot outlast the ferocity of the storm. If she releases the wheel, the ship will capsize with the next gust of wind. And if she doesn't release the wheel, the force of its rotation will throw her

Who will...

✱ take care of everything

How can...

I succeed, learn music, get gigs?

Should I...

✱ be doing more, pushing harder?

Can we...

✱ truly be happier in our careers? make enough $ doing what we love?

Where will...

✱ Josh thrive? What will bring him ultimate joy?

If I...

✱✱ Succeed, Will Josh be ok + not sink into a deeper depression?

to one side. It's a no-win situation. All she can do is leap back and let the ship go where it may—and fall to her knees to pray.

Ever been there? We have.

As much as we plan, organize, and attempt to keep things in order, life is not orderly. No, life is messy and volatile and full of change. There are definite times of calm seas, but the storms always come. You may even be one of the fortunate few who has enjoyed decades of calm seas. Be thankful for that gift, and continue to learn and prepare yourself, should storm clouds suddenly appear.

We cannot control the storms. We cannot control life. We can only lay claim to the peace that Jesus himself modeled for his disciples. Think about the boys in the boat on the Sea of Galilee (see Luke 8:22–25). They are panic-stricken, desperately trying to keep the boat from being swamped, fervently hoping the storm will cease, desperately hoping their leader will wake and tell them what to do.

What happens when they wake him? "Where is your faith?" he asks in exasperation.

Even when it appears God is sleeping through your storm, he is not. He is present, sitting in one of the most vulnerable parts of the ship, wanting you to trust him. With him in the boat, will it sink? Are you likely to capsize? If you capsize, who will haul you onto a floating barrel? It is an exercise for sure—mental, emotional, spiritual, almost a physical act—to so wholly trust in Jesus that we remain faithful, even in the storm. Rebecca and I have had weeks, months, and years so stressful that we prayed several times a day. Instead of worrying, pray. Turn your concerns over to Jesus as often as they come to mind. This is an exercise that leads to peace. Try it next time you're stewing over something. If you're not getting anywhere, "get it" to God.

HAND IT OVER TO GOD

Praying can be simple and fast—what a friend of ours calls "arrow prayers." To follow are some starters for you. Pick one and finish it with something you are struggling with right now. Don't write a paragraph, just a sentence or two will do. Get right to the point, and remember this is as easy as one-two: (1) state your case, and (2) ask for help. Eloquent or elementary, just lay on the line your thoughts and feelings. Talk to God!

Lord, I hate it that…

I put us in debt by being careless early on. Please help me release this guilt + find ways to spend wisely + pay our debts quickly.

Father, I am stressed over…

money, not suceeding, not knowing how to what is best for Josh.

Jesus, I am worried that…

I will never "make it," that I will fail +/or disapoint.

Christ, I need your help in…

budgeting, finding + releasing, to bu, focus + drive, determination + goals! following through

God, I can't do…

Commuting + UM ~ I'm sabotaging myself. Please Help.

Creator, I am lost. Show me…

how to help my husband be happy + find his ultimate dream.

Shepherd, help me let this go…

needing to please everybody + not staying true to myself.

Savior, rescue me from…

debt, fear + guilt.

When life gets scary, scoot on over toward God!

Lavita writes: When I was diagnosed with cancer and had to have a hysterectomy, everyone around me was worried. I felt that peace you read about in the Bible—the peace that passes all understanding. It was unexplainable. I felt loved, accepted. I knew I would be okay.

Yes, that's what we're after: peace, even in the midst of a terrifying storm.

Barbara Blankinship discovered this, too, during her storms. Barbara had four children in four years, and the last two were twins. When the twins were only a year old, an eye disease that had briefly visited her before came back with a vengeance, rendering her temporarily legally blind. Think on that for a minute! Barbara had four children under four years of age, and she found herself suddenly *blind*. Friends say that through it all she was the picture of serenity and calm. But Barbara has a different view.

"I was an independent woman, used to doing things for myself," she remembers. "And then I could not do anything on my own, from getting a haircut to buying a bra. I had to be totally dependent on others." But she found solace in her Lord. "I believe he allowed my illness so that all I could literally see was Jesus. I might not have seen him any other way, since I was not raised a Christian. But that time was a time of forced stillness for me—even in the midst of handling four children under four—when I could do nothing without sight. Instead, I learned to listen. I began to understand what it meant to be in communication with God, and it was then I learned about true peace. I learned that God could see me through everything—from dishes to diapering. Even blind."

I asked her in our interview if it ever happened again.

"It only came back again once," she said, "when the children were still young. But never since then. I know it could return any day, but I cannot live in the fear of the what-if. Doubt is always the shadow side of faith, but faith lives in the light. Living in fear of tomorrow diminishes the joy and peace of today. And sometimes the hard things in life are the best gifts. I wouldn't have ever chosen this path, but I'm so grateful. Those hard times were the making of my spiritual walk and my character."

Barbara credits Scripture, prayer, and actively setting time to *really* listen to God as factors for keeping peace in the midst of the storm. "That and marvelous Christian sisters and brothers who hold you accountable, love you, and guide you. My daughter Christina and I are best friends. She is such a support to me—and it's been my privilege to mentor her."

That mentorship has proven vital for Christina Harrell, Barbara's daughter. Just a few months after getting married, she was diagnosed with rheumatoid arthritis. "I was relieved on one front to know why I was so tired all the time," she says. "But then as I researched on the Internet, I began to get scared…really scared. I was scared I'd never lead an athletic, independent lifestyle again, scared about my ability to have children and care for them—I was worried that many of my dreams would have to change.

"My biggest mistake was not inviting God to the discussion from the start. I wanted to handle it on my own, and because of that, I did not hear from him like my mom did when she was blind. Gradually, my mother and my Christian sisters became like a mirror held up to my face—showing me that this was a really tough diagnosis, that it was okay to be sad, okay to grieve, okay to show weakness. And my mom, knowing she went through tragedy but didn't drag me through it too as a child, helped me keep my perspective. She asked me, 'Is this the worst thing that could happen to you? Well then, be thankful.'

"Sometimes it made me mad, because I wanted to be sad, but then it helped me to stand up again and deal with it. I took my cues from my mother, on how she lived out every day, did what had to be done, and focused on what was good rather than what was bad. This illness, in tandem with my mother and God, taught me the meaning of perseverance."

Illness and other hardships can hammer home what peace really looks like.

> Jacki writes: My sister was diagnosed with brain cancer, and my husband and I gave up a very lucrative business in order to care for her 24/7 until her death. I do not regret any of it. I went to help her and came away being helped and making lifelong changes. I was peaceful because I relied only on God to carry me through. I didn't know if she would live or die, but I knew that whatever happened was his plan for her, and so I accepted it as sovereign and didn't question it ever and still don't, although I miss her very much. God is always doing what is best for all of us. It taught me to trust in him who created us and not rely on my own understanding of things.

PEACE IN THE WHAT-IS

Jan Silvious, speaker and author of *Look at It This Way* teaches that "life is what it is. What might have been doesn't exist, so don't even go there."[1] This has been the single most important lesson to us over the last few years—to accept what is in our lives and not worry about what isn't. In caring for our families, leading in ministry, existing in relationships, life is full of longings for something different, something better and—we think—something easier. In accepting what is, rather than giving in to those longings, we find peace.

When you start to think about what might have been, the only healthy, life-giving response is to tell yourself, "This is a fantasy. It's a waste of time to think about it.... I need to move on."... Longing for what might have been is one of the most nonproductive, futile ways we can spend our time. Regret never changes what is.[2]

JAN SILVIOUS

To learn to think this way is a daily, sometimes hourly, process and discipline. Our vision gets so clouded. We stutter and stumble in trying to name what is good in our lives. We fall into longing for the *what-might-have-been*, playing it out in our minds like a movie reel. When we get to such a place, it's time to back up and focus on the *what-is*. We can't emphasize enough how this practice has helped us deal with enormous stress and strain! Concentrating on the what-is helps us see what is right, what is good, and what we can celebrate now. Remember how that Philippians verse at the beginning of this chapter began? "Rejoice!" It even bears repeating from Paul, a man who knew his share of heartache and struggle. Read it again: "Rejoice in the Lord always. I will say it again: Rejoice!" (Philippians 4:4). The more we strive to follow this command, the more often peace reigns in our hearts.

ATTITUDE OF GRATITUDE

"The inner righteousness we seek is not something that is poured on our heads," writes Richard Foster in his book *Celebration of Discipline*.[3]

You might have caught the notion that part of the magic formula in concentrating on the what-is has to do with being *thankful* for what is (and then rejoicing over it). Gratitude brings us back to center, back to the *what is*. It takes us out of fantasy and wishful thinking to a place of reality that reminds us of all that is right in our lives—even when we feel so much is wrong. Practicing this helps us prepare for days when life throws us the bigger curves—a phrase that is interesting. "When life throws you a curve…" is an analogy born of baseball. If you're at the plate, trying to make it to first or third or even home, what do you have to do? Hear the words of your coach in your ear: "Keep your eye on the ball. Remember all you've learned. Check your stance. Calm down. Concentrate. You can do this!"

> *Knowing that God loves*
> *me unconditionally has freed me*
> *from trying to live the Christian life by*
> *being perfect and trying to earn His love*
> *by performing. My understanding of*
> *God's constancy in His love encourages*
> *me to return His love by living a life*
> *which would bring honor to Him. I*
> *want to become a woman of excellence*
> *not because I have to perform, but*
> *because I choose to please God.*[4]
> CYNTHIA HEALD

If the pitcher throws you a curve ball, what do you think? *Can't get it past the infield! Other team's too tough! Go for the bunt! Outsmart 'em!* If you freak out, you'll be lucky to hit foul ball after foul ball or worse—strike out. How does a ballplayer learn how to hit a curve ball? She has to keep adjusting her stance and practicing her swing, remembering all that is good and right and true, remembering all she's learned already, all that has prepared her for this moment. She thinks about what this moment can teach her now, preparing her to be stronger, better at the game in the future.

By continuing to try and try and try until she connects bat to ball, she eventually sends it flying. She'll watch replay tapes to see what she did wrong in the last game, but she won't spend time berating herself for the mistakes she made. The best ballplayers are always looking for ways they can change what they're doing now, so they'll be better the next time.

The best ballplayers accept what was and what is, and they look forward to what will be. They're glad to be in the game, glad to be able to do what they love, glad for the opportunity to improve. Getting better at the game of life, too, is what brings us growth and makes us mature. Simply getting the chance to learn and experience

Thankful for What Is!

Do you have trouble practicing what *is*? Begin here! Use this as a prayer, adding some of your own thoughts on the facing page.

I'm thankful for…

⊙ *a bed with clean sheets.*

⊙ *warm water in my shower.*

⊙ *clothes (no matter how old or new).*

⊙ *a roof over my head.*

⊙ *a family (even if they're driving me crazy).*

⊙ *food in the fridge (or in lean months, for canned goods).*

⊙ *a car (even though it's not running right).*

⊙ *a job (even if it's not perfect).*

⊙ *friends to call or who call.*

⊙ *the opportunity to worship.*

⊙ *the ability to speak.*

⊙ *the ability to hear.*

⊙ *songs on the radio.*

something new is a reason for thanks. "Be joyful always; pray continually; give thanks in all circumstances, for this is God's will for you in Christ Jesus," says 1 Thessalonians 5:16–18. In everything? In illness, in strife, in pain, and in struggle, give God your heartfelt thanks. Gratitude is a choice.

My own thoughts of gratitude...

my cats (even if they add work all the time)
working appliances
lotion for my body
my parents
my voice
Martha
Betty Anne
my husband
anti-depressants for my husband
Sabina + Jonathan
my kitchen
my cell phone + internet
the energy to exercise
my health
our neighbors

In her excellent book *Basket of Blessings,* Karen O'Connor tells this story:

We must choose gratitude. Actor and comedian Bill Cosby exemplified this in a touching way at the graveside of his son, Ennis, murdered in January 1997. "We now want to give praise to God for allowing us to know him," he said, "not for giving him to us, but just for letting us know him."…

Cosby could have been enraged, silent or distant…. But Cosby chose, instead, to set his mind on a "higher thing"—on gratitude—to recognize that Ennis had been a gift, not a possession, not something he earned or deserved. And so he gave thanks. Will you?[5]

Choosing to give thanks in all things—in the midst of a cancer diagnosis, a divorce, a career change—signifies *trust,* the third hallmark of peace that follows joy and gratefulness. Romans 15:13 beams these words toward us in the dark: "May the God of hope fill you with all joy and peace as you trust in him, so that you may overflow with hope by the power of the Holy Spirit."

Ask God what he wants you to learn in the middle of your storms, and then listen for his answer. Sometimes it takes hours, days, months, or even years to hear it. But he is speaking. Are you listening?

PERFECTION OR EXCELLENCE?

My friend Kathy Boyles says, "There's a difference between seeking excellence and seeking perfection. Excellence is doing your best. Perfection is seeking to control something that cannot be controlled, or attempting to reach something unattainable."

This closely relates to accepting what is, rather than what isn't.

In an era of Martha Stewart–homemaking standards (never mind her stint in jail or staff of hundreds), magazine-model bodies, luxury vehicles, McMansions in suburbia, television channels dedicated to decorating or gardening, everywhere we look, there's something that calls us to work toward perfection and to wish for more. But God does not call us to perfection. He calls us to excellence.

The danger of the pursuit of perfection is that perfection is unattainable. You may be seen as the perfect golfer or cook or leader, but we all know the truth, don't we? While others may see you as perfect at something, you'd be unlikely to agree. On the inside, we see all the ways we fall short of the goal. What we project is partly illusion, at best. No one is perfect, at anything. Tiger Woods is perhaps the best golf player to date, but could he be even better? Certainly. Rachael Ray is adorable and a terrific chef, but is she perfect? Nah. Beth Moore is a fabulous Bible teacher. Could she be even more? Undoubtedly.

What we ought to admire is not how perfect these people are, but rather how they've pursued excellence, how they're living out who God created them to be (at least, in some measure). This is our calling as Christians—to be as excellent as possible, in all we do. As women of faith, our primary goal is to pursue excellence in faith. We learn to live out our beliefs, day in and day out. We learn to believe God—to take him at his word. And his Word says we are his, that he is our Creator. He has chosen to dwell within us!

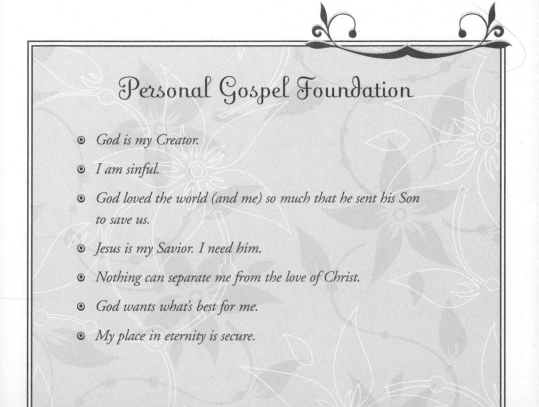

Personal Gospel Foundation

- ⦿ *God is my Creator.*
- ⦿ *I am sinful.*
- ⦿ *God loved the world (and me) so much that he sent his Son to save us.*
- ⦿ *Jesus is my Savior. I need him.*
- ⦿ *Nothing can separate me from the love of Christ.*
- ⦿ *God wants what's best for me.*
- ⦿ *My place in eternity is secure.*

UNDERSTAND GOD'S DESIRE

God loves you. God adores you. Even if you were the only woman on earth, Jesus would have died for you. He would have died only for you. Nothing you can do, will do, or could do will ever win his heart, because you have already won his heart.

This is the awe-inspiring, jaw-dropping, overwhelming message of grace: you've been claimed. No matter what you've done, where you've been, no matter how you think you have disappointed him, all God sees in you is your potential. Nothing you will do or have done will ever separate you from him. You are forgiven, free. God thinks you are fabulous. God knows you are phenomenal!

Pit Thoughts Versus His Thoughts

My life is out of control. I'm afraid.
God is in control and can give me peace and courage right now (John 14:27).

I'm worried about tomorrow.
My focus is on today—tomorrow is in God's hands (Matthew 6:34).

I can't do it.
I can do it, one step at a time (Hebrews 12:1).

I'm stressed, and there's no end in sight!
God can bring me peace in any circumstance (Philippians 4:6–7).

God has become silent.
God is speaking to me; I want to learn how to hear (Matthew 11:14–15).

Do we deserve such devotion? Absolutely not. This is the wonder of grace. By Christ's wounds, we are healed (see 1 Peter 2:24). By Christ's love, we can become all he created us to be. If we could hold up a full-length mirror that showed how we look in God's eyes, it would not just show the body we'll have in heaven, but it would also show our spirit—a heart shining in peace, joy, faith, fulfillment, and holy understanding.

HOW GOD SATISFIES

The offer is there, like a shiny gold ring in God's palm. "Go on," he seems to say. "Reach for it. Take it. I've paid for it. It's yours. Free." God wants us to be at peace, trusting him and waiting on him. He envisions for us to live in intimate relationship with him, full of contentment and fulfillment. To get into intimate relationship with him, we must understand that we are so thoroughly loved, so completely sought after, and constantly watched over by God that we cannot escape or lose him. There's nothing we have to do to earn it. It's the supreme *What Is* of them all!

Returning to the basics is the key for each of us; if we learn to rely on the core of the Word as the basis for how we live and view the world, everything else is easier to maneuver through. When we are strong within and strong in our knowledge of who God is and how much he loves us, we maintain our balance when the world tilts. When we find balance and rely on our foundation—returning to it again and again—we become women who embody peace.

Here's the paradox: sometimes the more we attempt to find margins in our lives—whether that means balance, time, contentment, satisfaction, or peace within ourselves—the more anxious we become. We cannot create holy contentment within us; we can only center on God's contentment already within us. It's been there all along! Author Becky Harling writes,

> God never fails, never changes, never grows weary, and never quits.
> When we trust in His character and abilities, we can rest because He is
> ever-present and everything we need. Change doesn't seem as daunting.
> Difficulties don't seem so monumental. Disappointments hurt but don't
> diffuse all hope.[6]

Focusing on God's presence and refusing to give in to panic… Talking to God about our problems, big or small… Becoming thankful for the what-is, even in the midst of saying good-bye to the what-might-have-been… Trusting and hoping in the God of light, even in the darkness…

If these phrases can describe us and our lives, we move closer to rest. We move closer to peace. We move closer to soul satisfaction.

Now may the Lord of peace himself
give you peace at all times and in every way.
The Lord be with all of you.
2 Thessalonians 3:16

The Hope at Life's Twists

A Chat with Carol Kent About the Peace You Crave

With one phone call in October 1999, Carol Kent's life changed forever, and her quest began for that peace that passes understanding (see Philippians 4:6–7).

The call was about her only son, then a twenty-five-year-old graduate of the U.S. Naval Academy and a lieutenant in the Navy with an impeccable military record. Carol and her husband were told that this dear child, the pride of their lives—an admired young husband and father of two girls by all who knew him—was now in jail on charges of first-degree murder. Several witnesses had seen him shoot and kill his wife's ex-husband.

How does one ever find peace after such heartbreak?

Here, Carol, a best-selling author *(When I Lay My Isaac Down, Becoming a Woman of Influence,* and her latest book, *A New Kind of Normal)* and founder-director of the national speakers' bureau, Speak Up with Confidence, talks about that. Perfect peace like Christ's can be yours, she says, even when your world's gone mad.

Lisa: You've suffered unspeakable tragedy in watching your only son sent to prison with a life sentence. Before you tell us about finding peace, tell us a little about the storm.

Carol: Many people have read about our journey with our son in my book *When I Lay My Isaac Down.* I'm the mother of an only child, Jason, and he was a joy to raise—president of the National Honor Society in high school, very focused and disciplined. He graduated from the U.S. Naval Academy in 1997, and my husband and I were looking forward to seeing our young son thrive.

On the day of his marriage to a previously married woman with two children, we became both in-laws and grandparents—and we loved being both. The next year became a whirlwind of activity as our son was involved in various training schools with the navy. But there was a matter that was bringing our son a lack of peace—multiple allegations of abuse against his wife's first husband who was trying to get unsupervised visitation with Jason's stepchildren. When our son felt his legal options for keeping supervision intact had run out, he did the unthinkable.

We received a middle-of-the-night call telling us our son had been arrested for the murder of his wife's first husband. The case was complicated, and while we were anticipating a trial for first-degree murder, the father, stepmother, and sister of the deceased were planning a funeral. The grief on both sides was palpable.

After two and a half years and seven postponements of his trial, our son was eventually convicted of first-degree murder and sentenced to life without the possibility of parole. He was twenty-five years old at the time of his crime. I went from walking around in a stupor to struggling with depression to finally realizing that I could never find peace on my own.

Lisa: What can anyone dealing with such heartbreak do?

Carol: In the middle of a tragedy, we are often crying too hard to read the Bible, so my peace arrived through concentrating on Scripture I'd memorized before the crisis. These verses from John 14:26–27 brought me enough peace to keep breathing: "The Counselor, the Holy Spirit, whom the Father will send in my name, will teach you all things and will remind you of everything I have said to you. Peace I leave with you; my peace I give you. I do not give to you as the world gives. Do not let your hearts be troubled and do not be afraid."

Another great source of peace came from people who reached out with tangible love and support. Three friends started a monthly e-mail update that listed ways people could pray for us and meet our specific, immediate needs. We soon knew we were not alone, and as frightening as our experience was, we felt surrounded by people who loved us and cared enough to walk this unlikely path with us. Some of those friends who brought the peace of Jesus to us were my funny friends, people who realized that even though I forgot how to laugh out loud for a while, I still needed humor in my life to survive. They sent me hilarious cards, silly gifts, and they surprised me with their presence when I wasn't expecting company. God used these friends to bring peace in the middle of the storm.

Lisa: What a reminder that we need to laugh in the storm, and what an encouragement that peace in the storm can be ours!

Carol: At the beginning of our crisis, living in a state of peace for even one minute at a time was a major accomplishment! What I've learned since is that too many of us, most Christian women, in fact, expect too much of ourselves.

Lisa: What do you mean?

Carol: In many ways peace and relinquishment go together. As long as we maintain control by trying to fix everything that goes wrong, we live in a constant state of turmoil. I grew up as the firstborn of six preacher's kids, so I was used to being in charge of my younger siblings, and I was good at anticipating problems and doing what was necessary to restore order and stability to a wide variety of situations. Going through this storm, though, I needed to learn that peace is not a permanent state, because we live in a fallen world where bad things happen to good people. I learned I have to pray multiple times a day—*Lord, please restore peace to my heart and to this situation*—not once a year or once a month or once a day.

Now I encourage women to have that prayer on their hearts at all times: *Lord, restore peace to my heart and to this situation.* The greatest benefit to requesting God's peace so often is that we have an ongoing dialogue with him as we live through each day.

Lisa: What do you think is the greatest barrier to peace?

Carol: Several sources—preoccupied husbands, uncooperative children, demanding jobs, irritable people, unexpected interruptions, relational conflicts, threats of terrorism, fears for the future, financial challenges, comparing ourselves with other women, fatigue, time control, obsessing about our weight, global unrest…the list goes on and on! We are by nature multitaskers, so we can juggle many of the aforementioned barriers to peace all at once. So in many ways, the easier question is: What isn't a barrier to peace for Christian women?

Lisa: [laughing] That's the point, isn't it? Living through the storms sure to come into *every* life.

Carol: Yes. That's why it's important to start with a definition of peace.

Lisa: Define it for us.

Carol: Definitely peace is a state of tranquility that stems from harmony in our relationships. But while many people think of peace as an absence of conflict, it's so much more. At a deeper level, it's freedom from disquieting or oppressive thoughts or emotions. As women we have an amazing ability to imagine a worst-case scenario for someone we love. If a family member is an hour late for dinner, we know they're probably wrapped around a tree following an automobile accident and they won't be coming home—ever! When they finally show up, long after the expected time, we're a little upset about that too, because we've wasted so much time planning their memorial service.

Lisa: Oh yeah. Been there.

Carol: See, fear is opposite of peace. We have phobic fears when our perception of the danger (for us or for our children) is much greater than the actual danger. We're afraid of losing control and revealing who we really are because inside our hearts we want people to like us and respect us. We're afraid of rejection and facing our past mistakes.

Lisa: What's the "new kind of normal" you're talking about these days?

Carol: That's actually the title of my latest book. *A New Kind of Normal* is all about making hope-filled choices when life doesn't turn out the way we planned—what's positive and moves us a step ahead in the middle of our "new normal."

Lisa: And this is something we all experience?

Carol: I get letters from women every day who have a need for peace, because their child was born with a disability, or they've been diagnosed with a serious illness, or they've lost a spouse or a child to death, or they've faced negative circumstances that they never could have anticipated. I like to remind myself and others: as Jesus brings peace to our lives, we're able to face these challenges with a better attitude and with a quiet confidence, knowing that the last chapter of our lives isn't written yet. When we embrace the unconditional love of our Father, we experience peace in the middle of the chaos—and peace changes everything. As we experience the peace that passes understanding, something surprising happens. We start providing encouragement, hands-on help, and genuine compassion when others are in need. The surprising result is that our own hearts are in turn flooded with genuine peace and joy.

Lisa: And that's a tangible thing?

Carol: Absolutely. You can see it, experience it—and pass it on. For me, it shows up this way: sometimes I write out prayers for friends and e-mail them to women I know who are struggling. I especially like to help women internalize the truth of a passage my mother asked me to memorize from The Living Bible when I was a teenager: "Don't worry about anything; instead, pray about everything; tell God your needs and don't forget to thank him for his answers. If you do this you will experience God's peace, which is far more wonderful than the human mind can understand. His peace will keep your thoughts and your hearts quiet and at rest as you trust in Christ Jesus" [Philippians 4:6–7]. And that's a formula for finding peace that always works!

The Path to Freedom

Your Financial Health

You can't take it with you—but you *can* send it on ahead.
RANDY ALCORN

When Rebecca and I started our business, Good Books & Company, we had visions of making an impact for eternity by spreading the good news through great Christian books, and, to be honest, we hoped for financial success. We thought we'd have more than enough and were ready to be generous to those in need, giving creatively. (I'd be a terrific rich person, I promise!)

These days, after pouring in savings, credit dollars, our 401(k)s and Roths—and then closing the company—all we're praying for now is financial peace.

What Rebecca learned long ago, and what has become particularly clear to me this last year, is that debt is bondage. It leads to things that aren't good for any of us: stress, doubt, fear. After building an impressive amount of credit-card debt, building a business, and taking a writing hiatus (no books = no income), things got rough. In fact, they got so rough that my husband and I had to cut up our credit cards and enter an agreement with a credit-counseling service in order to stop the pain (and the harassing phone calls).

Thankfully, in a few years, all our credit-card debts will be paid. It will take a few years beyond that to resolve all the business debt. Rebecca and I are each praying for wisdom—and for solid decisions that will get our financial feet on a firm path. We want to pay off all our debt and move onward. Our prayer is no longer for fabulous success (with a closet hope of wealth), but rather financial health. Tim and I want to find balance and peace in this realm of our life again.

Survey Says

More than any other area in our survey, a dividing line between women of different ages and stages showed up in desires for financial health. Also, those who face financial hardship rate financial security much higher as a priority than those who feel financially healthy—and the absence of financial peace is felt more acutely than its presence.

Perhaps you're on the opposite side of the financial spectrum, with a wealth of secure holdings. Are you trying to figure out how much to set aside for security and how much to give away? Perhaps you're listening to creditors' calls from morning until night. Or perhaps you're somewhere in between? What we want you to hear from us is that we know your concerns, because we've lived them. And so have others...

Jackie writes: We're self-employed and never know when the next check is coming. Today it's been three months since the last check, and I'm down to what's in the freezer to feed my family. I'm scared. When we have money, it's like a high for me. I have to fight the desire to spend it all. When we don't, it's like a torture chamber. I want it to change. I can't stay on this roller coaster and be the woman of God I want to be. It changes who I am, how I act.

Ellen writes: I'm not struggling with finances right now. But I've had some years in my life where I have and then found a way to get out of that situation by working hard, being financially disciplined, and doing things differently than most people. It worked, and I haven't had financial struggles for more than fifteen years.

Jordan writes: I am a compulsive spender and by nature pretty selfish. If I see something I want, I get it, even if it means that a bill may not get paid. My husband is the sole breadwinner, and I have made a commitment to the Lord and my accountability partner to get help to overcome this stronghold and to give back to God what's his all along. It's a small step, but it's a start.

Vivian writes: I know that our choices to put things on our credit card and borrow have led us to the position we are in now. It's a nightmare to repay with interest, and it's stressful to feel like we are constantly digging out. I look back and see that we were irresponsible. I know God doesn't want us to be unhappy or stressful, and he is truly all we need in this life. Every commercial would tell us differently, feeding our more, more, more thoughts. I have to constantly remind myself that God is More and that he is what I need to be truly happy.

These women expressed interesting points of view and used telling words in sharing with us:

- ◉ a high
- ◉ torture chamber
- ◉ discipline
- ◉ struggles
- ◉ compulsive
- ◉ selfish
- ◉ commitment
- ◉ irresponsible
- ◉ stressful

These are emotive words that deal with the *why* of finances more than the *how*. We're not financial experts by any means (for help, though, see the "Additional Resources" section in the back of the book). But we understand your concerns over provision, debt, and giving. We know your heart, because we've walked in your shoes in both good times and bad. We know how it changes your conversations and your responses to family and friends. We know that not knowing how you're going to pay the bills will hang over your head like the rain cloud over Linus in *Peanuts*.

If you're like us, deep down you want to get your head and heart straight about money and keep it straight. You want to know why you spend the way you do and why you should spend the way God tells you to.

So what do we *really* crave that we think money will provide? Most women hunger for security, and that drives them to either spend or hoard. Most of us would define financial security as this: enough to give freely, six months of living expenses saved for a rainy day, no credit-card debt, and a cash account to be used for unexpected expenses (that we build up again after we're forced to use it). That said, there is only so much security that money can buy.

In the same way that we know how to take off weight and keep it off (think calories = dollars), we also know the way to financial freedom. It's not rocket science. It's common sense—and the Kingdom Advisors (formerly the Christian Financial Professionals Network) can help us with five principles of financial security:

1. Spend less than you earn (Proverbs 13:11). Dishonest $ dwindles away, but he who gathers $ little by little, makes it grow.
2. Avoid the use of debt (Proverbs 22:7). The rich rule over the poor, + the borrower is servant to the lender.
3. Build liquidity (Proverbs 6:6–8). Ant → wise ways - no commander or ruler, yet it stores its provisions in summer + gathers its food at harvest.
4. Set long-term goals (Philippians 3:14). I press on toward the goal to win the prize for which God has called me heavenward in Christ Jesus.
5. Believe that God owns it all (Psalm 24:1). [1] The Earth is the Lord's, + everything in it, the world, + all who live in it

How Can You Spend Less Than You Earn?

Budgets: I call this the *B*-word. *B* also is the starting letter for behemoth, belch, and barf. (Rebecca is cringing right now; those are crass words in her southern upbringing.) Tim and I never did a budget until we went to see a financial planner to see how our gobs of money seemed to vanish into thin air. Then we saw.

Like most of our survey respondents, Tim and I are not extravagant spenders. We clothe our children mostly at Target. We live in a middle-class, cookie-cutter suburban neighborhood. We drive two cars, one that's paid off, and one that we pay for monthly. We keep our thermostat set at sixty-five degrees and tell the kids to wear a sweater when they're cold. We don't have air conditioning. Most of our vacations are to see family in lovely settings like Montana, Washington, California, or Arizona.

Not so crazy, right? Our biggest financial problem is a mental one. To be honest, I'm the financial mental case. Tim and I are dually deadly—we're both entrepreneurial. Because of that, we always have a potential windfall around the corner—a fat royalty check, a new contract, a big sculpture deal. Somehow the money is always spent before we get it. Our income is not static, so it's either feast or famine in our household. But we're both positive-thinking dreamers, so we always think *feast* when we think of next week. And since feast is right around the corner, why not spend what we have now, right? Alene finds herself in a somewhat similar position:

> I'm what people would classify as a "life gambler." I am overly optimistic and always know that things will work out, and they always have, but I have a tendency to spend money on things that I just think will pan out. Most of them do. Some would classify that as struggling—I classify it as life!

The discipline of budgeting and saving keeps a person out of this terrible cycle of spending and then wondering how to pay the bills. Spending more than we earn is a form of gambling—something we all want to avoid. To be frank, Tim and I really had no discipline at all in this regard. Cutting up our credit cards was merely the first step on the road to getting out of the crazy cycle. As hard as it is, and even though I don't know how I'll pay what I currently owe, I am a much happier woman knowing that things are not getting *worse*.

The point is to stop the downward spiral. Do it now. Do it wherever you are. Figure out why you're in a less-than-healthy place financially. Spend some time on it, and pray about it. Most of the financial experts say that our finances really begin with how we see money—what we think money will buy us. For me, my principal *whys,* on the personal side of spending, are control and instant gratification.

If you're one of our financially healthy sisters, still spend a little time discovering why you are financially healthy and why you want to stay there. Whatever your situation, draw the line in the sand and say, "I want health. I want peace. I want financial security. I want to know I can live on what I can earn. I want to live within the means that God himself has given me." Make a budget and start saving, and if it's not on the budget, learn to say "no" or "later."

How Can You Steer Clear of the Debt Trap?

It's a charming campaign, really: the major credit-card company advertising something on the order of: "Soccer shoes: $70. League dues: $150. Travel to the state tournament: $500. Time with your son after the losing game: Priceless."

It pulls at the heartstrings, doesn't it? But what is it telling us? Think about it for a second. My immediate thought is, *It doesn't matter what it costs. It's worth it.* But the true underlying message is this: Memories are all that matters. If you love someone, you'll spend money on him whether you have it or not.

This is a dangerous message, a very dangerous message.

It wasn't until Rebecca and I began writing this chapter that we even thought about that hidden message, because messages like that are abundant in our culture.

The Treasure Principle

You can't take it with you—but you *can* send it on ahead with these six keys from Randy Alcorn's book *The Treasure Principle:*

1. *God owns everything. I'm His money manager.*

2. *My heart always goes where I put God's money.*

3. *Heaven, not earth, is my home.*

4. *I should live not for the dot but for the line.*

5. *Giving is the only antidote to materialism.*

6. *God prospers me not to raise my standard of living, but to raise my standard of giving.*[2]

We are what we spend, whether it's on the right school for our kids, the right home in the right neighborhood, the right car, clothes, purse, shoes, trip, league for the kids' sports, charities, or toys. How we spend defines us, doesn't it?

Do you experience peer pressure? How about a top-of-the-line car with six air bags? If you love your family, you want to spend the money to protect them, right? Or what about living in the right neighborhood with the best schools? You don't want your child to be shortchanged, do you? How about that spendy Christian school? You want your child exposed to only the finest aspects of our culture and faith, right?

Everywhere we look, we feel the pressure to spend money. All right, we hear you; in actuality, we feel the call to *spend* it because it makes us feel good. If I go into a store today and spend one hundred dollars, I feel a temporary rush, an instant gratification in fulfilling a need or desire. I come home with something bright, shiny, and new. Then later I feel guilt and worry as I wonder if it was foolish. *Was I simply being greedy, a simpleton mastered by her desires?* That guilt is probably God nibbling at my toes, saying, *Remember. This is uncomfortable for a reason. I'm trying to talk to you. You know what you're supposed to do. Why don't you do it, Lisa?*

We need to live within our means and deal with our cravings for achievement, freedom, respect, power, security, and happiness in other ways besides accruing debt. Did you know that the average American consumer will spend twice their credit-card balances by paying the minimum payment on a credit card with a 17 percent interest rate? Did you know that if you fall behind on one bank's card, or even miss a payment by a few days, the bank can raise your rate, and other banks then have the right to raise their rates on your balances as well? It's a tightrope you're walking!

Mary Hunt outlines her Rapid Debt-Repayment Plan in her great book *Debt-Proof Your Marriage.* When referring to debt, we're speaking mostly of unsecured debt like credit-card debt. Here are Hunt's rules:

- Rule 1: No more new debt. If you're unwilling to subscribe to this rule, you could be on a downward spiral. Reflect and pray over this.
- Rule 2: Pay the same amount every month until all your unsecured debts (credit cards) are paid.

- ◉ Rule 3: Arrange your debts so that the one with the shortest payoff time is at the top and the longest payoff at the bottom.
- ◉ Rule 4: As one debt is paid, take that payment and redirect it to the regular payment of the next debt in line.[3]

Tim and I had to go the credit-counseling route, but you can do the same thing by following Hunt's rules and cutting up all your credit cards. You'll rebuild your credit score at the same time you're getting out of debt.

HOW YOU CAN BUILD
A SAFETY NET?

Just before Tim and I headed to Montana for our annual vacation with my folks at their lake home last summer, the air conditioning in our car went kaput. (This is our "new" car, the one-hundred-thousand-mile Sequoia that we still pay on monthly.) The estimate for fixing the air conditioning was three thousand dollars, but given that we could feed our family for months on that amount, we elected to pass on fixing it.

Did I mention the midday temperature was ninety-eight degrees? And that our intent was to make the eighteen-hour trek in one day?

My ingenious hubby hopped online, convinced he could come up with a temporary solution. He found an old-fashioned system of air blowing across ice to create rudimentary refrigeration (read: cold air). He promptly bought a picnic cooler and a ten-dollar fan, then cut a rectangle in a wood slab and fit it on top of the cooler. He loaded five dollars worth of ice into the cooler, plugged the fan into our retrofitted cigarette lighter, and voilà—a meager amount of cool air resulted that helped Tim only a smidge (and didn't help our sweltering kids in the back at all).

The point is this: without liquidity offering access to handle life's emergencies (or the need for a car air conditioner), life is bound to get uncomfortable. With some cash at your fingertips, to be used only when necessary, one would never have to fret (or sweat) again.

Mary Hunt suggests establishing a Freedom Account that's part of her 80-10-10 Plan (80 percent to living expenses, 10 percent to giving, 10 percent to this

Freedom Account). This is a fund to be used to fix that air conditioning, replace the hot-water heater, pay an unexpected medical bill, or buy the kids' winter coats—household cash-flow issues that typically force most of us to use credit cards. At first the Freedom Account begins as a contingency fund to help us stop our descent-into-debt spiral, then grows to feed several dream accounts, then pays off the rest of revolving debt, and finally funds an investment portfolio. Financial expert Dave Ramsey recommends something similar. He says the first thing you do toward becoming debt free is to set aside one thousand dollars for these types of needs. Take a step back, and it begins to make sense. Talk about power! Respect! Achievement! Freedom!

WHAT ARE YOUR LONG-TERM GOALS?

Kay Arthur once said to Rebecca, "There is no retirement in times of war."

Don't you love that concept? My husband is also a firm believer in planning for nonretirement—to work until you can work no longer. He feels that our society's concept of the golden years is all wet, creating a false sense of entitlement for an unending vacation just because you've worked for forty years. But there are physical limitations in the elder years, and it may be tough to serve God, whether it be at McDonald's or on the mission field.

We don't want to worry, so one of our long-term goals is to be debt free. Another is to rebuild our retirement savings.

Long-term goals are particularly difficult to embrace when you're young and healthy. You can't imagine your life without health and a chance to work. Tim is a wood sculptor, and at age forty-two his back and wrists are showing signs of wear and tear. We have to be thinking more about the future. *Where is he going with his business? How can we spin his business in ways that don't entail his actually laying chisel to wood? How will that impact our finances?* These things are the reality of our lives. We don't want to hit our sixties and wonder what we're going to do to survive financially. We agree with Kay Arthur that life and mission don't end until we're sitting with Jesus in heaven, but there are some particulars you can prepare for.

Hunt advocates that you create subaccounts in a Freedom Account dedicated to things, such as a new car or college education. The point is to begin planning for the future, right now. We know some of the things that are coming down the pike. Why avoid saving for them until it's too late?

> Danya writes: I want to start saving for retirement, but my husband would rather spend our extra money on toys—a speed boat, new car, skis. I like those things too, but I'd rather be secure.

We're guessing Danya's husband isn't a long-term thinker. Instant gratification is a powerful pull. And sometimes, thinking about getting old and not being able to take care of ourselves is something we'd rather avoid. Tackle why you might not be thinking long term yourself.

Pit Thoughts Versus His Thoughts

If I have enough money, I'll have achieved a lot and do well.
Only what I am through Christ counts (Philippians 3:8–9).

If I have enough money, I can have what I want, when I want it.
I already have so much, compared to so many. I can be content with what I have (Hebrews 13:5).

If I have enough money, people will respect and like me.
I will devote myself to God and not money (Matthew 6:24).

Having enough money gives me power over my life.
The gospel gives me the only true power in this world (Romans 1:16).

Having enough money means I will always be safe.
I can't take my money with me—but I have an inheritance in heaven (Matthew 6:19–21).

Do You Really Believe That God Owns It All?

If I'm a PCOG and he is my God, then it all came from him, right? Every smidgen of the bounty comes from him and will return to him. This whole grand mess of my life is just the temporary reality, and I have to stay focused on keeping it in perspective. If we live within our means and trust our God, we can take steps to make the world a better place in his name. From this perspective, giving leads to financial freedom.

My wise friend Sarah said in Bible study, "I'm pretty sure God's not going to bless us with more until we prove ourselves with what we've got."

I love that, even though it's not easy. If I practice radical giving, I'm testifying to God that I believe he will take care of me, and that everything I have is because of how he made me and what opportunities he's given me.

Sarah's right. Giving to others in need helps keep the mind focused on financial realities. True, I'd like a bigger house, but most of the world lives in housing a fraction the size of mine. I'd like new clothes, but most of the world lives with no more than two outfits. I'd like a new car, but many people in the world don't even own shoes. This is about perspective, perspective, perspective. All we have is a gift from God; giving is a way to acknowledge that gift and show God we're grateful.

My grandfather used to tell the story of having a dime of his own when he went to church. Faced with an offering plate and no way to split the coin, he put it in. It was painful for him. (Even as an eighty-year-old man, he remembered it vividly.) The next day, driving along a country road, he picked up a hitchhiker (think country road in the 1930s). When Granddad dropped off the hitchhiker, he saw the man had left "two bits," or twenty-five cents on the seat. It was a treasure at that time, something like your ten-year-old finding a ten-dollar bill. The point in my grandfather's story was that if we freely give, God will take care of us.

In Malachi 3:8–12, Scripture is very overt on this front:

"Will a man rob God? Yet you rob me.

"But you ask, 'How do we rob you?'

"In tithes and offerings. You are under a curse—the whole nation of you—because you are robbing me. Bring the whole tithe into the storehouse, that there may be food in my house. Test me in this," says the LORD

Almighty, "and see if I will not throw open the floodgates of heaven and pour out so much blessing that you will not have room enough for it. I will prevent pests from devouring your crops, and the vines in your fields will not cast their fruit," says the LORD Almighty. "Then all the nations will call you blessed, for yours will be a delightful land."

Operating under this reestablishment-of-covenant direction, Tim and I are striving to hit that 10 percent tithe, even in the middle of our ten-year plan to get entirely out of debt and reestablish our retirement savings.

Again, we must figure out *why* we don't give: because we don't believe we're to do so, or we won't control those dollars, or we'd rather spend on something personal? Only when we face that answer can we come to a point of decision on why we should tithe and more. Giving, then, is the first step away from greed.

SO YOU HAVE IT ALL TOGETHER?

Is all of this sounding obvious? Do you give as much as you can, perhaps more than 10 percent, put extra into your savings account, and live within your means? Good for you! We applaud you and encourage you to encourage your sisters along that track to financial health. You might consider looking at your mortgage and how you can pay it off early, saving tons in interest, or how you can ramp up to even more radical giving.

Take another look at your savings too. Catastrophes happen all the time, even to the financially secure. Rebecca invested in a Texas condo at the top of a real-estate boom with skyrocketing prices. When the bottom fell out of the market and she had to move, she lost thousands of dollars. My dad retired after thirty-five years with United Airlines only to discover that the pension fund he invested in and counted on was no longer there when the company declared bankruptcy. My folks will be okay in retirement, but they've had to put the lid on many things they wanted to do with that money—the things you save, hope, and dream of for later in life.

Kate writes: We've always been good financial planners and lived within our means. But our plan had always been for my husband to work until he was sixty-five and then retire. He's fifty-five now and was supposed to have his greatest earning potential ahead of him, earning more than a million dollars in the next ten years. But he's come down with a rare, undiagnosed disease, and we're spending money on doctors in thousand-dollar increments. He cannot work. The insurance company doesn't want to pay on an undiagnosed disease. Now our marriage is suffering. There's no such thing as too much money saved.

Amen to that, Kate. As in most areas of life, there's always room for improvement. Get wise counsel regardless of your financial situation. Expect the unexpected. Train yourself to see money as a tool for basic needs, not as the tool toward achievement, freedom, respect, power, security, and happiness. Only a God-filled, love-filled life can bring you satisfaction on those fronts.

Do not store up for yourselves treasures on earth,
where moth and rust destroy, and where thieves
break in and steal. But store up for yourselves treasures
in heaven, where moth and rust do not destroy, and
where thieves do not break in and steal. For where your
treasure is, there your heart will be also.
Matthew 6:19–21

The Hope-Filled Choices at Life's Crossroads

A Chat with Ellie Kay
About the Financial Security You Crave

Known as "America's Family Financial Expert," Ellie Kay is the best-selling author of eleven books including *Half-Price Living,* and a popular national speaker and media veteran with more than six hundred radio and television appearances under her belt, including spots on CNBC, CNN, and Fox News. She's an international radio commentator for *Money Matters* and a columnist for five national magazines as well as a spokesperson-consultant for clients such as Visa, Mastercard, and Entertainment.com. Ellie Kay is married to Bob, a test pilot, and they have seven children.

Rebecca: How did you learn about managing finances? Were you always so savvy about money?

Ellie: As a young child, I was dubbed Moneybags by my dad because I was an entrepreneur. I had my first home-based business at the age of seven. I got one of those handshaking buzzers from a box of cereal and charged the girls in my second-grade class five cents to shake their hand. I charged boys fifteen cents—extra for the added agony of having to touch a boy's hand. I made ten dollars in two weeks.

Rebecca: That's a lot of handshakes!

Ellie: My parents told me that one dollar of that was the Lord's tithe. I still remember the feeling I had when I put that dollar in the Sunday-school offering plate. I learned that the sweetest dollar I ever made was the dollar I could give away. By middle school, I had a baby-sitting business where I played with the children, fed them dinner, gave them baths, kept the house as clean as I found it, and never talked on the phone to friends. I had a sliding scale for those party animals, where I would end up charging double after midnight.

Rebecca: You were tough!

Ellie: You better believe it! My clients had to book me at least two weeks in advance to get on my calendar, and if they cancelled, they paid for the night anyway (because I likely turned down other jobs to accommodate them). I earned enough money by age fourteen to pay cash for my first car and regularly support Eastern European Missions in addition to my tithe.

Rebecca: That's quite a start.

Ellie: And I kept going—I majored in business in college and became a broker. When I married my husband, I left my business to be a wife and mom. Financially it probably didn't look like this made sense: My husband had two daughters when I married him and was forty thousand dollars in debt because of a nasty divorce. I stayed home with the five children we had in the first seven years of marriage, and Bob took a pay cut of fifteen thousand dollars a year to go fly jets in the air force. But we committed our finances to God's way of stewardship, and amazingly enough we were completely debt free in two and a half years. During this time, I put my business background and Moneybags attitude to work and learned a variety of painless ways to save money. That is how my ministry to families started.

Rebecca: What have you seen as women's greatest craving when it comes to spending?

Ellie: Women want to be loved and feel valued and accepted. Ask any woman who has purchased that Vera Wang suit, Prada sunglasses, or Dolce & Gabbana bag how she felt when she was buying it; she'll likely say she felt good, satisfied, or happy. But after a short time, she needs another purchase to get those endorphins pinging again, and so she's off to the mall. The funny thing about spending money to gain acceptance is that you're never satisfied for very long with those items you've purchased. Only God can fill the void that lies within a woman's heart, not Vera or Coach or Ralph.

Rebecca: What's the number one fallacy about money that Christian women need to conquer?

Ellie: Women don't take enough of an active role in budgeting. Most women don't have a budget, or if they do, they don't stick to it. Budgeting is a habit like any other healthy habit: do it for thirty days, and you're more likely to do it forever. Put it off, week after week, and you're more than likely to have debt, money worries, and a lack of funds.

Rebecca: What can women do to get on the road to financial health?

Ellie: First, be a Budget Babe: Go to crown.org and use their interactive tool to set up your own budget. Then follow the steps in order to stick to it! Next, be accountable for your finances. Have a money buddy, or join a group such as Crown Financial Ministries small groups. Go over your budget, set up a way to pay down debt, and let someone ask you accountability questions about your finances each month. This is Proverbs 27:23–24 for the twenty-first century.

Rebecca: It's not as easy as it sounds, is it?

Ellie: It's not! We have to be realistic. It's important to take small steps toward financial health and not feel as if you have to go on a money crash diet in order to succeed. Depriving yourself or trying to make too many changes at one time often leads to failure. Set up a realistic budget, and pay a small amount down on your debt load each month. As you become more adept at saving money and stretching those dollars, increase your debt pay down. Don't forget to budget fun as well as regular splurges. If those treats are in the budget, then you won't feel as if you're cheating when you pamper yourself!

Rebecca: Did you encounter any other surprises you've learned about women tackling their finances like this?

Ellie: Definitely—women need encouragement to become "givers." Proverbs 3:9–10 says you can give generously and it will come back to you. That's a promise. So I encourage women to tithe or give away

10 percent of everything they have: their paychecks, groceries, household goods, cars, clothing, and their time.

Rebecca: And that's hard for most women?

Ellie: Women are usually feeling stretched, so if they can give in one area, they consider their work done. But if our lives and possessions belong to the Lord, shouldn't we be tithing from every aspect?

Rebecca: I'd never thought of it that way. I like it.

Ellie: It is surprising. Another surprising thing I've seen is that women aren't the ones who usually make a family go into tremendous debt. Sure, women can contribute to the debt load, but a woman's splurges are usually for clothes or toys for kids. On the other hand, a man's splurges are big-boy toys: a boat, car, plasma TV, expensive hobbies. That's why communication between women and their men is so important, especially when it comes to money matters.

Rebecca: What do you wish every woman would know about money?

Ellie: That you can live a life that's meaningful, fun-filled, and satisfying without going into debt in order to achieve that kind of a lifestyle. If you want to become debt free, share more with others than you have in the past, and hear God say, in reference to the way you handled money, "Well done, good and faithful servant!… Come and share your master's happiness!" [Matthew 25:23]. God is El Roi, the God who sees, and he knows where we are right now. He is Jehovah Rapha, the God who heals, and he wants to heal not only our finances, but also our emotions, our desire for love, and our need for acceptance. So call upon him today, and he will heal all of you. Finally, remember that he is Jehovah Jireh, the God who provides. He's already made provision for us to get financially healthy and stay that way! Just take the first step and he will meet you where you are so that you can become the financially confident woman you were designed to be.

The Smile Within

Joy and Happiness in Your Life

> The secret of a satisfied heart is not the pursuit of satisfaction or happiness. Satisfaction and happiness are by-products of the pursuit of God. Discovering God and His love not just in our minds but also in our actual experience—this is the basis of true joy in life.
>
> RUTH MYERS

M y friend sat beside me on the couch, sobbing. Her heart was breaking as the last nail was driven into the coffin that contained her marriage. She was lost and flailing. "I just want to be happy," she said in a plaintive wail.

I hugged her, held her, wept with her, and consoled her as well as I could. But I felt powerless to connect her deepest desire to my most obvious answer, Christ. I'd told her about Jesus, about how he brought me joy on a daily basis, but she refused to commit to him in order to get there. Until she connected the dots, my nonbelieving friend would never discover the root of true happiness—joy—because she did not know Jesus. She was trusting in herself to make her life work.

Not that being a Christian makes every day easy. Rebecca became a Christian in college, drawn to the promise of Jesus, as he told his disciples, "I came that they may have life, and have it abundantly" (John 10:10, NASB).

For a college sophomore, that sounded like a good plan. But Rebecca thought it meant life was going to be easier somehow, that things were going to work out just right. A few years later, while trying to survive her first year of full-time work, she threw her Bible against the wall and told the Lord, "If this is the abundant life, I don't want it!"

She's more mature now. She doesn't throw her Bible. But she still gets frustrated and angry at God for his timing, "and I just ignore him instead."

Survey Says

The younger respondents to our survey (twentysomethings) ranked joy and happiness as their number two priority, just behind the priority of relationship with God. However, joy and happiness as a goal seems to move down the list of needs for each successive age bracket. As one, more "mature" woman said on her survey, "I've concluded that joy and happiness is a by-product of everything else."

I've been angry at God plenty of times as well, irritated to full-blown furious by how he moves (or doesn't). Just like everything else in my life, I want to control him, which, of course, is impossible.

But the journey each of us takes toward and with Christ is an ongoing story, unfolding each day, and when I consider the great joy-versus-happiness conundrum, I often think of my brokenhearted friend and that moment on the couch. Conversely, when my own heart was broken, in the midst of devastation, fear, and bewilderment, I had a curious strength, assuredness at my core. Even in tears, I could cling to the joy that never ends. I knew that it would all be okay. Although it was hard at that time, I knew it would get better. I had strength within me that could not be put down.

We're not alone in this experience.

Beth writes: He gives me joy in life. Without him, life isn't worth living. Things get me down, kids aggravate me, my family disappoints me, but the Lord is there, is true, is always with me. He is forgiving, understanding, loving, caring and everything else we could want in another. He fills the gaps and in doing so, brings me joy.

In *Lord of My Rocking Boat,* Carole Mayhall writes of two women, a friend of hers and her sister, Joye, who each faced serious problems. "Yet one's walking in despair," Mayhall writes, "and the other in joy. What makes the difference?… My friend's heart was occupied with her problems; my sister's heart was occupied with the Living God."[1]

Most of us know the difference between joy and happiness. We all desire to be happy, but the only way we can get there is to understand the path toward true joy: a heart fully occupied by God. Happiness is rooted in the temporal. Joy is rooted in the eternal. Happiness is fleeting, shifting from day to day. Joy remains, regardless of circumstances.

THE FRAGRANCE OF JOY

When Rebecca was a young girl, her grandmother had a bottle of perfume she received as a special gift. Rebecca loved going into her grandmother's bedroom and lifting the stopper to just get a whiff of jasmine and roses. (Why is it that grandmothers seem to have such a distinct scent? I think I'd know my beloved grandmother was present in a crowd even with my eyes closed. And I associate that scent with good things, happy things: love, joy, peace, and homemade donuts!)

But do you know people who seem to give off a sort of *joy* aroma? They're the people you always feel good being around. You can see joy in their smiling eyes, quick grins, and inclination to laugh. They're the ones who can spot the flower on a pile of manure. Their joy seems to emanate from them and flow into you.

Now think about their lives, their circumstances and struggles. Do you believe they are joyful because they have it easy? Are they free of real troubles? Are they joyful because they have no issues or have never gone through anything difficult?

The unshakably joyful people who we know are those who have a deep, abiding relationship with God, who trust him no matter the stakes and no matter the cost, and often they're people who have looked to him through very dark days and emerged on the other side with faith intact. The *Holman Bible Dictionary* defines joy this way: "in direct proportion [to the] believer's walk with the Lord…[who helps them] rejoice even when troubles come." Are you one of those people? If not, how can you get to be?

> *We are a fragrance*
> *of Christ to God among those*
> *who are being saved*
> *and among those*
> *who are perishing.*
> 2 CORINTHIANS 2:15, NASB

Psalm 43:3–4 says, "Send forth your light and your truth, let them guide me; let them bring me to your holy mountain, to the place where you dwell. Then will I go to the altar of God, to God, my joy and my delight." If God is our joy and delight, then the more we live in communion with him, the more we will find what we seek.

In Beth Moore's excellent teaching on the fruit of the Spirit, she calls this saving, intimate knowledge of God (and his intimate knowledge of us) "joy's bedrock":

God is telling us, "If you only understood what grace means and what you have received by way of it, you would never cease to rejoice!"… I believe the main reason we lack an awareness of joy in our salvation is because we are unaware or seldom reminded to what and from what we have been saved. In this way, we have neglected "so great a salvation" (Hebrews 2:3, NKJV). We need to consistently focus on our great salvation so that our joy might be full.

You may have noted another facet of "God's salvation." Recognizing that salvation belongs to Christ helps to get us out of ourselves…. Salvation is His. It's about Him. Following Christ breaks the stranglehold of self in our lives as He becomes the center of our universe. We decrease; He increases (see John 3:30). Joy results.[2]

We decrease; he increases. Joy results. Those fascinating words are the key to our study and contemplation of joy. Psalm 39:5 tells us that our time on earth is "a mere handbreadth." Time is short, girls. We've got to get this straight—and fast. We have no time to waste! With our names written in the Book of Life (see Philippians 4:3), a book belonging to the Lamb, our salvation is assured by God's grace and through our faith in Christ. If we allow God to pull us close, whisper in our ear, comfort and guide, we will find continual joy.

SURPRISED BY JOY

C. S. Lewis maintained that God _is_ joy. "All joy…emphasizes our pilgrim status;" he wrote, "always reminds, beckons, awakens desire."[3] He seems to write about the life of faith as if it's a giant treasure hunt, with magnificent signposts and subtle symbols that, combined, take us along the route we were always meant to take toward the joy of all joys.

Many of the references to joy in the New Testament have to do with something hidden and something found. Jesus himself, "full of joy through the Holy Spirit," says in Luke 10:21, "I praise you, Father, Lord of heaven and earth, because you have hidden these things from the wise and learned, and revealed them to little children. Yes, Father, for this was your good pleasure."

You don't have to make your way through a complex math matrix to find joy. The treasure is yours for the asking! We don't have to have a comprehensive knowledge of the Bible or read many fabulous books to come to a place where we smell of joy. If we approach faith as directed—as little children—we'll be delighted by the surprises God lays in our path. We'll begin to discover his surprising us with joy each and every day; as we abide in Christ, we begin to be fed by an internal, eternal spring of joy that flows even when we're in life's deserts.

> Lissa writes: Seventeen years ago my baby daughter was stillborn. It was by far the most difficult thing I've ever gone through in my life. One night, sleepless and unable to stop crying, I was suddenly filled with this inexplicable joy as the Lord showed me how he had spared my daughter the pain in this life. She would never have to experience physical pain, emotional turmoil, or mental distress. My tragedy in this life was an eternal victory.

JOY IN THE DESERT

"Consider it pure joy, my brothers, whenever you face trials of many kinds," wrote the apostle James in his letter, "because you know that the testing of your faith develops perseverance" (1:2–3). Perseverance and trust are built only as we grow in maturity in our faith. Our Christian witness in this regard is vital.

Though you have made me
see troubles, many and bitter,
you will restore my life again;...
My lips will shout for joy
when I sing praise to you.
PSALM 71:20, 23

Paul and Silas free a slave girl of her evil spirit and shortly thereafter are stripped, beaten, and then jailed. Acts 16:25–34 records that, in response, Paul and Silas sing hymns and pray. Other prisoners hear them. In that heart-stopping biblical scene, the chains fall away, the doors open and—the result? Many hear the truth. The jailer and his family are saved! Note that Paul and Silas didn't find happiness only when God busted them out—no, they had joy in the midst of and *in spite of* their circumstances. What God wants us to see is that the boys remained faithful to him even in jail. And because of that, the jailer and his family were saved.

Is it possible that God allowed Paul and Silas to be humiliated and to suffer physical and emotional punishment in order that the jailer might hear the good news and witness God's power? Those who hold the joy of Christ in their hearts

Pit Thoughts Versus His Thoughts

I'll never be able to find joy.
Seek me and you will find me. In him, I can find true joy
(Matthew 7:7).

One day I'm up, the next I'm down. I'll never find true happiness.
I can find joy as I trust in him, day by day (Psalm 16:5–11).

I'm so worried and anxious about everything, there's no room for joy.
He consoles my soul and brings me peace (Psalm 94:18–19).

My dream has shattered. I am in despair.
God can make things whole again (Romans 8:28–39).

My sorrow is too great.
He will restore me and sustain me (Psalm 51:12).

Nothing I do really gives me joy.
My joy is complete in him (2 Corinthians 2:14–15).

believe that God can and will work through all things. Our purpose in our temporal life is always to serve the Eternal One, even when we do not understand what he is doing or why. If Paul and Silas had cowered in the corner of their jail cell and cried, what would have happened? Would the jailer have been inspired? poised to listen to them?

> Blaire writes: Twenty years ago my father-in-law died suddenly from an aneurism. My husband didn't deal with it well and withdrew from God and from our family, me especially, for a time. Unfortunately, the men of our church didn't support him, and the unsaved men at the steel mill did. Our marriage suffered because our relationship became only physical for a while—there was no emotional bond, and we just sort of coexisted. But God sustained me during that time with his unspeakable joy and peace. I came to realize who I am: a child of God, loved with an amazing love. Eventually, my husband and I rediscovered our first love of each other and God, but that earlier, difficult time grounded me and gave me a firmer foundation of joy.

Carole Mayhall writes of her sister, Joye, who, with a swath of bandages encasing her throat from a biopsy, talked to a student nurse. The nurse, Jan, was interviewing terminally ill people to see how she might help them. Joye answered, "Oh, Jan, I'm a bit fearful of the pain and process of dying—but I'm not afraid of death! It'll just be a change of residence for me." Mayhall continues, "I heard my sister [speak], her face radiant from within.... And for forty-five minutes, Joye explained the good news of Jesus Christ to Jan."[4]

Mayhall's sister wasn't concentrating on her pain, frustration, or fears. She was concentrating on her Savior and the joy within because of him.

We hope we're not called to such extreme places in order to serve him, but our call is to serve God wherever we are, regardless of our circumstances. Our charge is to be so filled with him that nothing else can take his place.

Beth Moore writes, "Paul's joy in tribulation was motivated by his knowledge that the 'best' of God's presence, purpose, and power was undoubtedly discovered in the worst of circumstances."[5]

RESTORATION HARDWARE

In liturgical churches, we sing, "Restore unto me the joy of your salvation and uphold me with your Holy Spirit" (see Psalm 51:12). But what does it mean to be restored?

> Amy writes: I thought I knew what joy was and considered myself a "good Christian." But it was only when I lost my job and my marriage over the course of two years that I truly understood what it meant to walk so closely to Jesus, day by day, hour by hour, that God's joy somehow flowed from him and into me. Did God want me to divorce? I don't think so. But did he use that really tough time in my life to teach me, shape me? Absolutely.

Amy gets it that we have a choice when we face hardship: we can choose to believe that God allowed hardship to achieve a greater good we might not otherwise discover, or we can believe he has forgotten us and then wallow in bitterness.

Rebecca and I have faced this. Through the course of building our business and then dismantling it, we've become used to difficulty, challenges. We've often

When Joy Disappears

When joy disappears, it may be because...

- ⊙ we're serving more than we're seeking.
- ⊙ we're talking more than we're walking.
- ⊙ we're more impressed by miracles than his still, small voice.
- ⊙ we're weary and not taking adequate care of ourselves.
- ⊙ we think we're spiritually superior and set apart.[6]

mused that God uses struggles because nothing takes us off our desk chairs and down to the carpet in prayer faster. Do these struggles ruin our lives? Certainly not. They make life harder, for sure, but also…priceless—because knowing that God hears our prayers, is who he says he is in his Word, and is active in our lives draws us closer to our precious Savior, the One who suffered for and cried over us before we were born. He feels our pain with us and remains ready to see us through.

WILL MY LIFE ALWAYS BE THIS HARD?

Whether you skate through life with few mishaps or seem to be called to endure a life of searing pain, please do trust that God will see you and yours through. You might be miserable like Gina, who has to clean toilets five days a week, 8:00 a.m. to 5:00 p.m., at her job. Or you may be suffering like Hannah, who has terminal cancer, a husband who abandoned her, and three kids with no one to care for them when she dies. But there is a purpose in all things. God can use every moment of our lives, if we only allow it.

The apostle Peter wrote that we must suffer "a little while." What follows, he said, will be restoration—making you "strong, firm and steadfast" (1 Peter 5:10). The prophet Jeremiah (see chapter 31) and the entire book of Job also promise many things as part of the joy of restoration: favor, rest, dancing, comfort, and bounty.

As we learn to hold on and watch, God reveals what he wishes to teach us; since he's always after the best for us, he will do whatever it takes to get us closer to it. The Bible uses analogies of pruning our dead branches, refining us by fire, molding us like clay. Those are physical analogies that suggest the idea of pain. God's ultimate goal is to see us reach his vision of who we were created to be. This process can eat up years, even decades, or it may largely occur overnight. What would you choose?

Rebecca and I are constantly praying, *Help us to learn what you want us to learn here, Lord,* now. *We're willing. We just can't see it. Show us the way.* We've come to recognize that the sooner we own up to sin or laziness or fear, the sooner God may release us…or at least move on to other ways of teaching us.

HOW GOD SATISFIES OUR HUNGER FOR JOY

Julie writes: I'm surprised at my survey choices. I honestly mean to have God be my number one priority, but I let him get squeezed out by so many other things that only matter in this life. I also thought I would have put love and influencing others higher on the list, but they're apparently not on my radar. As a stay-at-home mom of a seventeen-month-old with another on the way, sometimes just remaining vertical is a major accomplishment. I go to a Bible study where my group leader is the mom of six—the youngest, thirteen-week-old twins—and she seems to have it all together. I can barely manage my one! What I really want is for Jesus to come to my house and literally take over.

We hear you, sister. Day-to-day life can be hard, even when we're not facing something extreme like illness, divorce, abuse, or death. Tim and I often say that the hardest job in the world is a day of kid duty. But this stay-at-home mom is onto something: maybe even her Bible-study leader, who appears to have it all together, may not have grasped the need for Jesus in everything.

What would it mean for Jesus to literally take over in our lives? If we could see Jesus in the corner of our kitchens, living rooms, backyards, church, and riding shotgun in the car, what would he be directing us to do? Where and when would he confront us? How would he cheer or encourage us? What would he have us ignore or pay special attention to? Would he show us new ways to serve him or point us in the direction of people who need to hear about him? How would our new, Christ-in-charge lives help us shine his light in a way that speaks to others?

Life doesn't suddenly become easy when God, instead of us, has his hands on the steering wheel. But it becomes more directed. We're trusting in the Holy One, the One who created us, who knows us through and through, loves us, and died for us. We're not acting on our own feeble intuition or smarts.

Can this happen overnight? For most of us, no. It takes months and years of discipline (or if you're stubborn like us, decades). It takes lesson after lesson to form within us enough history and knowledge that we finally see that life is really not about us; it's about him.

Abide with Me

Abide with me, fast falls the eventide.
The darkness deepens; Lord, with me abide.
When other helpers fail and comforts flee,
Help of the helpless, oh, abide with me.
I fear no foe, with thee at hand to bless;
Ills have no weight, and tears no bitterness.
Where is death's sting? Where, grave, thy victory?
I triumph still, if thou abide with me! [7]

Ultimately, our unmitigated, unending joy can only be found in true, constant, and deepening relationship with Christ, serving him in any way we may be led. Abiding with him, we catch glimpses of the path where he's leading, but we recognize that all we really need to know is where to place our next footstep. We understand there's a feast set ahead, even if we hunger now. We understand that if we allow him to prune us and shape us, we'll one day bear fruit that will bring others a measure of joy, and in turn know joy ourselves.

As the Father has loved me, so have I loved you.
Now remain in my love. If you obey my commands,
you will remain in my love, just as I have obeyed
my Father's commands and remain in his love.
I have told you this so that my joy may be in you
and that your joy may be complete.
John 15:9–11

In the Beginning Was Acceptance

A Chat with Jan Silvious About the Joy You Crave

Last year found speaker Jan Silvious on the road with the Women of Faith team and leading women's retreats in churches across the country. Jan, the author of *Look at It This Way* and *Big Girls Don't Whine,* has always had a heart for helping women turn their heads in the right direction. But where does *she* find joy when life gets tough? And how does she align both heart and brain to choose joy when things are hard?

Rebecca: As a counselor, speaker, and Bible teacher for twenty-five years now, you must have met many women who have experienced heartache that the rest of us can only imagine.

Jan: Yes. I'm never surprised when I hear some new thing more troubling than the last. Life on this planet is hard and can be stunningly harsh.

Rebecca: How do you encourage people in the midst of trouble or suffering, then, to find joy?

Jan: The truth is, there's something eternal in each of us that wants to know that Someone bigger and more powerful is calling the shots; even when there seems to be a rift with God, our ultimate hope is that he really is in control and really did have the last word, even though it's painful. So I offer reminders that referencing God's involvement in every hard situation never fails to bring comfort.

Rebecca: How is joy different from happiness?

Jan: I find it hard to separate the two. The classic definition of happiness relates to "happenstance" or feelings about what has "happened." In other words, we can be happy when things are going well—and that's true to a point—but happiness is a choice we make in the face of circumstances we wouldn't choose for ourselves. Happiness is a feeling based on what you choose to believe, and so is joy. There's choice involved. Joy is a confident, peaceful acceptance that there is a God and that he is deeply and wonderfully at work in all that happens. It's the willingness, the choice, to see that even though today's events may bring sorrow or may leave me reeling, there is always tomorrow and the unshakable belief that good will ultimately win. That fact makes me happy!

Rebecca: I've heard you mention some medical and psychological studies you've been looking at on this. What have they shown you?

Jan: I love learning new things, and the new brain research is fascinating. Medical science now has the capacity to "see" our emotions on certain high-tech brain scans, which show that our outlook affects our bodies. What I've learned—and stick with me here; I promise this applies— is that certain areas of our brains "fire" when we feel joy or sorrow or fear or peace. The area of the brain where emotional-response memories are stored, the amygdala, is connected to our limbic system, which releases hormones like adrenaline and cortisol, which cause us to respond to what's going on around us. They also affect the health of our bodies; all of that interaction is pretty involuntary.

So consider that and the fact that our brains also have a neocortex, where we make the decision to believe what our memories have generated. This means we can choose memories to take us in one direction, such as: *A dog bit me when I was two. I see a dog just like that dog. It's going to bite me. I have to scream and run.* Or we can decide to think: *A dog bit me when I was two. I see a dog just like that dog. It may or may not bite me. I'm an adult, and it's a very little dog; I can defend myself if it becomes aggressive. It's probably not aggressive, because I've never been bitten by any dog since I was two. I think I'll just keep walking and forget it.* That kind of reasoning is the work of the neocortex.

Rebecca: And that's also where our reasoning gets off track.

Jan: Right. We end up thinking like the two-year-old who was once hurt, rather than the adult who has survived decades longer with no further hurt.

Rebecca: At least we all battle this tendency together.

Jan: Oh yes! We are far from alone. In fact, lately I've been studying the children of Israel from the time of their captivity in Egypt to the time of their deliverance by Moses and their wilderness wanderings. It's so interesting to me that the children of Israel struggled, using their own reasoning, and wandered until almost that whole generation died in the wilderness.

Rebecca: We really are all in it together, then—we've been struggling on this front since the dawn of time.

Jan: Yes. The Israelites liked the idea of reaching the Promised Land, but as soon as they came upon hard times in the wilderness, they were totally unable or unwilling to control their thoughts. They flipped into blame, accusations, whining, immorality, idolatry, and just all-around bad thought patterns. This behavior did nothing to forward their progress or health, and ultimately, God allowed all but two of them to die. The two who survived were Joshua and Caleb.

Rebecca: And he chose them because…

Jan: They were men who made the choice to believe God. They chose with their neocortexes to believe him.

Rebecca: Despite suffering, despite pain.

Jan: Yes, and the other Israelites chose to let their memories run wild, while their reasoning lay dormant or was perverted. Joshua and Caleb lived through the same hard times as the others, but they refused to let their minds run wild. They chose to believe what God said, not what they were experiencing.

Rebecca: And because of that, they received what God had promised.

Jan: Yes! And remember what we said earlier? *Joy is a confident, peaceful acceptance that there is a God and that he is deeply and wonderfully at work in all that happens. It's the willingness, the choice, to see that even though today's events may bring sorrow or may leave me reeling, there is always tomorrow and the unshakable belief that good will ultimately win.*

Rebecca: The Israelites weren't confident or at peace. They saw nothing but doom, not enough of their God.

Jan: Which is so much like us! We crave the mountaintop experiences and shun the desert. So, too, were the children of Israel who became so brainwashed by their experiences in Egypt that they just couldn't get past seeing themselves as "grasshoppers" [Numbers 13:33] in their own eyes. Even though God promised—and they'd seen first-hand how he could deliver—they just couldn't or wouldn't make their minds believe that his promises were true.

Rebecca: They lost sight of the greater story, the bigger truth.

Jan: They had no vision for a future where good—and God—ultimately wins.

Rebecca: They lost hope just as we lose hope at times. I want to be full of joy, but sometimes it's just hard! It's much easier to throw a first-class pity party. How do we avoid that? How do we keep from being like those children of Israel, lost in our own sorrows?

Jan: Obviously, since Jesus promises that my joy will be "full" [John 15:11, KJV], then he's bringing an additive that I need in order to be complete. Granted, it's hard in many situations to feel joy. It can be challenging to experience anything but fatigue and depression when you're physically ill or facing a situation that seems way beyond your ability to cope. Those are the times you choose to believe that Jesus knows what we don't, that Jesus has what we don't, and that Jesus is willing to give us what we need.

Rebecca: When we need it.

Jan: Indeed. I love this definition of grace: grace is what God does in you, through you, and to you that you cannot do for yourself. So my joy can be full when I just rest and let God, by his grace, fill me with joy.

Rebecca: And yet we women tend to think of joy as being in a locked chest we just need to decode and then the treasure will be ours!

Jan: And it's really not locked away at all. There's nothing to be done to receive it other than right thinking and properly placed trust. Joy is not something we can work up or pretend to have. We can only real-ize it as we find ourselves experiencing it.

Rebecca: Usually the experience happens when you least expect it and when you truly believe you can't have it.

Jan: Then, all of a sudden, there it is—joy!

Rebecca: One of the things I love about you is your ability to cut through the fluff to the true heart of the matter. What do you say to someone who asks, "Will my life always be this hard?"

Jan: If a person continues to see her life as hard, it will continue to be hard. It's the old axiom, "It's not what happens to you but what you think about what happens to you that matters." I've never seen anyone focused on her hard life ever get past it. But I have seen many people focused on the "violet in the mud" of their lives and somehow always make it so. Attitude is everything when it comes to predicting how a person's life will turn out. Circumstances are varied, but a positive attitude is the same no matter what.

A Life in Balance

Your Emotional Health

> Be filled with the Holy Spirit and be willing to allow the Holy
> Spirit to have control. Evaluate your life and see if you are
> doing anything that may be blocking the Holy Spirit from
> filling you or working in your life. Sometimes a stubborn atti-
> tude can block the Spirit's work. You must invite Him to work
> without limit in every area of your life. Full control depends
> on being completely influenced by the Spirit!
>
> *Life Under Control,* First Place Bible Study

I magine yourself actually bearing the weight across your shoulders of a curved wood yoke, like the oxen of old. Whether your yoke feels light, or heavy and driving splinters into your neck, depends on who shares the load with you.

The Bible talks about being yoked to fellow believers and to the Savior whose burden is light. Above all, the apostle Paul warns us: don't be yoked in slavery (see Galatians 5:1). What does Paul mean?

Paul was writing to believers in Galatia, people not actually enslaved, but burdened by the belief that they can be saved by observing the Law instead of by faith in Christ. How hard is that? To have to gain God's favor by adhering to the complicated Jewish laws—an impossible task for sinful beings—is, in Paul's words, slavery, not freedom. Or, in the classical Greek Paul used, "to be burdened" meant "to be caught or entangled in."

Survey Says

Even in this more open day and time—where confessions seem to be the norm in media and books, a surprising number of women who face serious issues are reluctant to share their stories or painful situations with others, even with their otherwise loyal confidantes. How are you more open and supportive (or not) with the spiritual sisters in your life?

As you read this, ask yourself, *To what am I enslaved and yoked? What do I find myself burdened by—depression, abuse, loneliness, skewed perspective, anger, an eating disorder, an addiction? How is my life in balance or out of control?*

Rebecca and I aren't counselors, therapists, psychologists, or psychiatrists, but we've learned from the truth of the gospel that health and wholeness can be ours. The only prescription we offer is one all believers can take to get on the road to freedom, one that leads to balance, peace, and love. It might be your first step or your ten thousandth step. The point is to take small steps. Get going, and keep going in the right direction, knowing that others are ahead waiting for you, and others are behind, rooting for you.

A LIFE IN FOCUS

One thing that surprised us from our survey of what Christian women think about balance was how much they talked about emotional health by using words that have to do with *vision* and *focus*.

Connie writes: My mind and emotions must stay stable and *clear* to do my ministry and relationships. It's a fight sometimes to combat the crush of information and noise and demands that sap me mentally and emotionally.

Paula writes: I have bipolar disorder, so I know the impact that poor emotional and mental health can have on a person. A sound mind is essential—it's the *lens* through which you perceive your world, and it affects how you live out every aspect of your life.

Kirsten writes: I'm at a point in my life where everything seems in a frenzy. If I could just slow down and find a few minutes of peace, I could better *focus* on the other things in my life.

We all want to view life with the healthy perspective of one living a life in balance. Learning to see things like the One who is perfect will help us get there. Gaining that holy perspective takes years. Each of us has "junk in the trunk" or things we must deal with and get beyond. But what happens when day-to-day life is too much, when you feel on the verge of collapse? What happens when you just can't cope? Are there limits you can set or behaviors you can change to make life better? How do any of us move from frenzy to focus?

Lynne writes: I am exhausted physically and emotionally. I ask God daily for strength and "copability."

Copability is a wonderful term. Our lives demand this ability—to flex, to flow, and cope. But sometimes we make choices that make coping seem impossible! And sometimes life seems to bring things we didn't choose, making it harder than ever.

Paul wrote, "When we came into Macedonia, this body of ours had no rest, but we were harassed at every turn—conflicts on the outside, fears within" (2 Corinthians 7:5). We can easily become as overwhelmed by life as Paul seems to be at this moment. But Paul goes on to say that God comforted them by bringing them Titus—and the love and concern of others (see 2 Corinthians 7:6–7).

That's one key to getting a grip on balance: we may feel alone, but we're never alone!

THE BEAUTY OF SELF-CONTROL

Another key is self-control. I discovered this when I entered the last chapter in Beth Moore's *Living Beyond Yourself* Bible study with fear and trepidation. "What do you think when you hear the topic of self-control?" she asks. The options were "dread, excited, confused, condemned" or "other." I chose *dread*.

But Beth's study artfully confronted whatever feeling was chosen with a presentation on our need for walls. She likened each of us, every person, to a city with a temple and palace within and, in the best of scenarios, a strong wall surrounding it. The study reminded us: "Like a city whose walls are broken down is a man who lacks self-control" (Proverbs 25:28). Beth wrote that a city is only as safe as the walls around it.[1]

Her point is good. Don't we all live with walls in need of minor or major repair? Some of us have some old walls that need to be rebuilt, others have disintegrating sections, and yet others have gaping holes where the Enemy can enter and exit at will. Since we're essentially portable temples of the Holy Spirit (see 1 Corinthians 6:19–20), self-control is our modern wall of protection. When we build strong walls to keep out evil, we find increased freedom to live out the fruit of the Holy Spirit: love, joy, peace, patience, kindness, goodness, faithfulness, gentleness, and—you guessed it—self-control (see Galatians 5:22–23). The more we live within proper boundaries, the more we're at ease with the fruit, learning more and more about their power and strength, where they can ebb and flow in our lives.

Dr. Henry Cloud and Dr. John Townsend struck this chord when they published their perennial bestseller *Boundaries,* one of the nonfiction books we recommend (see "Additional Resources" in the back of this book). In a related article, Cloud writes, "Simply stated…: people have a need to be in control of their own lives, and they have a need to know that God is behind that idea…. God created us to be free, and to act responsibly with our freedom. He wanted us to be in control of ourselves, and to have a good existence. He was behind that idea all along. But as we all know, we misused our freedom and as a result, lost it. And the big fruit of this loss of freedom was the loss of self-control. We have felt the results of that ever since in a wide variety of misery."[2]

When self-control is absent, we see a world full of people trying to control one another. We're motivated by guilt, anger, and fear instead of love. We see rampant evil in relationships and entire cultures, along with the inability to solve problems, addictions of various kinds, and a generational cycle of sin. Cloud writes, "Jesus died to set us free: from sin, from the devil, from the world around us. And that is the essence of what *Boundaries* teach—freedom."[3]

These strong boundary walls aren't about simply saying no to demands. Boundaries are meant to establish perimeters that give us freedom to grow and flourish within and then find strength to push outward, inviting others into Christ's light of love and hope.

Think of boundaries in your life like a queen thinks of life within her castle with its towering, unbroken strong walls. Does the queen invite evil through her gates? Not knowingly. Who is invited to live within the walls? Her most trusted friends and people. Does she ever leave her castle? Of course, but under guard and with her eyes wide open.

WHEN THE DAMAGE HAS BEEN GREAT

The quest for balance, boundaries, and emotional health requires more than encouragement from others, self-control, and some know-how. Our survey showed that many women are struggling to survive some horrific situations and heal.

> Heather writes: I'm in counseling right now, working through sexual abuse from my past, trying not to let it take over and destroy my marriage to a good man.

We exhort you to seek a Christian counselor if you've suffered and are still struggling to heal, need someone to help you through a current crisis, or are wrestling with a particular issue. Sometimes, a woman just needs a safe person to listen to her. Find no shame in asking for help. Pat yourself on the back for taking charge of your pain, taking steps to rid yourself of your burdens, and to move toward health.

Nina writes: I know I've had depression over the years and wish I had spoken to someone, but I've never sought a counselor because of the cost, and I was taught to handle your problems yourself.

Change takes risk and work, and it's not usually fun. Peter Gabriel sings that we have to dig "in the dirt to find the places we got hurt." It's a lot like digging in a deep, muddy mess. Often what we think is hard will undoubtedly get harder the deeper we dig. It's like taking care of an infection; we can't simply take care of surface wounds. We have to dig to the bottom to fully rid ourselves of that infection and begin to heal from the bottom up. It may take two, twenty, or two hundred sessions. Commit to the healing, dear sister. Commit to the work. You are meant to be whole.

Patti writes: The effect of an abusive, neglectful childhood rears its ugly head periodically. Surrounded now by caring and concerned people, though, is somewhat overwhelming…painful instead of comforting, because my emotional wires got crossed when I was very young. Instead of being hurt by isolation and lack of love, I became accustomed to them. It's like my emotions have been asleep, much like a limb that falls asleep. Recent experiences have seemed like the sensation of pins and needles when the blood once again flows in that limb. I look forward to being fully, completely awake, all parts of me. But until the connectors are back in the positions for which God designed them, healing is uncomfortable and painful.

Before you begin digging, you may want to find a Christian therapist as a guide (see www.cloudtownsend.com for advice on choosing the right one), or join a program at your church like Celebrate Recovery, helping you determine where to dig, how deep, how wide, and how long. Think of your counselor as your guide on an archaeological expedition. You could dig in the wrong place if you don't have a wise guide. Friends can fill the role of listening and empathizing, but a counselor will help you take steps forward. Good listening skills are great, but we often need a guide for the journey, someone who will help us get to the destination we want to reach.

Ultimately, we cannot heal ourselves, no matter how hard we dig, how good our counselor is, or how great our spiritual mentors are. The ultimate source of our healing is the Great Physician. Kay Arthur writes,

> Beloved, to whom have you run for healing? Make sure that you get godly counsel—that which has its very foundation in the Word of God, that which points you to God and all that He is—rather than counsel that is apart from Him and His precepts of life. Don't think that the spiritual part of you belongs to God and thus, can be healed by God, while the psychological part must be healed through man's wisdom. The One who created you, who formed you—body, soul, and spirit—is not only your creator, He is also your sustainer.[4]

Sometimes there is a medical condition that can only be addressed by professionals. We believe that God can heal anyone—he is the Almighty after all—but he also has given us the gift of medicine when the body and even the mind betray us.

Margie writes: During my very hard time, I would cry all the time. A dear friend told me I needed help. I went into a clinic that my church referred me to where I was prayed over, loved, and cared for. The counselors took care of me, body, mind, and soul. What followed was a great healing time.

Heal me, O Lord,
and I will be healed;
save me and I will be saved,
for you are the one I praise.
Jeremiah 17:14

I learned a lot and met a lot of wonderful people and counselors. I don't share this with everyone, because they just don't understand.

What a difference support, understanding, and treatment can make! Ask yourself, *How can I celebrate and support someone trying to get stronger, healthier, and whole?*

FINDING BALANCE IN OUR LIVES

It may not be a deep, dark issue that's causing you to suffer emotionally. Maybe your struggle is simply the constant everyday chaos of life that threatens your equilibrium. Maybe you're a soccer mom taking three kids in ten different directions, or a retired senior who has overextended herself in volunteer work, or a woman who thinks she's not doing as much as she would like but *feels* overwhelmed, exhausted, and depleted.

Gail writes: I'm constantly struggling to balance my life. As a mother of five (ages two to eighteen), the activities I have to attend keep me running; in addition, I face a minimum of two loads of laundry each day, keeping our house clean despite being outnumbered by mess makers, paying the bills, shopping.... I work hard to keep my marriage fresh: I go on regular dates with my husband and have my own career as an editor and novelist. And yes, I'm occasionally frustrated, often tired, and much of the time overwhelmed. But I'm also fulfilled. I love my kids and want to be a good mother. I have talents and gifts that I can use and feel a strong sense of purpose in those arenas as well. I want to teach my kids to pursue their dreams, and that means sometimes living in a messy house, sometimes scrambling to get a meal on the table. It's a juggle, that's for sure, but I remind myself it's a choice that I make willingly.

I understand Gail's conflicting calls and desires because her story reflects my own. But nowhere in my life is there a decent amount of time to delve into God's Word or pray, and I wonder if Gail has similar struggles. There is not time for me to be adequately rested so I can be at my best for my family and friends. I'm running myself ragged. Somewhere I messed up, procrastinated too long, committed to too much. As Gail wrote, they were choices I made willingly. No one forced me into them. I need to pull it together and get done with some of my responsibilities. Then I resolve, once again, to be careful to not overcommit myself.

Becky writes: I'm just too busy. I don't say no to much of anything. But right now I'm too tired to summon up the energy to change anything.

We both have friends who overcommit, because they get a sense of love and worth out of meeting other people's needs (and we group ourselves with those

Pit Thoughts Versus His Thoughts

This feels like the worst situation I've ever been in.
I can give thanks in all my circumstances since he is in control (1 Thessalonians 5:18).

I'm too tired to move.
I find rest in the Holy One (Matthew 11:28).

I'm so overwhelmed.
I'm overflowing with hope! (Romans 15:13).

This is never going to get better.
I will concentrate on, and find inspiration in, whatever is true, noble, right, pure, lovely, and admirable! (Philippians 4:8).

I can't do it all.
I am nothing without God—and everything with him (Romans 12:3).

friends). Rebecca says she's one of the "pleasers," trying to make everybody happy; I get strokes from people who say of me, "How does she do it all?" I like the admiration, the sense of stature. But how crazy is that? Why do we get ourselves into such messes? Why can't I get enough stature out of simply knowing myself as a PCOG?

Dr. Richard Swenson, in his book *A Minute of Margin*, writes, "Consciously slow the pace of life. Take your foot off the accelerator pedal. Throttle back. Put on the brakes and obey the speed limit of the soul. The green pastures and still waters yet await us—but not in the direction the treadmill is spinning."[5]

> Cassie writes: I run all day long so I can justify to my husband why I need
> to stay home with the kids. I'm president of the PTO, team mom for three
> sports teams, teach Sunday school, volunteer in three classrooms weekly,
> and run carpool. Every day I pack four lunches and make a gourmet din-
> ner, as well as clean my house. My husband doesn't want to do all these
> things and seems to be okay with my staying home if I do all this. But the
> thing is, I feel like I'm on a hamster wheel, condemned to run and run and
> run…and I want off. But then my husband will want me to go back to
> work. Help!

Perhaps this woman is overdue for a heart-to-heart talk with her hubby. Perhaps she needs to tell him she's overcommitted, exhausted, and unhappy but feels she must continue in order to justify her staying home. Should she let him know she needs his support, even if it turns out she needs to simply keep house and make dinner for a few months? What would happen if she finally finds out she can be truthful and vulnerable—and that he's a safe person? What would happen if she finally learns to decipher what *she* needs and wants?

This woman wants peace, balance, and health just as we do. Shouldn't we all examine our castle walls, repair the holes, and make sure we're healthy (or on the road to health)? Shouldn't we prepare the grand dining hall for a feast of peace, and enjoy the preparations? Take heart in this promise from Isaiah 58:12: "Your people will rebuild the ancient ruins and will raise up the age-old foundations; you will be called Repairer of Broken Walls, Restorer of Streets with Dwellings."

We can set proper boundaries, add a measure of margin in our lives, and discover that true peace is abiding with the Prince of Peace in the great dining hall of our castles-in-good-repair. And there, my fellow queen, sitting with him, we will feast.

It is for freedom that Christ has set us free.
Stand firm, then, and do not let yourselves
be burdened again by a yoke of slavery.
Galatians 5:1

Room to Breathe

A Chat with Joanna Weaver
About the Balance You Crave

When Joanna Weaver isn't busy in her duties as a pastor's wife, Bible-study leader, mother, and writer (her books include the best-selling *Having a Mary Heart in a Martha World* and *Having a Mary Spirit*), she likes to have coffee with friends, read, pray, and enjoy her beautiful surroundings in northwestern Montana. She's one of the women we're aiming to be like— shining Jesus with her eyes and exuding the fragrance of Christ. But does her sense of balance and emotional health come from her serene surroundings? Lisa asked the woman who has tapped into the Mary-versus-Martha spirit.

Lisa: Okay, we both love the Flathead Valley in northwest Montana. Does it take living in a more slow-paced region to find balance in one's life?

Joanna: I'm sure it helps, but the overwhelming pace of busyness is epidemic in America no matter where you live.

Lisa: So how do we find that Mary-heart-in-a-Martha-world mentality?

Joanna: The basic premise is knowing that God longs to know us and be known by us! But the sort of living-room intimacy that Mary had, that we long for with God, is never found in Martha's sort of kitchen service for God. Christ offers the same intense relationship Mary found at his feet to every one of us, Marys and Marthas alike, no matter our personality type or giftings.

Lisa: How are you finding balance in your life these days? You're in the throes of seeing your two eldest children off to college and adult life, and at the same time you're the mother of a special-needs preschooler (a surprise baby!) and filling your role as a pastor's wife. Oh, and writing too!

Joanna: Balance is such an ethereal concept. Just when I think I may have found it, it somehow gets lost in all the demands of life. I don't think there's a secret formula except making ourselves available to the Lord. Unless I spend time with him on a consistent basis, I end up living my life in my own strength, and it isn't long before that strength is depleted and I'm one snippy, uptight mama! But when I take time to invite Christ to take the throne of my heart, to lead and direct me through my day, things tend to go more smoothly.

Lisa: When your youngest son, Joshua, was born and you found out he would have some challenges ahead, that must have rocked your boat. How did you regain your balance?

Joanna: Finding out I was pregnant at forty was what really rocked my boat! I didn't handle it at all well. But as I hammered out surrender in that area, God released grace for the actual mothering. I can honestly say I have more energy, patience, and joy now than I had with my first two—and I know that is a gift from God. It really is true: God gives us grace sufficient for the day. Josh's low-muscle tone and motor and speech delays are hard to deal with at times, though not nearly as difficult as the challenges many other people face. But God has really helped me to live in the moment rather than in fear of the future or regret from the past—to accept Joshua where he is (and love him there!) while still challenging him to go beyond his limitations. There are times when fear wants to claw at my mind: How will he cope in school? Will he be accepted or teased? Is there something more I should be doing, and what in the world would that be? But I'm learning I can't go into fear. There are no answers there, only turmoil. God has given me a space of grace, and that's where I need to stay. He will lead and guide my husband and me as we seek God's best for Joshua.

Lisa: How does that transformation, living in that space of grace, give you balance?

Joanna: A Mary spirit is really at the very heart of the matter.

Lisa: Explain what you mean by a Mary spirit.

Joanna: It's a willing spirit. We see it displayed in Mary of Bethany as she spilled her treasure; in Mary the mother of Jesus when she said, "May it be to me as you have said"; and in Mary Magdalene when, after being delivered of seven demons, she left all to follow and minister to Jesus for the remainder of his life. But it's also displayed in Martha's teachable heart when she received the rebuke of Jesus in Luke 10 and chose to change. We must participate in the process of transforming, changing, if we're ever to be like Jesus. The only way to bring true balance to our outer lives is to give God access to our inner lives, to be willing to ask the hard questions: *Why do I have these destructive patterns in my life? Why do I so desperately need people's approval?* We have to take time to quiet our souls, so we can hear the still, small voice of the Spirit pointing out the things we need to see. For God only reveals to heal!

Lisa: I like that… God reveals to heal.

Joanna: Yes, that's the purpose. Correction isn't rejection—it's life, life more abundant, life as it was meant to be lived! But such vulnerability before God can be hard to face, let alone welcome. I'm coming to the place in my life where I'm saying, "Bring it on, God. Break me, shake me, challenge me, change me! Whatever it takes, make me like you!"

Lisa: How much does having a Mary spirit apply to the average woman's daily grind?

Joanna: There are so many facets that directly affect daily life—living victoriously in the battlefield of our mind, choosing humility as an antidote to pride, rooting out bitterness and unforgiveness. But I think the most important part is the realization that there's a war going on inside of us, a war in the members of our body, as the apostle Paul puts it in Romans 7:23. My Flesh Woman, as I call my lower nature, doesn't want to give up her influence in my life. As a result, there's a tug-of-war going on inside of me, in all of us. The flesh wars against the Spirit.

Lisa: I can relate to that!

Joanna: Here's the kicker. Only we can determine which side will win, which side we'll give in to. We are either Spirit led or flesh driven. It's up to us. But as we make these daily choices to die to the flesh and live by the Spirit, we are changed! Not a *poof!* magic-wand overnight transformation, but a deep inside-out renovation that eventually works its way out from our inner life to affect our outer life—changing the way we live, walk, and talk.

Lisa: It's a process.

Joanna: Yes, one of constantly putting first things first. Make Christ the center of your life, and let everything move around that. But please don't worry about doing that perfectly! We tend to be such all-or-nothing people that if we can't do the spiritual part of our lives with absolute excellence, we tend to do nothing. I used to dedicate myself to reading through the Bible in a year, but by the middle of February, around the third chapter of Leviticus, I'd slip into a coma. Well, not a real coma, but spiritually speaking, what felt like one. I've since learned to set reasonable goals for myself—set myself up to succeed rather than fail, because God isn't looking for perfection. He desires consistency, and sometimes consistency is nothing more than the refusal to give up trying. So when I go for a week without having my time with the Lord (or, I'm embarrassed to admit, even longer!), rather than throwing up my hands and deciding I'm not the spiritual sort, I repent and return. And Jesus is always there waiting—with open arms and a loving heart, longing to pour himself into me so I can be poured out to my world.

Lisa: That's living in the space of grace.

Joanna: Yes, and it starts wherever you are. If I could give one piece of advice, I would echo the words of the Quakers: "Start small, but begin." Put God in the center. Make him your priority, and make his presence your heart's desire. Your life will never be the same!

Really, Truly Happy at Home

Your Marriage, Home Life, and Intimacy

I'd like to suggest a motto for Christian family life: "God is in the room."

While God is *always* there, so often we act and think and behave and speak as if he were not. We fight, we argue, we laugh; we play games, watch movies, make love, and do just about everything without even thinking about the implication that *God is in the room.*

Even though we pray before our common meals, it amazes me how quickly I can slip back into thinking and acting as if the word *Amen* is a kind of curtain that I pull down in front of heaven. I've said my obligatory piece, and now I can carry on as if God has passed over us rather than taken up residence among us.

GARY L. THOMAS

R omans 12:10 tells us to "honor one another above yourselves." But can you imagine living in a home where honor, true honor, was actually in play 24/7? Have you ever seen such a home or family? Most women in our survey admitted not.

I've had glimpses, and in those homes peace and joy seem to reign with greater frequency than in my own household. If we could learn to love one another as much as we love ourselves and truly honor each of our family members, we might just transform our households, marriages, parent-child relationships, communities, even our nation.

We're not wishing for androidlike behavior and relationships—just the respect, love, grace, and honor that author Tim Kimmel describes:

> Homes of honor see the other person's time, their gifts, their uniqueness, and their dreams as gifts to be cherished and stewarded. Homes of honor still have room for sibling rivalry…[and] occasionally entertain arguments and disappointments, but for the most part, these homes give children a deep sense of being loved in a secure environment. All children are important, along with their opinions and concerns. Their time…ideas…space…and their vulnerabilities are respected. There is a present-tense commitment to making each day an asset that builds on the day before.[1]

The key to modeling grace, honor, hope, and love for our children seems to be in getting our hearts and minds straight on what we believe and how we want

Survey Says

Whether married or single, divorced or widowed, younger or older, the desire for a happy home life topped nearly everyone's list of wants, needs, and priorities. How did you rate your desire for this in Your Five-Minute Survey (page 6).

to live out our beliefs. This begins with the parents' individual relationship with God and a healthy husband-wife relationship.

Perhaps you're a young woman still living with your parents, or a divorced or widowed woman living with children. You may be an empty-nest parent getting used to a quiet house, or a woman who has taken in her elderly parents. Regardless of your home situation, these principles apply.

A Happy Home Begins with You

"If Mama ain't happy, ain't nobody happy," a bumper sticker proclaimed on the freeway. The words rang through my head, and I began to notice mothers in cars all around me. Some mamas looked stressed. Many were talking on cell phones or singing along with their radios, seemingly oblivious to the chaos in the backseat. A few were in animated or happy conversation with their kids. I wondered what was going on inside each vehicle as we sped along at seventy miles an hour. I imagined a freeway full of a thousand mamas trying to buy off their children with McDonald's, or promises of McDonald's, threats, admonishments, singing, or cajoling.

Any day of the week can find me playing any of those mama-behind-the-wheel scenarios I just described. Too often, the pressure of getting the kids all ready, into a vehicle, and to some destination on time makes me a crazy woman. Every Sunday is an example. Since my husband plays with the contemporary-worship team, it's up to me every Sunday to get four of us bathed, coiffed, dressed, and out the door. Without going into the details of how that works (or doesn't), let's just say that too often I'm not modeling grace to my children or setting the tone for us to enter into worship with open minds and hearts.

Our survey encouraged me that I'm not alone.

Bobbie writes: I often joke that my fantasy is to be bored…not that I ever want to be bored, but I wonder what it would feel like to actually get to the end of your lists of things you have to do and things you want to do. I'm pretty exhausted by the time I fall into bed each night. Balancing my work and other responsibilities, it pretty much feels like everything could come crashing down at any time.

Leanna writes: I have four kids and I often feel overwhelmed with everything going on. One of my biggest sins is not turning over my worries to Christ. I am a HUGE worrywart, and there is no need—I simply need to ask Christ to take it away from me and show me the direction in which I should go. In the same way, life itself tends to overwhelm me. I never can say no. So then I don't have time or energy to create the kind of home I want for my family!

So what is it about us? Why can't we get it all together? Why are we always so rushed, short on time and energy? Why do we sometimes wish for children who obey our every command, are quiet, still, and obedient? I know I wouldn't be happy with such children for long—I want children who are free to express who they are by smiling, laughing, eager to learn, and at peace with themselves. And yet…secretly many a mom does wish for androids so that life might be *easier.*

Is it I who has constructed an impossible schedule, expectations, and goals? I do consistently set myself up for partial failure; when I don't hit the A+ mark, I live under a silent barrage of self-incrimination: *Why can't I keep a perfect house? meet all my deadlines? make more money? spend less? return all my telephone calls? e-mail everyone back? write letters to friends? keep my children from getting sick? attend every parenting option at school? put in hours on the PTO? exercise every day? lose weight? make a great meal every night? write a better book?* On and on it goes: lack of grace for me, and when I can't treat myself with grace, it's hard for me to treat my husband or children with an ample measure of it either.

I usually come to the brink of collapse and meltdown before I reassess and return to Scripture. The wise sages tell me what I need to know: Slow down. Rest. Love yourself. Forgive yourself. It's a juggling act, managing a family.

Getting this grace and love thing straight in our own heads and hearts is the first step to a happy home. When we do give and receive grace and love, we begin to set the tone for the household. Who wouldn't want to be married to a woman (or want a parent or daughter) exhibiting joy, peace, grace, honor, respect, and love? Do you want to be a woman who eagerly greets each day as a gift to be embraced and an adventure about to unfold? I do.

The Power of Time

Just as our God demands a portion of our time, so does a healthy marriage or family life. I was reminded of this when a preteen neighbor was locked out of her house one evening and we invited her to come in and have dinner with us. We were having barbequed chicken, a tossed salad, and bread at our kitchen table. A

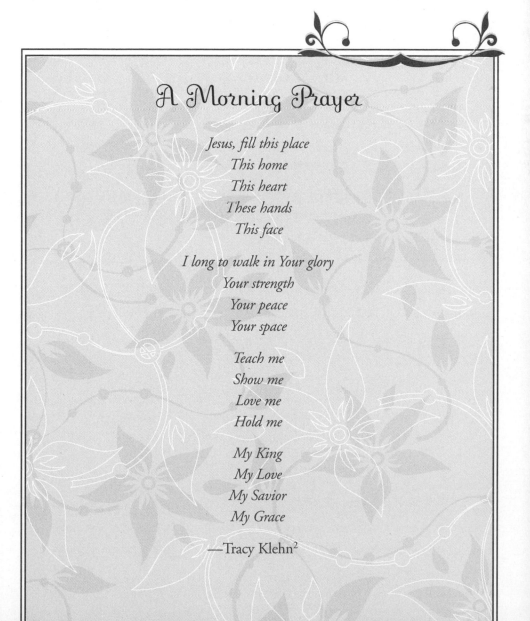

A Morning Prayer

Jesus, fill this place
This home
This heart
These hands
This face

I long to walk in Your glory
Your strength
Your peace
Your space

Teach me
Show me
Love me
Hold me

My King
My Love
My Savior
My Grace

—Tracy Klehn[2]

couple of candles were lit. Hands were washed. Grace was said. It was just din-ner…and yet more. To hear our young neighbor talk, you would have thought we'd pulled out the linens, china, and crystal. She told us she rarely had dinner with her parents and, when she did, it was usually pizza or frozen food in front of the television.

The Power of Play

The families that play together are some of the most attractive families around. Here are some ideas to bring the spirit of fun back into your household:

- ◉ Keep a running score during a month of marathon card games; winner gets a week off from chores (whether Mom, Dad, or a child).

- ◉ Make a block-long hopscotch trail in chalk, and invite everyone in the family to attempt it; neighbors on the block are bound to join in!

- ◉ Use plastic Easter eggs to hide love notes to your kids all over the house.

- ◉ Blow off homework, and go to a movie on a week night.

- ◉ Read a daily joke or riddle—laughter releases endorphins into the blood stream—and everyone will feel better!

- ◉ Watch silly and funny old television shows together.

- ◉ Try every board game in your cabinet.

- ◉ Go to a department store or video-rental store and try the video-game aisle together; choose a game rated E for Everyone. Master it as a family.

I was reminded that there is power in the simple things, the rituals of home life. Dinner is an easy and important time to draw together. Cooking, even if you aren't a great cook, sends a message of care. I'm not talking become a virtual Rachael Ray. Nicer grocery stores often offer meals-to-go (as does your frozen-food section); dinner doesn't have to be fancy. It just has to be dinner. Two or more items are all you need. And time together to review the day, talk, and share.

Another way to live out grace and love at home is to limit your kids' extracurricular activities each season. If you have two or more children, just attending to school and church is quite a bit to handle. Add a sport for each child and your schedules really get crazy. Add more and you have potential chaos and stress. No matter how much the kids want to be involved in everything, remember, you're the parent. You're looking out for them as well as the health of your entire family. Consider joining a local league rather than the stellar traveling league. (What are the chances of your child really getting a scholarship or going pro?) Consider encouraging your child to pursue one seasonal sport a year rather than one each season.

Besides, being selective about activities to join reminds our children that time to relax and play are as important as anything else on the family calendar. After all, each family member's activities affect the rest of the family. We all want our children to grow and experience new things and to excel at a talent. Ask yourself, *Will my child get more out of trying a new league this quarter or a weekend away as a family where we all try something new together? What is going to make a memory? What kinds of experiences will my children rely on for decades to come?*

Don't think of this as limiting your children, but protecting them. You're preserving your children's youth, saving them from stress, helping them discover what they need to say yes to, and what they can decline. You are parenting!

Donna writes: I don't work outside the home, but I'm still exhausted. With two kids in four activities combined, we're always on the run. It seems like I'm always running around, getting the kids to practices, usually one every night, sometimes two. On weekends, we have three or four games. I'm team mom for both boys, so I have to pick up snacks, buy uniforms, and arrange for field time. When we're home, it's only to grab a quick bite or a change of clothes. I think it's healthy for the boys to be in sports, but I'm missing my family. I want our home life back.

If you can't cut back any more than you already have, car time can be valuable time. Turn off your cell phone and radio, and tune in to your child. If your children are grown and gone, spend that time chatting with your husband. If you're single or alone, spend that time talking to God and celebrating the fact that you have a bit of time for yourself! Remember that a happy home life begins with you, so take care of yourself, and pay attention to how God is leading you to make changes or adjustments.

Parenting Your Parents

Of course, some of us have vastly changed home landscapes, because we're trapped between generations or suddenly caring for aging parents. It's a fact of life in our society that many of us are going to be taking care of our parents, and our elders deserve our love and help, just as our children do.

> Joni writes: People say that taking care of a parent is like taking care of kids. But it's not. Raising children, you have hope, something to look forward to and aim for. Caring for my mom is different. It's the end. She feels she's of no use. She has no hope. She just wants to die.

A situation like Joni's can be sad and taxing, which is why it's more important than ever for caregivers to think about how to draw boundaries for themselves, as discussed in the previous chapter.

Another help is to create a way to involve your parents in your family's normal activities. If grandparents live nearby, they'll enjoy being around you and the children even if they're not able to be active participants in every event.

Embrace time with your parents as a gift, even when they're stubborn and crotchety! Endeavor to connect with them (and all of your children's grandparents as much as possible), involving the children in nurturing the relationships. The elderly gain by leaving a legacy; the young gain by the framework of heritage. Take lots of pictures; write down stories. Try to keep an eternal perspective while you shelter your parents through this last season of their lives.

Rebecca moved home to Arkansas, primarily because she wanted to be nearer to her mother. "I was fortunate that I was able to transition workwise so I could relocate—it was my choice, not something circumstances demanded," she says. "After decades of being a plane ride away, I love having the chance to enjoy my mom. Though there's added responsibility that comes with the territory, nothing can replace this time."

INTO-ME-SEE: INTIMACY

It's a point of interest that we Christians are no better at keeping our marriages together than our non-Christian counterparts in the world. In fact, according to some researchers, we're actually worse at keeping our marriages together. Why is that? Is it because we're reluctant to seek counseling when we need it, because we're supposed to have it all together? Is it because we're reluctant to admit failure? Or is it because we're not investing the time necessary to keep moving toward a more intimate relationship with our spouses? Over and over, we've seen couples who've drifted apart, or where one spends time "working on the relationship," while the other spouse is seemingly disengaged.

Many great books have been written about the unique needs of a man and a woman, and if you want to delve deeper into the sometimes-complex marriage relationship, please see "Additional Resources" in the back of this book for recommendations. But what we want to address here is their mutual need for intimacy. Man or woman, we're all seeking this vital aspect of a relationship.

Part of intimacy is fulfilled through sex, to be sure. A satisfying sexual relationship is vital for any growing, maturing, stable marital relationship...within reason. Sometimes, of course, it's hard to maintain with screaming infants, exhaustion, and physical ailments. Stressorama? Remember grace! Women often deny their husbands physical intimacy because of day-to-day stress or because they don't feel attractive (even if their husbands tell them they are). As we said before, sex is more mental and emotional than physical. For a lot of us, it doesn't take much to keep us from being in the mood.

We can pray for desire, pray for energy and time, and pray for the proper mental picture of ourselves as PCOGs, wearing the scars of our pregnancies and age as medals of honor instead of trying to hide them. We need to tell our husbands to talk to us, because we need words and not only kisses to communicate the message that we're beautiful, desirable, and wanted.

Angie writes: Although my husband and I are best friends, we have no intimacy. I am cognizant that the intimate side of our relationship will never be like it was when we met, but I pray daily for some sort of spark beyond friendship.

Some of us are reluctant to explore in a married sexual relationship. It takes *vulnerability* with your husband to tell him how to touch you, where to touch you, when to touch you. It takes a willingness to be vulnerable to tell him you want to try other positions, or even other rooms of the house. According to authors on Christian sexuality, this is the most exciting thing you can do for your husband—talk to him about your desires, needs, and ways you can be closer. He wants to please you. He wants your sexual life to be satisfying. So help him out! Intimacy requires a willingness to be vulnerable.

Women also want an intimacy that goes beyond the marital bed. In her great idea book, *Prayer Starters for Busy Moms,* Tracy Klehn writes,

Before my first writers' conference I felt that the Lord wanted me to ask Russ [my husband] to pray over me specifically for the conference. It was a very humbling and intimate thing for me to ask of him. I've heard the word *intimacy* explained as "into-me-see." When a specific circumstance or issue comes up in your life, humbly ask your husband if he would pray with you.[3]

This is a fabulous idea. First, it honors your husband with your trust and respect. Two, it ties you together through prayer. Three, it builds the intimacy you crave! If you've been married long enough, I'd wager that you've either struggled with a loss of intimacy for a period of time or are currently struggling with a loss of intimacy.

Here's what survey respondents had to say about that:

Eileen writes: My marriage seems to be at a plateau. I don't feel that either of us knows which way to turn to take it to a higher plane. Our relationship seems to be taking up a lot of my energy, and I worry about how it affects the children.

Marsha writes: My marriage is very important to me—I have a great husband! I know he loves me and I adore him—but if we are not connecting with each other, it colors every part of my life. Even when I am exhausted as a mother, I know that this relationship, next to the one with God, is of utmost importance to maintain and grow.

Jen writes: I don't feel loved. I feel secure. I feel needed. But I don't feel wanted, appreciated, or desired. My children look to me for their very existence (e.g., food, clothing, shelter), and my husband just seems to want a maid, chef, and all-around house manager. I do not get together with close friends for one-on-one time anymore; it's always with our children, and they are all that we talk about.

Our first two friends are casting about, trying to figure out how to get more on track with their husbands. And they're exactly right—a healthy marital relationship, not the parent-child relationship, is consistently marked by psychologists as the most important relationship in a child's emotional life. So this is important for us to get right in order to meet our own needs as women—and also to meet the needs of our children.

Our third friend is aching for intimacy on about every front of her life. We wish we could take her to lunch right now, listen to her heart, tell her she's valued, loved, and cherished, and then encourage her to reach out and take action, to sit her loved one down and tell him what she needs. To risk asking! The worst he can say is no. But it is even worse to not tell him at all. We become contributors to the problem rather than part of the solution when we are unwilling to put our hearts on the line.

Joelle writes: We do not share as intimate a relationship as I would like to. At times, he seems indifferent. He is very respectful and caring, but not a person who shows love readily. I believe we need to work on intimacy, and togetherness. Our son is often the focus of attention instead of each other.

We heard from women who have a good sense of intimacy in their lives too:

Teresa writes: My husband works a lot to make ends meet. We try to find time to talk, just the two of us. I find the times we are most intimate is when we share our struggles with each other and pray together.

Denise writes: We are best friends, as well as husband and wife and lovers. We laugh every day!

Best friends… That's what we're seeking in our marriages, right? A deep, abiding sense of knowing and being known. That's what we women want. Remember that we each express and receive love in different ways. In Dr. Gary Chapman's excellent, classic book *The Five Love Languages,* he identifies the five: quality time, words of affirmation, gifts, acts of service, and physical touch.[4] If a wife doesn't express love in a way her spouse understands, he may not realize she has expressed love at all. Think of a man speaking words of love to you in Croatian (assuming you don't speak Croatian); how much would you understand, absorb, and feel?

We sometimes need an interpreter to help us understand our spouses and help them understand us. This concept can also be applied to every other relationship in our lives—whether with a parent, a sibling, a child, or a friend. Find the bridge!

INTIMACY IS NOT JUST ABOUT SEX

Intimate moments happen any time we are sharing on a deep, emotional level with a friend. Such intimacy is what helps take a Class III friendship to a Class IV or even Class V. Whether or not you're married, Klehn's into-me-see scenario is something you could do with anyone you wish you were closer to. Next time a friend is going through a crisis, stop and ask, "Would you mind if I said a quick prayer for you right now?" Too often, we promise to pray for a friend, and it seems like an airy dismissal. Make it a priority, right then. Live out your faith. Be brave. Be courageous and ask her. Who would refuse?

Then, next time you're going through something, say to a friend, "It would help me if you could pray for me, even briefly. Would you mind? I need to know my pals are praying for me right now, and it will help ease my heart." Talk about connection on a holy level! (By the way, prayer works over a phone line too. Rebecca and I have become quite adept at this. When one of us is on the road heading to an important meeting, that person drives while the other one prays! We have come to know the power of praying unceasingly—for us as business partners as well as sisters, that can be five or six times a day!)

What would it do for our children if we were to ask them to pray for us? I know my daughters would be thrilled and honored by such a request. We need to be vulnerable, humble with our children, and model for them what we want them to be—open and honest and eager to grow.

Pit Thoughts Versus His Thoughts

We don't accept each other just as we are.
Christ accepts me just as I am, so I can accept others (Romans 15:7).

I feel like others take me for granted.
I can model selfless service and then mentor others to do the same (Galatians 5:13).

We're constantly irritated with each other.
I want to practice patience and can encourage others to be patient as well (Ephesians 4:2).

There's not enough kindness or compassion in this house.
I can learn to be kind and compassionate in all things, and show them how nice it is (Ephesians 4:32).

We hold grudges instead of forgiving each other.
I must forgive every offense, even if the offender doesn't ask me to (Colossians 3:13).

Finally (which should be the first point), we want a deep, abiding intimacy with our Savior, who is available to us day or night, whether we're young or old, married or unmarried. He is ready to meet us, to hear about our most desperate desires, concerns, and worries. God wants to hold us close. Author Angela Thomas Guffey writes about this:

> I am not finished with occasional indulgence and personal retreats.... But I have come to realize, from the ache in my heart, that my soul needs more. I need more than a few hours in church on Sunday and an hour of Bible study on Wednesday....
>
> I need a love that is deeper, lasts longer, and satisfies the hunger inside me. I need a relationship that is consistent and pure.... I need oceans of strength and mountains of grace. I desperately need Jesus Christ, not just hearing about Jesus, reading about Jesus, or singing about Jesus. I need the Son of God to come and do the Bible in my life....
>
> I am so needy that this cannot wait until the children are older or until our lives are "settled." I must finally come to the end of myself and cry aloud, "Dear God Almighty, I cannot possibly make it apart from You."
>
> To begin to care for my soul is to admit that my vision has become blurry...and I am spinning. I can't see God anymore. I can't feel anything except someone tugging on my jeans.... I am empty. There must be more to living for God. I am tired of spiritually squinting and pretending. I am weary from overcompensating and acting as if I can see the board from the back of the room, when in truth it has become one big blur....
>
> I can't bear the thought of living like this for the rest of my life. I want to walk with God and enjoy His presence. I want to be filled by His love and commitment to me.... I want His love to spill out of my life and onto the ones I adore.[5]

We love that last line—"I want His love to spill out of my life and onto the ones I adore." As Guffey explains in her book, it begins with a true, vital, growing, and intimate relationship with your Savior. Regardless of whether you're strapped for time because of young children, aging parents, work, or all three, take time to be by yourself with your God. Steal ten minutes beside a park on the way home from the grocery store. Go ten minutes early to pick up a child from soccer prac-tice or to a meeting or appointment. Make those stolen moments your prayer parking lot. You can make time for an intimate relationship with God—if you want it badly enough.

When there is opportunity for retreat, leap! On your own, with friends, with a church group, just go. (See WhatWomenWantBook.com for personal and group retreat plans.) I'm constantly amazed at how hesitant women are to leave their fami-lies for a weekend of retreat. Your husband, children, and parents in the retirement home will all benefit by your taking care of yourself. Yes, if you have a young fam-ily, you're bound to come home to a frazzled husband, messy house, and kids who all want to sit on your lap at once. But that short-term angst will be won over by long-term gain. Think with eternal perspective. Think of yourself as a heroine in an epic battle. Does she deny the call of her King because the house might fall apart after a weekend without her or because she has an appointment she's unwill-ing to reschedule? Does she give in to her fears of not knowing what will be planned for her, where she'll sleep, if she'll know anyone? Or does she cry, "You call, my King, and I shall answer!"

Listen to your heart. Delve deep. Come away, and know your King as your own beloved. This, above all else, will bring you joy and peace and intimacy, right where you are.

Finally, all of you, live in harmony
with one another; be sympathetic, love as brothers,
be compassionate and humble.
1 Peter 3:8

In the Beginning Was Relationship

A Chat with Barbara Rainey
About the Intimacy You Crave

After marrying her best friend from college, Barbara Rainey and her new husband, Dennis, traveled to seminary (where, he says, he wanted to "major in Howard Hendricks," the teaching of a gifted professor), learned all they could about marriage and raising a Christian family from Hendricks, then ended up in the FamilyLife ministry "by default." Moving to Little Rock, Arkansas, the Raineys joined other couples in founding a ministry with the primary goal of assisting Campus Crusade missionaries preserve and save their marriages. This venture that Barbara says she and Dennis thought would last just a few years has turned into a thirty-"and counting"-year-old ministry. Now an empty nester with six grown children, Barbara is as busy as ever in a thriving ministry, speaking, and writing career. Rebecca asks her, in the midst of it all, how does she invest in her marriage?

Rebecca: I've known you forever, it seems, from our college days. But how long have you been married now, Barbara?

Barbara: Thirty-four years, a lot longer than we thought we'd make it—not because we thought we'd get divorced, but because I thought Jesus would come back!

Rebecca: [laughing] I keep hoping for the same, especially when I'm under a deadline. What have you discovered about your own marriage through these years of ministry?

Barbara: If you'd asked me that question sixteen years ago, I'd have given you the delusional answer—that sometime soon we'd "arrive," that it would get easier. But the reality is marriage is hard work, and you never arrive at the finish line. There are things that get easier because we know each other so well, but it always remains work.

Rebecca: Sounds a little like the Christian life, doesn't it?

Barbara: Yes!

Rebecca: Through FamilyLife you've had the opportunity to see many, many marriage relationships, some great and some troubled. What's the number one need you see in Christian marriages today?

Barbara: Communication! An old answer, but honestly, so much of the struggle in marriage is because we're not hearing what our spouses are really saying, or not accurately saying what we need our spouses to hear. We have to stick with it and grow past those differences in communication styles. We're so different as men and women, and we underestimate the impact of those differences.

Rebecca: The women in our survey expressed a need for intimacy—what do you think that tells us about communication in their marriages?

Barbara: Communication reflects what's really going on in your relationship. If you're having trouble communicating, hitting roadblocks, it's hard to be intimate, because intimacy is really about knowing another person.

Rebecca: That sounds like a principle that relates to more than just marriage.

Barbara: The same issues and principles apply to any relationship. If two friends love and care about each other and one gets hurt, she tends to withdraw rather than work through the issue. If one or both people withdraw, then intimacy dries up.

Rebecca: We've all experienced one of those rifts in some relationship. What causes it?

Barbara: Feeling left out, like you're not a priority, like you're not understood, rejection—hurt feelings of any sort can drive a wedge. Any intimacy is based on communication; you have to follow through and get down to naming what offends and what you need, so that the next time it happens, you can point it out, and both parties can begin to learn, fight through the pain, and figure out the tools they need to work it through so they can go on in their relationship. People need training and skills to fight through obstacles rather than run away. Our divorce culture tells us to bail. But if you always bail, you never achieve intimacy with anyone.

Rebecca: "Fight through" is an interesting choice of words. What do you mean by that?

Barbara: I don't mean fight in the literal sense, but rather do the work necessary in order to come through on the other side. It's a battle; it takes courage to go forward into something that's difficult. It takes stamina and commitment to engage, name the struggle, and apply forgiveness or whatever is needed. If you do these things, your relationship will prosper.

Rebecca: Many of us don't have a clue on how to do these things well, do we?

Barbara: No. It's not natural; even if we've been raised in good homes and taught good skills, we still have miles to go as adults. We think we're prepared, and then we realize there is still much to learn.

Rebecca: What happens if the woman wants to fight through, work at her marriage, and her husband doesn't?

Barbara: The real solution in a marriage, or a friendship for that matter, is to find your true hope and security in the Lord. This will not be the only or last time you feel lonely and rejected. The Enemy whispers, "You're the only one who's married to a guy, or has a friend like her, who doesn't meet your needs." It's so easy to buy that and feel sorry for ourselves! During seasons of difficulty, though, it helps to grow in our relationship with the Lord…if a spouse or friend isn't interested in resolving an issue or growing closer together. We never face that with God. He's always interested, always pursuing.

Rebecca: I love that about him. What one thing would you suggest for women who want to pursue a relationship with God?

Barbara: I'm a huge advocate of women being in small-group Bible study.

I've seen what it does for me. I have to be in a study group because I need accountability to do my homework and show up in class—and I've learned so much. It's really helped me develop a relationship with the Lord that sustains me during the hard times.

Rebecca: Practically speaking, how do we women let God really meet our needs?

Barbara: Relationship with God begins with study of his Word. The Bible is his letter to us. It's where he relates to us about who he is, who we really are, and how we relate and experience him. Not too long ago, I left a study after learning about how "God is my strength." I remember thinking, *If God is my strength, how can I apply that today?*

When we were going through a difficult time with one of our kids, I prayed that God would give me strength, and I experienced it in a way I never had before. It's not that God meets all my needs all the time. God is not a vending machine or fairy godmother or magician. So when he doesn't meet my needs immediately, it's human nature to get disappointed in him. But if we continue to go back to him and say, *Okay, Lord, this is not working out the way I thought it would,* or, *You aren't going about this the way I thought you would,* and then add, *but I trust you, and I will not go away,* oh, our God loves that.

Rebecca: There's that communication principle again that applies back to intimacy in a marriage or friendship!

Barbara: Exactly. Everyone in relationship with me needs to know I will not abandon them or go away. It may not be pretty or the way I like, but there are seasons where we just gut it out. It's not going to kill me to live with less-than-ideal circumstances for a while. I've learned that suffering actually is good for us.

Rebecca: Good for us, but I hate it!

Barbara: You're not the only one. As Americans, we run from it. We try to alleviate all pain, discomfort, and difficulty from our lives, and we try to do that for our kids too! So God has to whack us a good one to get us to go through some difficulties that will grow our relationship. We don't realize that we're missing opportunities to know him better.

Rebecca: Yes, nothing like a little pain to push us back into God's arms. That's intimacy.

Barbara: It really is a good thing, even though we fight it tooth and nail.

Rebecca: What do you say to women about sexual intimacy?

Barbara: The interesting thing about sex is that God wired men and women so differently. Sometimes it feels like a cruel joke, because we have such different needs and different abilities to express them. In the whole grand scheme of things, God designed us to complement each other. So I need my husband and everything he is as a male, because I am not. And he needs me for the same reason. We couldn't be more opposite, and that's true in our sexual relationship. It's been *very* hard, because we're so different. But we've learned to appreciate our differences, even though it took years; in doing so, we've reached a level of intimacy we never could have imagined in our first twenty years together. There's a level of acceptance and appreciation and understanding in each other, rather than trying to change each other. Our vast differences are not a mistake.

Rebecca: There's a level of service and sacrifice that are part and parcel of any true intimacy, isn't there?

Barbara: Paul said that a marriage is a reflection of Christ's relationship to the church. There's not a relationship that involves more sacrifice and service than that, is there? And it's true about any relationship in our lives. It's about appreciating how God has created another person and getting to know everything about them. The trouble with many marriages and friendships is that people forget to have a sense of adventure and a spirit of discovery about their loved ones.

Rebecca: What if you're too tired for sex?

Barbara: [laughing] There are definitely months, years, or even decades when you spend a good deal of your time and energy on other things, such as raising children. But even when the children are young, it's important to spend time and energy on your marriage. It's actually the best thing you can do for everyone—being close to your husband.

Rebecca: Because then you're modeling a good relationship.

Barbara: Absolutely. And if couples can just make it through that stage to this stage in life, where Dennis and I are as empty nesters, it can be a new beginning. Too many couples miss out on the reward because they don't stick it out.

Rebecca: It's worth going the extra mile?

Barbara: Every time. We can't let our relationships lapse, even in the face of laundry and children and jobs. We have to do the work to keep them healthy, growing. Don't settle. Ever. If you're unhappy, ask yourself, *What am I going to do about this?* Life is full of choices—choose everything you can to help grow your relationships with a friend, a spouse, with God himself.

Rebecca: Why do you think God created us with this deep need for intimacy?

Barbara: God is relationship. He has a relationship with the Son and the Holy Spirit, they're unified, and we're created in his image with that kind of need for intimacy. He wants us to know him, intimately, and he gives us a glimpse of himself in others. We cannot ignore the call to intimacy, to relationship, to love. It's who we are.

Body by God

Your Physical Health and Appearance

> *Physically, no one comforts better than Christ.* In the midst
> of your deepest physical pain, His presence brings comfort
> and strength. He may choose to restore your physical
> health, but frankly, He may not. Regardless, His grace is
> abundantly sufficient for you. His hand is on your life at
> this time of your affliction. It's better than the hand of
> any friend, any partner, any parent, or any child, because
> when He touches, He brings great compassion and lasting
> relief. No one comforts better than Christ.
>
> CHARLES R. SWINDOLL

We're killing ourselves. Across the country, we're dying from lack of nutrition and physical exercise, along with overdoses of sugar, alcohol, and stress, or all three. We're addicted to more painkillers than ever before in history, and we're afraid—afraid we're not going to be able to do all we want to in the future, afraid we'll be housebound, afraid that our weight issues will keep us from jobs or friends, afraid we might not be able to walk a mile, let alone take a hike in new territory.

What we Christian women want is to look good and, even more, to feel good;

to live every day our God has given us and not leave on the table any day we could have taken; to deal with the issues that contribute to our ill health (if any) and get on to the rest of our lives. We want to learn how to live with chronic illness—or fight the disease that threatens to destroy us—with grace and without fear; we want to make peace with our bodies, and accept and embrace who we are and how we were made.

AMERICA'S TOP HEALTH ISSUE

Unless you've been hiding under a rock, you know the facts. Open any magazine and you'll realize that more than 66 percent of adults over the age of twenty struggle with weight issues—most of us on the gotta-lose-it side, a few of us on the need-to-gain-it side. The survey consensus was overwhelming: comments on physical health were focused on weight.

I (Lisa) am in yet another chapter of my life bent on losing weight; Rebecca, as a diabetic, shares my concerns—it's even more critical that she watch what happens with her body. I'll turn forty as this book goes to press, and I want to be the healthiest I've been in years.

Rebecca encourages me, "Do it now because it just gets harder!"

With my childbirth years behind me, I can no longer use pregnancy as an excuse for the forty pounds I've gained since marriage. My weight issue is between me and God. Unfortunately, as Rebecca says, though my weight issue may be between me and God, the rest of the world notices. Being overweight is the last culturally acceptable prejudice.

Rebecca and I have each tried diet after diet, but the fact is we both love to eat, along with all the things that go with dining in or out.

My aunt relates. "I spend my whole day thinking about food," she quips.

We do too! We love planning for meals, shopping at an excellent store (I *feel happy* entering Whole Foods), cooking, gathering friends or family members around the table, and enjoying a meal together. And now there's a twenty-four-hour food channel!

Sally writes: I'm not obese, but I'm close to it. I've tried pretty much any diet out there. I lose weight and then gain it back again. It gets harder each time, partly because I think I'm defeated before I even start. I don't know where to turn.

In our own efforts over the years, we've come to understand what every successful eater who truly loves food knows: the only thing that works in weight control is portion control, healthful eating, and working off enough calories to justify what you're taking in. We just don't burn enough calories during our sedentary, daily tasks. In order to eat what we want, we need to get our bodies moving. And walking from one side of the house to the other or going up and down the office entry stairs just doesn't cut it.

Let's think about what we eat every day. Let's decide to take in the kinds of calories our bodies can process most efficiently. I lost a lot of weight on the South Beach Diet last year, but then gained half of it back when I began eating white carbohydrates again. I want to eat the occasional white carb, so I do. (I'm sorry, but I just can't do whole-wheat spaghetti or say no to every slice of Italian bread offered me!) If I don't allow myself occasional splurges, I'm afraid I'll go off the deep end and throw my entire eating plan out the window. But the splurges in my diet need to be fewer and farther between. I need to eat more veggies than I really want every day. I need to stay away from sugars and junk food. It all boils down to daily choices, self-respect, and self-care more than it does to self-control.

When we're overweight, it can interfere with our sleep (overweight people struggle more often with sleep apnea and snoring), our activity level (we avoid fun activities that take physical effort), our sex lives (isn't it hard to feel sexy when carrying extra pounds?), and our overall satisfaction with life. Obesity often leads to diabetes, heart disease, and other illnesses too. We are trading our days, weeks, months, even years of our lives for something we can largely change. Yes, there are

When Something's Got to Give

When people try to fix a lifetime of food and weight problems, many changes become necessary. Check any of the following that apply to you.

In order to lose weight and keep it off, I might be changing...

○ *a comfortable way of life.*

○ *my best and most acceptable form of distraction.*

○ *a way to satisfy needs.*

○ *protection from my own sexual impulses.*

○ *protection from the sexual advances of others.*

○ *a way to control my life with false structure.*

○ *a major coping mechanism for life's stresses.*

○ *my tried-and-true way to deal with boredom.*

○ *my best or most acceptable numbing device used for emotional pain and anger.*

○ *a way of thinking that reinforces those feelings of not being good enough.*

○ *a way of pretending I have no problems.*[1]

hereditary issues or underlying medical conditions that make it more difficult for some of us. But for most, weight issues are a result of our choices. So why do we avoid the right ones?

Rebecca says, "One of the many weight-loss counselors I saw (pick a diet—I've done it *and* paid for it) told our group that we were all eating to fill our emotional holes. There is some truth to that for all of us who are in this war. Sometimes I'm bored, sometimes I'm thirsty, but sometimes I'm just hungry!" Discerning why we're overeating or eating the wrong things and why we want to eat differently seem to be two of the key factors to getting on target with our weight.

> Geneva writes: I'm winning the war on weight. My doctor told me two
> years ago that I was prediabetic. I needed to lose weight and exercise. I'd
> heard that before! But she took time to describe what was happening to
> my body and what could happen if I became a full-fledged diabetic, and
> she said she wanted to see me in four months, twenty-eight pounds lighter.
> I changed the way I thought about food (more as fuel, less as pleasure),
> learned to regulate my food, and walked everywhere, logging twenty-five
> miles a week. I hit my doctor's goal and more! My present goal is to gain
> pleasure from things that aren't food and learn to like what I eat (veggies,
> whole grains) rather than eat what I like. The good news? My blood sugar
> numbers are normal, and I hope I dodged the diabetes bullet.

A NOTE TO OUR SKINNY SISTERS

Maybe you're one of our fortunate sisters, blessed with a fabulous metabolism or an internal setting that never allows you to overeat. In our survey, very few women responded that weight was not an issue for them. But we know you're out there!

We challenge you, too, to ensure you are making wise food choices for the right reasons. No matter what our bodies look like, it's a universal challenge to exercise consistently, eat healthily, and respect our bodies as "God's temple (His sanctuary),… God's spirit has His permanent dwelling in you" (1 Corinthians 3:16, AMP). We all want to accept our bodies as God made them, but we want them to be *all* that God made them: We want to be strong. We want healthy hearts. We want to be able to climb stairs and mountains without keeling over!

Women want to be healthy—physically, emotionally, mentally, spiritually. And all of those are intertwined. So what is it that keeps you from making the right choices?

> Ilene writes: I only have to walk around the block to go to Curves, but do I make it? No.

> Anita writes: It seems the more I want to lose weight, the more I want to eat.

> Nicole writes: I am a compulsive eater! I have to surrender this area to God.

Some of us give up for a time or are "refusing to fight," as our friend Suzy puts it. She goes on:

> I could stand to lose twenty pounds, but I refuse to live my life under restriction or in gluttony. I want balance here too! I try not to obsess on my appearance. I look decent enough even if a bit heavier than I'd like. To me the outside of the cup isn't as important as the inside. It helps that I'm twenty years younger than my dh [dear husband], and he thinks I'm a hot chick and tells me that all the time. He really means it, so that helps me relax about how I look.

We love Suzy's "dh"! We wish every one of you out there had a husband—or someone—calling you a hot chick (if you don't), but we wish even more that every one of us could learn to truly love and accept ourselves and see what comes of it. We women put so much energy into caring for others and oftentimes shortchange ourselves. Story after story in our survey shows us a world of women who work like crazy all day, caring for their families or friends or working overtime, only to fall into bed, utterly exhausted.

We want to be thankful for what we do have. We want to be able to tackle change and hope that our physical health can improve. What will it take for you? Daily walks? Praying with a weight-loss buddy? Seeking godly counsel to help you untangle the emotional issues that may be holding you back? Are you afraid of change? If so, why?

Be kind to yourself and spend some time considering what is good about your body—there's got to be something! List ten things about your body you're grateful for. Then think about what you can do to get your body moving. You may never be the size you were a decade ago, but what is a realistic and healthy chal-

Minigoals for Shaping Up

Check three or more things you could do this week to get closer to your goal of being healthy.

○ Drink lots of water—often we mistake thirst for hunger.

○ Go all-organic for one grocery run per month.

○ Lose one pound at a time.

○ Walk today and the day after tomorrow.

○ Explore a path in a park you've never tried.

○ Cut down caffeine intake by one-half cup per day.

○ Skip dessert every other night.

○ Eat an apple before you go to the grocery store.

○ Shop at the grocery store with cash, and keep to your list.

○ When you're tempted to snack, polish your nails (think about it!).

○ Wait fifteen minutes before heading to the refrigerator.

○ Clean up the kitchen after dinner, turn out the light, and don't go back in until morning.

○ Other: _____

lenge to set for yourself? Can you set a minichallenge for yourself, and then define the next challenge when you reach the first goal?

It's easier for me to think about taking off weight five pounds at a time. Most of us are big on instant gratification, but a huge health goal can take a while to reach. Give yourself time, set minigoals—celebrate them, and we guarantee you'll get closer to your goal.

THE CALLS OF THE WILD

Rebecca and I are encouraging each other to lose twenty pounds over five months. Just four pounds a month, one pound a week—that doesn't sound daunting, does it? It's more important for me to focus on feeling *better* than feeling skinnier. It's far more gratifying, and it's actually making me think more about *why* I eat rather than just *what* I eat. We're both praying about the things that drive us toward unhealthy choices in the first place, asking God to reveal them to us. I call them "the calls of the wild." No, this isn't a whisper in my ear to go trekking in the Himalayas. When speaking of "the wild" here, I'm referring to those calls of our world that are often louder than our heavenly call.

The greatest call of the wild is the idea that *we can control our own destiny.* To enjoy a body by God—at least on the healthy-weight front—we focus on the power of submission to him and trust him in all things. We take responsibility for our actions and our choices but recognize that we cannot control everything in our wild world. If we honestly approach our loving Savior, he will gently but firmly set us on the right path. If I'm holding a doughnut in one hand and an apple in the other, and I ask God which one to eat, he'll make clear what I don't want to hear. It's a lesson in control and giving it *all* to El Roi, our God who sees. It's about giving him control rather than our own self-control.

The call of the wild, however, asks us to put off responsibility until later. It tells us to *indulge now.* It reminds us that we *deserve* the doughnut because it will make us happy and content. The wild whispers that we'll feel the rush of control, when actually it represents no control at all. For our underweight sisters, this is the same call and the same promises—just from the other direction: "Abstain. Withdraw. Say no, even if your body is in starvation mode."

The reality is that anything that smacks of the call of the wild is to be avoided. Sin speaks to us in a variety of ways, preying upon us where we are weak. There is so much more to us than what we eat or don't eat! We need to figure out *why* we eat the way we do and *why* we listen to the voice of the wild rather than the voice of truth. Yes, those french fries taste good, but what is the reason we're stuffing them into our mouths even after our stomachs tell us we're full?

Stephen Arterburn and Dr. Linda Mintle write, "Losing weight and keeping it off has more to do with changing how you think, feel, and act at any given moment rather than what you eat or whether you take part in a regular exercise program."[2] So we must begin there.

Pit Thoughts Versus His Thoughts

Why did he make my body this way?
I can praise him because I am wonderfully made (Psalm 139:14).

I have no self-control; I don't have the power to change anything on my own.
His power works in me. He is my strength (Ephesians 1:19).

I'm really anxious about my health and what will happen later in my life.
He will give me peace about the future when I talk to him about it
(1 Peter 5:7).

This illness is too much for me to bear.
Even if my body fails me completely, he is all I really need (Psalm 73:25–26).

I've tried this before. Why should this time be any different?
As I trust him, he will fill me with hope (Romans 15:13).

An Affair of the Heart

Cardiovascular disease is the number one killer of women.[3] Carrying extra weight makes us like heart attacks waiting to happen. Many treatments advised by doctors for people suffering heart disease can benefit the rest of us who are trying to avoid it or even those who simply want to live more healthfully. What can you do to save your heart? Follow these ten methods:

1. *Choose the most convenient way to get active.* If it's hard, you're less likely to get to it. So begin with three times a week. Work up to five.

2. *Gradually eat less saturated fat.* For example, change from drinking whole milk to 2 percent, then 1 percent, then nonfat.

3. *Think color.* Truly work on getting five to seven servings of fruits and vegetables each day, and try to make them all different colors to keep things interesting (and even more nutritious!).

4. *Increase the fiber content in your diet.* If one loaf of bread that you choose at the grocery store has less than three grams of fiber per slice, put it back on the shelf and find another. The first ingredient should be "whole wheat flour." Think white = bad; brown = good.

5. *Stop smoking.* But then you knew that. Isn't it time? And the hype about second-hand smoke isn't just hype—it's truly bad for us. Send smokers in your life outside, and encourage them to quit too!

6. *Check your cholesterol.* You want your HDL to be high and your LDL to be low. Have your cholesterol rechecked in three months, then six months, to make sure you're on the road toward better health.

7. *Get a pedometer and walk one thousand steps a day.* You can do it! Gradually work toward higher goals, including walks around the block—or multi-milers.

8. *Confront what's stressing you out—because stress kills.* You really can make changes: change jobs, reduce hours, cut back on volunteer work, go to family and/or marital counseling, and so on. Do whatever you need to reduce your stress. Begin now. Not later.

9. *Find a friend.* Preferably, find someone you can confide in about the stress in your life, and someone who will help you map out a health plan and encourage you as you pursue it.

10. *Pray daily.* Daily meditation and prayer helps keep you calm and your blood pressure low.

STRESSORAMA: IT KILLS

Stress is a literal killer. Scientists found a long period of stress can literally age human cells by ten years or more.[4] Look at pictures of departing prime minister of England Tony Blair (who has said he will step down from his role in September 2007) or former president Bill Clinton at age forty-eight and then again at age fifty-three. Both men bear the scars of more than five years worth of aging—every wrinkle and gray hair is born of bearing both personal and national trauma. But it doesn't require a leading position in a superpower country to age beyond our years. Many of us are in trenches of our own making, trenches we need to soon exit.

> Alexandra writes: I work twelve hours a day, stop at the store on the way home, make dinner at eight o'clock for the family, help the kids with home- work, and then clean up. I fall into bed exhausted around eleven o'clock and wake, exhausted, at five o'clock in the morning. But I'm afraid I can't stop. I've worked so hard to get here. I'm afraid of what I could lose: stature, prestige, money.

> Colette writes: Your question, "Why are you afraid to change?" took me aback. With all the stresses in my life, I haven't had time to stop and think. I'm starting to think about changes I need to make to reduce the stress in my life. I cannot change how things are, but my attitudes and outlook can.

We agree with Colette to some extent. Some stresses in life are just a part of life, the nonnegotiables, and it helps if we take them on with a right attitude. But just as God designed good and healthy foods to eat, he gives us opportunities to experience joy and peace on a daily basis, opportunities to find satisfaction rather than continual striving. You and I want to find contentment within a life lived in communication with the Holy One, where we never need to feel alone.

CHRONIC ILLNESS

Some of you are thinking, *I wish my only health problem was my weight or my stress.* For those of you facing a chronic or life-threatening illness, being too heavy or too thin sounds like kindergarten stuff. Do nurses and lab techs know you by name?

> Marcy writes: I had a bad accident when my youngest child (of three) was still an infant. Learning to deal with the daily struggles as a result of the accident has been hard. I am on the road to recovery, working on getting full mobility and strength back, so I can be the mother I want to be.

You may be living with constant back pain or an autoimmune disease. You may be facing one more round of chemotherapy for breast cancer or struggling with issues of fear or depression. Handling your chronic illness on mental and emotional and spiritual levels—as well as the physical—can become your most important ally. Rebecca has dealt with diabetes for years and gone through multiple treatments for thyroid cancer (happily in remission). My mom, Karen, has rheumatoid arthritis. Your illness might bring annual, monthly, weekly or even hourly battles with the Dark One who wishes to use it for his purposes, not for God's glory. Do you believe that you are "fearfully and wonderfully made" (see Psalm 139)? Do you believe that God is well aware of your struggle? Rebecca says that ultimately it's still a matter of trust.

> Mom writes: Living with the fear that chronic disease almost always generates requires trust and faith that God will be with me no matter what lies ahead. It also requires getting up every day and being thankful for what I do have rather than fretting about what I *don't*. I thank God every day for the wisdom of doctors, medications, and procedures that have brought me quality of life.

Most women gain a sense of empowerment (versus powerlessness) by becoming fully informed about their illness. Be aware that if you hop on the Internet, you will find a plethora of information (not all of it trustworthy and all of it possibly overwhelming). Begin a page of notes and a second page of questions for your doctors so you can begin building your own knowledge base. One of the greatest fears about chronic illness is how it may affect lifestyle or life goals. Find a support group through your hospital or church.

Remember that no matter how dark the hour, how frightened you are, or how much pain you are suffering, you are not alone. God is constantly present, holding your hand or even holding you in his lap when you are at your most needy. Ask for help from your Savior and your friends. We know it can be difficult to ask, but when you don't, you are passing over possible support, guidance, and hope. Allow your friends and God to do what they want to do most—express love to you through their support. And find inspiration in Joni Eareckson Tada, a quadriplegic, and her words:

> When I was on my feet, big boisterous pleasures provided only fleeting satisfaction. In a wheelchair, satisfaction settles in as I sit under an oak tree on a windy day and delight in the rustle of leaves or sit by a fire and enjoy the soothing strains of a symphony. These smaller, less noisy pleasures are rich because, unlike the fun on my feet, these things yield patience, endurance, and a spirit of gratitude, all of which fits me further for eternity.
> It is this yieldedness that gains you the most here on earth.[5]

We find ourselves asking, even without physical trauma, how can we find such yieldedness?

SISTER, LET IT SHINE

Physical health obviously relates to our appearance. We often try to conceal our shortcomings by things we put on the outside. We women spend an inordinate amount of time making ourselves look as good as possible, don't we? We spend money on hair for things men would never consider doing—highlighting, lowlighting, extending, cutting, curling, straightening. We spend more cash on nails and makeup. We pour over clothing catalogs and take hours trying on clothes to see what makes us look best. And shoes? Don't get us started on shoes. We all love

Just Ask: Questions for a Friend with Chronic Illness

- "What events in your life are changing and how are you coping with the changes?"

- "Can I help you talk through a decision you are weighing right now? I know you are constantly seeking answers, with no guarantees."

- "What kind of meal would your family enjoy this week?" (Take it over in disposable dishes, if possible.)

- "Do you want company the day that you wait for the test results? I could come over for a couple of hours."

- "How do you feel God is working through—or despite—this illness in your life? I'm interested."

- "What do you wish people understood about your illness?"

- "Would you be comfortable having your name on a prayer list, so that others can pray for you?" (Don't assume she's okay with that.)

- "I'd like to pray for you right now, is that okay?"

- "Do you have an errand I can run for you before coming over?"

- "Would you like to go with me to a concert (a walk in the park/a drive to a scenic location) today?" (She's more likely to participate if you ask at the last minute depending on whether it's a good day or a bad day.)

- "What are your top three indulgences?" (and then spoil her soon).[6]

them, because regardless of what we weigh, shoes always fit. And the only thing you have to look at in the store mirror is your feet!

Regardless of your shape or features, whether you are a long-distance runner or in a wheelchair, you are already beautiful. God longs to shine through you! When you allow him to do so, you instantly become attractive.

I read somewhere that men claim the sexiest thing a woman can do is smile. Look around you in a crowded room and see if you agree. Who are your eyes drawn to? The beautiful face looking tired and troubled or the average-looking woman engaged in smiling conversation? Think of three women you consider average in looks but who seem happy. Then think of three above-average-looking women who seem unhappy. Which group would you be more apt to call beautiful? Add a fragrance-of-God attribute to that smile, and you're a beauty that can't be beat!

We know women who have outward beauty, and then we know true beauties, women who know they belong to God and celebrate life. They understand that every moment is a moment of potential joy. They exude love and joy and peace. If someone embodied all of that, even if she were outwardly less than perfect, who could resist her?

Now stop and reflect on the fact that within you lies a potential true beauty. Secure in your knowledge that God loves you, you are eager to celebrate every moment of life. As you mirror God's love and joy and peace to the world, imagine that flowing back into you, through you, then out of you! God can rock our world. God can work through each of us. God can show the world what beauty truly is!

Hear it again from us. You are a PCOG. You have an inner beauty, an inner healthy person, just waiting to shine through your body, which was designed by God himself. Will you let her shine?

Offer yourselves to God, as those who have been
brought from death to life; and offer the parts of
your body to him as instruments of righteousness.

Romans 6:13

In the Beginning Was Body, Soul, and Spirit

A Chat with *Dr. Linda Mintle*
About the Body and Appearance You Crave

Thousands in need have responded to Dr. Linda Mintle's warm style and compassion. She is the epitome of a woman living on purpose—using her gifts, talents, and passion for God—in her role of helping people who are struggling with issues that range from marriage trauma to eating disorders to infertility. Dr. Linda is a licensed clinical social worker, therapist, and author of *Lose It for Life, Overweight Kids,* and *Making Peace with Your Thighs,* among others. We thought a woman who wrote a book about how to make peace with our thighs was the perfect one for us to talk to about body image. What follows is an exclusive chat between Lisa and Linda, as Lisa seeks Linda's core advice on having a healthy body, soul, and spirit.

Lisa: From a psychological perspective, how important is it for women to approach health on a mental/emotional/spiritual as well as a physical front?

Linda: Since we were each created with a body, soul, and spirit, to ignore any one part results in an unbalanced life. But because our culture focuses so much on our bodies, it's difficult to develop a holistic view of who we are. Weight obsession and physical fitness are national

192 ⊕ Body By God

pastimes. Beauty and thinness are idolized and worshiped. And we abuse our bodies with lack of sleep—

Lisa: Oh yeah, that could be its own book!

Linda: —as well as self-induced stress, alcohol, tobacco, and unhealthy sexual practices. So to live a balanced life, we must resist the pull toward body obsession or neglect and instead attend to all parts of who we are. Since we are body, we must eat healthy, exercise, get enough rest, and guard what is sacred.

Lisa: And because we have a soul?

Linda: We must daily renew our minds with God's truth, manage our emotions and stress, and work through relationship difficulties.

Lisa: And because we are spirit?

Linda: We must know how to satisfy our spiritual hunger and longings through an intimate relationship with God.

Lisa: What are the top cultural lies that women believe about their physical form?

Linda: The "I can never be thin enough" lie, which keeps us on a weight-loss roller coaster, constantly in need of more diets and weight-loss plans. This is one of the reasons that body dissatisfaction is at an all-time high. Then there's the "there's always more that could be done" lie, which sets up the need for constant physical improvement like cosmetic surgeries, anti-aging strategies, and the use of more products and pills—all of which are costly and distract us from other parts of our lives.

Lisa: What else plagues us?

Linda: Oh, of course, there's the "you have to have big breasts (or some other body part) to be successful" lie. Perfection is our goal and can be found through cosmetic surgery or other forms of alteration. Whether it's a larger booty, fuller lips, smaller nose, or bigger breasts, someone else (besides God) is defining who we are supposed to be. Do we really want to clone ourselves into someone else's idea of how we should look?

Lisa: I hope I don't, but it's hard! Suddenly I've hit forty and everything is changing in my body. I'll admit that when I stare in the mirror, I have Botox fantasies. The wrinkles… Good grief, the new wrinkles and spots! How can we combat society's spiral?

Linda: I can think of six ways right off the bat. First, be intentional in defying the cultural body myths. Question the sanity of such claims as "thin is in" and ask yourself if those views drive you to your checkbook, to obsession, or to God.

Next, don't accept narrow cultural prescriptions for beauty. In a day and age in which we celebrate diversity, something is wrong with the one-size-fits-all mentality. Reclaim your body as unique and individually created. You aren't a mistake in need of a fix! Broaden your definition of beauty. Go beyond what's skin deep.

Third, rethink your values. Make the choice to bring back wholeness by embracing the spiritual (as in *God looks at the heart*) and the emotional (as in *physical beauty doesn't bring peace and contentment*).

Fourth, stop comparing yourself to unrealistic media images of how you are "supposed" to look. Supermodels are typically not the epitome of healthy eating and living. And they represent the smallest fraction of women. Most often their images are airbrushed, computer altered, professionally lighted, and attended to by fashion experts and professional hairstylists.

Lisa: I often wish I had a whole team to help me get ready in the morning!

Linda: You and me both, but we have to fight that urge.

The fifth way to combat the lies the world tells us is to be around other women who don't obsess about their bodies. It will help you refocus.

Sixth, change conversations away from the physical to the emotional and spiritual parts of people's lives. Bring back the needed balance. Discuss character and spiritual experiences.

Lisa: What are the spiritual lies the devil would like us to believe? How do we combat those?

Linda: It's interesting that the original sin involved food and body image! Think about it. After sin entered the picture, the first couple's perfect physical bodies didn't change, but their reactions to them changed immensely. They were naked, ashamed, and hid from God. None of this was true before the Fall. See how sin distorts our ability to see ourselves the way God sees us? The Enemy knows this and does everything in his power to distract us from our true identity and power. The Father of Lies tells us we are shamed, inadequate, unworthy of God's love. He wants us to doubt God. But when we repent and accept God's forgiveness and grace, we are changed. A spiritual transformation takes place that impacts all parts of our lives. As we daily renew our minds with Christ's truth, we are healed from lies and can see ourselves through God's eyes—beautiful, changed, and forgiven.

Lisa: What are the greatest gifts that God has given us in our physical form?

Linda: Our bodies are the temples that house his Holy Spirit. The fact that all of God is in Christ and all of Christ is in me gives me a power and authority I would never have on my own. My identity is secure. My acceptance is sealed. Our bodies give life, and through them, we give life. They provide movement, touch, postures of worship, and a dwelling place for God.

Lisa: What's the most important thing a woman who is suffering from chronic illness can do to help combat her disease and health issues?

Linda: She should keep her mind renewed with the love and promises of God; not allow the Enemy to deceive her with ungodly thoughts; remind herself that she isn't forgotten or unimportant, punished and unloved. The body may fail, but God never does. While we don't always understand our physical struggles, we can be assured that God is using them to bring glory to his name. Christ knows our suffering firsthand. By staying intimate with him and believing his Word, we can make it to the other side of grief and pain.

Lisa: Anything else you'd like to share with women who are eager to improve their physical health?

Linda: The toll that stress, trauma, and disease take on a women's health is well documented. Make it a goal to better manage and eliminate stress. Learn to relax, slow down, eat well, exercise, and know God and what he says about you. Attend to your emotional, interpersonal, and spiritual states. Whatever you can do to bring peace and resolution to problematic relationships, do it. Forgive often, offer grace to others, be intimate with God, and be mindful of the connection between body, soul, and spirit.

On God's Road

Meaning and Purpose in Your Life

> Purpose in life is not just something we do. It involves
> who we are and our way of being in this world.
>
> JAN JOHNSON

W e long to know what our purpose in life is: *Does my life count? Is my life important? Is there a reason to get up each day, take a shower, put on makeup, run the kids around, work? If so, what is it?* Indeed we get confused about what our purpose truly is, thinking that if only God would send us an e-mail, we'd be happy to follow his direction and, ultimately, be happy. We've confused purpose with role and meaning and call, often blending them into one.

Wouldn't it be great if we had a sign ever in front of us that gave us a constant reminder of the different meanings of these words?

- Our *purpose* in life is…to worship and serve God in every aspect of our lives, seeking to become more like Christ every day.
- Our *role* in life is…to accept ourselves as PCOGs wherever we find ourselves.
- We find *meaning* in our lives by…seeing God at work all around us, in everyone around us, in everything we do.
- Our *call* in life is…to use our gifts and talents for God's good purposes.

Tina has confused *call* with *purpose:* At forty, I still do not know where I best fit in the world. I know I am an alien until I get to heaven, but I still don't know what job, etc., is right for me. What is my purpose in this life?

Joaquina has confused *purpose* with *meaning:* As a forty-five-year-old single adult woman, I wonder more and more if my life will count for anything when I'm gone. Will I leave any kind of legacy? Am I just going through the motions for a paycheck?

Gemma has confused *role* with *purpose:* I feel like all I do is pick up the house, haul in groceries, make meals, pick up some more, and then begin it all over again the next morning. I know I'm *important* to my family, but is that really equal to *purpose?* That's a very big word for my small, little life.

Rhonda is more on track (we think!): The more I open up to God and risk doing things for God, the more I become aware of my purpose in this life. As I am much more open and become aware of my gifts from God, my purpose also is further revealed.

Survey Says

We call the result on this topic the "halftime effect." Having a purpose in life rated highest as a driving want, need, and priority for women age forty-five and older. Younger women appeared more focused on their families. How did you rate this need?

We can see why they're confused. We get confused too! And all four factors: purpose, meaning, role, and call intertwine to form the most important aspects of our lives—the things that drive us and feed us and stimulate us, the things that give us satisfaction and significance in life. (Stay with me, here. I don't want to lose you in semantics. But I do want you to break down the factors into separate categories, because I think it will help you get to what you're hungering for—purpose and meaning.)

Think of them as different pieces of colored film, like those used by light technicians on a movie set. *Purpose* might be the white light, illuminating all the color, the backdrop that makes a flat piece of film luminous. If *meaning* was the yellow piece of film, *call* was blue, *role* was red, and *gifting* was green, each one, when set upon the *purpose* flood light, would be special. But when we combine the colors, something extraordinary occurs. Combining Call Blue with Meaning Yellow? We get a tantalizing spring green. Combine Meaning Yellow with Role Red? We get

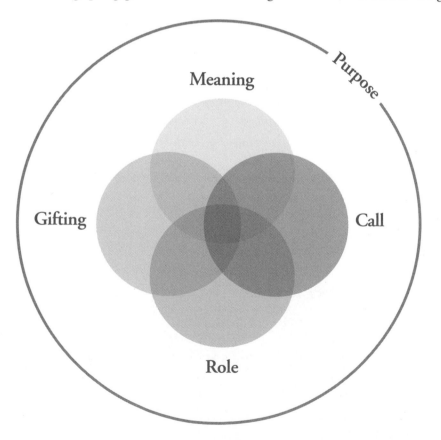

an inviting tangerine. Gifting Green with Call Blue? A fabulous purple. Any one of those combinations, overlaid on top of *purpose*—to love and serve and worship our God and become more like Christ—adds depth of color to our lives. And when all colors are in play, the Master Lighter can really do his best work, using us to be all we were made to be and serving him on all fronts. This is the ultimate path to satisfaction, God's road for us.

Jan Johnson says, "A purpose in life must be much bigger than any role. Roles change because life circumstances change."[1] This is why the mother suddenly facing an empty nest or a career woman handed a pink slip tends to associate *role* with *purpose*. Each woman is asking herself: *What am I supposed to do now? What's going to fill my days? What's the reason I should get up in the morning? Where does God want me?* She thinks that because her role and circumstances have changed, her purpose has changed.

But it hasn't. It's been the same all along. The woman confident in her purpose,

Rick Warren's Five Purposes for Life

Since we are...

- ⊙ planned for God's pleasure, our number one purpose is to offer real worship to him.

- ⊙ formed for God's family, our number two purpose is to enjoy real Christian fellowship.

- ⊙ created to become like Christ, our number three purpose is to learn real discipleship.

- ⊙ shaped for serving God, our number four purpose is to practice real ministry.

- ⊙ made for a mission, our number five purpose is to live out real evangelism.[3]

truly confident, is ready to serve and worship God wherever she is. Regardless of her circumstances and role, she has the same purpose.

This constant, never-changing purpose fuels meaning in her life. "Meaning in life is not found in fulfilling divine purposes, but in a relationship with God," writes Johnson.[2] In relationship with him, she begins to see God at work all around her, in others, in herself. She is in communication with the Divine, and everything about her is infused by a holy light, a secondary color altogether.

Now, we believe *call* is where things begin to solidify, because it's more tangible. If we're putting forth effort in our lives—whether in the workplace, home, or community—and that effort utilizes the gifts that God has given us, we're fulfilling something holy, and we find fulfillment. Our roles in answering that call may change, but the *call* remains.

Our gifting might be clear and present, or slowly emerging. By *gifting,* we mean how you've been created as a unique person—from spiritual gifts to talents. Are you a leader? a servant? a worker? Do you work well with others, or do best on your own? Are you creative? insightful? a team player? What do you love? hate? Where do you excel? shine? It may take eight years in college, nine jobs, or fifty years to ascertain your gifting. The more fortunate among us know it straight out of high school. There are personality tests and career centers that can help you, but

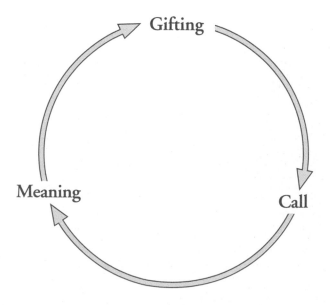

deep inside, you have an inkling, if not full understanding of your gifts. What is your temperament? What are your talents? What are your passions?

Rick Warren says, "God never wastes anything. He would not give you abilities, interests, talents, gifts, personality, and life experiences unless he intended to use them for his glory."[4] We all have giftings that grow, if nurtured, and spread like flowering groundcover as we go through life. It's part of discovering all that God created us to be. We're never to stop growing, exploring, learning. If we do, we stagnate.

So gifting hopefully flows into call, which hopefully flows into meaning, which fuels our gifts and helps us grow. This is the Circle of Purpose, as we see it. What are we longing for? What do we want? We want to inhale a healthy daily serving of the eternal in our average, everyday lives. We want to be counted as PCOGs who truly get it—understanding that the eternal is accessible, tangible, and happening right here, right now.

So What?

Where do worship, fellowship, discipleship, ministry, and evangelism have the most impact? Out in the world! We need every available man, woman, and child out on the streets, in schools, in cubicles, in conference centers, on the phone, or wherever we find ourselves. We also have a holy calling upon our lives, one that will bring each of us ultimate satisfaction. But how do we find it? What if we cannot sense that holy calling in the midst of our ordinary, mundane lives?

Author and teacher John Eldredge teaches that we need to begin to see ourselves as heroines in an epic story.[5] (Quit shaking your head. That includes you.) *Me? A heroine?* Yes, you are a mighty important, admirable heroine we all can learn from.

But let's back up. We typically see our world in three dimensions, with time as the fourth dimension. Perhaps we need to begin to see a fifth dimension: the unseen world. To get a fifth-dimensional Christian perspective, we must begin to see that there is much going on in our world that cannot be seen with our eyes. Think of the people along the road to Emmaus. The crucifixion is over, Christ has left them, and they are heading home, shattered and dejected. Who shows up alongside them? Who joins in their conversation? It is Christ himself, of course, and they initially don't recognize him.

As believers in the Christ who died, rose again, and now lives within us, as believers who know ourselves as forgiven and restored people covered in grace, as believers who have been given the Holy Spirit as our confidant, counselor, and friend, why do we, like the Emmaus disciples, keep missing this vast, extravagant, exhilarating, profound unseen dimension?

Regardless of circumstances or roles we play in our seen world, we have an exciting and meaningful purpose in the unseen world. As PCOGs and heroines in the epic story, we have been called to put it all on the line, to answer God's call to war against the dark. Eldredge writes, "Christianity isn't a religion about going to Sunday school, potluck suppers, being nice, holding car washes, sending our secondhand clothes off to Mexico—as good as those things might be. This is a world at war. Something large and immensely dangerous is unfolding all around us, we are caught up in it, and above all we doubt we have been given a key role to play."[6]

> *We give an offering to God when we surrender, but he gives us far more in return. As we surrender to God, he begins to transform our lives. The result of a transformed life is that we experience the precious blessings of his Spirit: "love, joy, peace, patience, kindness, goodness, faithfulness, gentleness and self-control." The more we surrender, the more we are transformed, and the more these blessings flow from the Spirit to us.… Consider the thank-you bonus that comes when you surrender your day-to-day comings and goings, your problems, and your concerns to the Magnificent Counselor. He will give you all the wisdom and focus needed to live a life of worship, gratitude, service, and purpose.[7]*
> KATIE BRAZELTON

Doubting that we could ever play key roles as heroines in this epic battle is the Enemy's most effective strategy against us. He wants to lull us into the idea that it is all about us, that there is not any more about us than meets the eye, that there is no fifth dimension. Come out of your dreamscape, and hear the trumpeter's call! Ephesians 5:14–16 tells us, " 'Wake up, O sleeper, rise from the dead, and Christ will shine on you.' Be very careful, then, how you live—not as unwise but as wise, making the most of every opportunity, because the days are evil."

Shantal writes: God has placed passions and desires on my life. When I'm not living and flowing from those passions and desires, there's a piece of me that's stagnant or paralyzed. God promised life to the full.… I believe that and refuse to accept the "life as usual" mentality. God is writing a story, and he has a role for me to play in his story. That's huge and overwhelming! I don't want to miss out! I love it!

Pit Thoughts Versus His Thoughts

I've tried, but I don't seem to be making any difference.
I am a PCOG. I will persevere (Hebrews 10:35–36).

God has no special purpose for me.
I am here to serve and worship him! I am here to become like Jesus! (Colossians 3:12–13).

I have nothing to add to the world.
He has created me and is preparing me to do his good work (Ephesians 2:10).

I'm afraid of what others will think.
The Lord is my helper, I don't need to be afraid; what can anyone do to me? (Hebrews 13:6).

I don't trust God. He will fail me.
God is faithful and loving—with me always (Psalm 145:13).

Scripture abounds with unlikely heroes. Moses spoke with a stutter but led the Israelites out of slavery. Esther, a forbidden Jew, became a king's wife and saved her people. Rahab was a prostitute who recognized truth and risked her life for it. Samuel was a child who heard God in the night and answered the call, later becoming a great prophet. Christ himself was not the mighty warrior king the Jews expected. If we believe that all these people were used by God, and we believe Christ lives within us, then how can we not see that we might be used to accomplish something great for God? John Eldredge writes, "The story of your life is the story of the long and brutal assault on your heart by the one [Satan] who knows what you could be and fears it."[8]

Who will rule *your* heart and *your* story? Will you dare to believe what Scripture tells you? Or do you prefer the lies of the world? This is not about trying harder. Hear that again: *This is not about trying harder.* This is about accepting truth. This is about opening our eyes and beginning to see in the fifth dimension.

SERVE WHERE YOU ARE

In every battle, there are a hundred foot soldiers to every leader. Leaders are important, but without the foot soldiers, the battle cannot be won. If we accept that we are in the midst of an epic fifth-dimension battle and that we play important roles as those foot soldiers, let's embrace the reality that together we form an unbeatable army. (Unless the Enemy convinces us there is no battle at all.)

We are called to be Jesus in the world. Whew! That's a tall order. We're called to be living out our faith in Christ wherever we are: in the carpool, the grocery-store line, our cubicle or office at work, or the elevator; on the phone, in the mall, on the plane, when we're happy, when we're sad, when we're irritated, when we're at peace. We live out Jesus in us, Jesus in the world.

Let's stop thinking of ourselves as Christian workers. Instead, begin to think of ourselves as workers of Christ. This is not about doing; this is about being. We are all Jesus, all the time. The more we do this, the closer we get to giving off the fragrance of Christ, and the more others will be drawn to him and want to know what we've got goin' on. Christ in you is the hope of glory. Wow!

It is not just our hearts that we must enfold in the truths of Christ; we must also engage our minds, spending time in Scripture, reading favorite authors whether they be C. S. Lewis, Max Lucado, Beth Moore, or anyone else on our lists. If we are immersing our hearts, minds, and souls in this endeavor, we become even more valuable when we are called to arms.

Women tend to concentrate on the heart. God loves our hearts, but he also gave us good minds with which we can plan, reason, and create sound arguments for our faith and way of life. Think of a medieval noblewoman who trains with her knights. At first, she might not even be able to lift a sword. But with practice and understanding about tactics she can meet an oncoming strike. As she builds strength, she can pick up a sword and defend herself when her knights fall. Ever stronger, with time and training, she becomes a warrior, a leader, a Joan of Arc. She engages and utilizes all that she has learned, using everything within: her heart, strength, and mind.

If this claim is valid—if Christianity is true—then it cannot be simply a file drawer in our crowded lives. It must be the central truth from which all our behavior, relationships, and philosophy flow.... As a result of our failure to apply Christian truth to all of life, the secular mind-set monopolizes public debate....

The problem is that Christians often allow this [defensive, hysterical] reaction to intimidate them. We withdraw from the battle, spending most of our time safely talking with each other, venturing out of our burrows only to conduct evangelistic outreach. And thus we fail to bring the Christian mind or perspective as a counterpoint to the prevailing secular assumptions. We allow them to define modern values unchallenged....

"There is no [longer a] Christian mind," asserts Harry Blamires. Nothing could more profoundly alter the character of our culture than for the millions who claim to be Christians to demonstrate the contrary."[9]

—Charles Colson

206 ● On God's Road

WHAT'S HOLDING YOU BACK?

We don't know about you, but Rebecca and I find that we can tolerate a lot of in-conveniences, hurdles, challenges, and setbacks when we keep our fifth-dimension goggles on. Inconveniences, hurdles, challenges, and setbacks are minor occurrences in the grand scheme of things. But what if something from your past is holding you back? What if something is actually keeping you from climbing on your noble steed and becoming a heroine? We urge you to go forward with your goggles on.

> Elizabeth writes: I grew up in an abusive household, and I married an abu-sive man. For my entire life, I've been told I'm nothing. Now that I know Christ, I know I am something. But something special? That's altogether something else.

> Bobbi Louise writes: I know in my head that I am special to God. Having been told many times as a child that I was ugly, I have struggled with feel-ings of inferiority all my life. I often miss out on affirmations from the peo-ple in my life, dismissing them if they do come. It's difficult to truly grasp the fact in my heart that I am special.

The fact is that we all are damaged goods. Some of us have little scratches, oth-ers have big dents, and still others are missing limbs. The longer we live, the more wounds we might carry. We live in a fallen and sinful world and are often impacted by other sinful people (or we're immersed in our own special sins). We are con-stantly in a state of healing and regeneration. One of the greatest gifts of the Chris-tian faith is the ability to begin again each and every day.

Rebecca says, "There are times when I want a 'do over'—I've done something stupid or made a wrong choice or just plain sinned, and I want another chance. Although I can't erase the effects of my actions or thoughts and often suffer the consequences of sin, I know that God loves me—he says, 'I have redeemed you; I have called you by name; you are Mine!'" (Isaiah 43:1, NASB).

Paul wrote, "Forgetting what is behind and straining toward what is ahead, I press on toward the goal to win the prize for which God has called me heavenward in Christ Jesus" (Philippians 3:13–14). Paul didn't literally mean to *forget;* he meant he left the past behind him as settled and done. Our ultimate prize will be like Paul's, claimed in heaven. Seeing heaven before us, whether we see it tomorrow, in ten years, or in fifty, is part of living with our fifth-dimension goggles on. We see ourselves as PCOGs greeted by Jesus in the light. We see him patting us on the back and saying, "Well done, my good and faithful sister."

My grandmother used to dismiss those who obsessed about heaven. She would say, "They're so heavenly minded they're no earthly good." She was a devoted believer but grew up in a time when work was primary, the first goal of any person. To be sure, James says, "You see that a person is justified by what he does and not by faith alone" (2:24).

Alexa writes: Sometimes I struggle with this because, on the one hand, my life is quite peaceful and content, but on the other hand, there is a lot of need in the world. My struggle is to get out of my comfort zone to meet some of those needs. It's easy to stay in a bubble of comfort and peace rather than to move out and minister.

We like how Alexa thinks. We are meant to be Christ's body in the world. A body lives and breathes and moves—runs, skips, jumps, ducks, relaxes. We're meant to spread his love and light to everyone we meet.

> *Forgetting the past so that we can press on toward the future isn't an instant, one-step event; it is a multifaceted process. Psychologists tell us that we really can't forget something (except through dangerous repression of it) until we have experienced some type of healing. So before we launch full-steam ahead down the pathway to purpose, we need to allow healing to be a legitimate life focus for a period of time. It really is okay to give yourself permission to slow your pursuit of purpose in order to concentrate on healing and to put behind you whatever could overwhelm or immobilize you on the journey ahead.*[10]
> KATIE BRAZELTON

But some of us aren't ready for that. We cannot shine outwardly until we shine within. Some of us are smoldering embers. Others are huge bonfires. If your light has been doused or neglected and you have issues that need to be dealt with, please be encouraged. You can do this. You can find healing. Go back and dig it all up, and work it through. It may take a few weeks, a few months, or a few years, but it will be worth it. When you reach a place of healing, you'll discover your light is already a nice hurricane lamp, and you'll be set to glow from there.

WHEN GOD DOESN'T TAKE YOU WHERE YOU THINK HE OUGHT

Sometimes God allows us to wander for a time before we discover the call on our lives, our gifts, our unique roles and how that all fits in with our purpose. Sometimes he changes our direction. Once or fifteen times. The point is, we always need to follow his lead, surrender to him, and trust him—and act on what we *do* know. *The idea is to keep moving, always following his lead.* Obedience is the hallmark of a surrendered life.

If we want to discover where he's taking us, we will constantly seek his direction, praying for signals and a definable whisper in our hearts. I don't do camping, so of course, I'm terrified that he'll call me to serve as a missionary in Africa. (My husband tells friends that I consider Motel 6 camping. And he's right.) Then I'm afraid because I know that God knows I don't want to go to Africa, and so I expect that's exactly where he'll send me. He probably expects me to learn some fantastic lessons out there on the Serengeti. I go about trying to convince him that I'm doing excellent missionary work right here at home, working away on my computer. Half the time I think I'm doing a passable job at snowing the Big Guy.

Do you hear me laughing at myself? After all this time, after all I've learned, I still have so far to go. But the point is, we all need to be eager learners, eager to be molded, shaped, and sent where he wills—even to the Serengeti. *(Oh please, Lord! Not that!)*

Finally, we have to be willing to risk, to try anything he urges us to do. I read about a church a while ago that every week asks people to stand up and tell of their failures on the road of faith, and afterward everyone claps for them, applauding their efforts. Some stand up and tell how they tried to reach out and invite a neighbor to church and got shot down. Others tell of how they tried to give a friend a

Christian book and were told it was the most stupid thing they'd ever read. Still others write letters to editors, make speeches… Whatever you do in your line of kingdom work (and we're *all* in kingdom work!), it's important. No matter how you've failed, no matter how you fear failure, God applauds you *for trying*. Olympic hurdlers sometimes miss a hurdle and come crashing and rolling to the ground, *but they are on an Olympic field.* They're in the game, playing it for all they're worth.

This is not about doing more. This is about serving where we are, when we are called. This is about living out our God-given potential and letting it unfold in his timing. Let's be very clear on this: you could sit back and do nothing and still be welcomed into heaven. God makes no further requirement of us other than to accept Christ as our Savior. That's what grace is all about. You are completely loved, covered, sanctified by grace.

Your bill has been paid. You do not need to do anything—that's grace. But if you love Jesus, if you are grateful…don't you want to?

It's in Christ that we find out who we are and what
we are living for. Long before we first heard
of Christ and got our hopes up, he had his eye
on us, had designs on us for glorious living.
Ephesians 1:11–12 (MSG)

In the Beginning Was God

A Chat with Valorie Burton
About the Meaning and Purpose You Crave

A sought-after life coach and speaker, Valorie Burton is the author of *Listen to Your Life; What's Really Holding You Back?; Rich Minds, Rich Rewards;* and *Why Not You? 28 Days to Build Authentic Confidence.* She's a professional certified coach, coaches entrepreneurs with multimillion-dollar businesses and professionals seeking a more purposeful path, and has spoken before the nation's largest churches and organizations. She is a former Miss Black Texas USA and a runner-up to Miss Texas. She is creator of the annual Texas Trailblazer Award luncheon, which honors trailblazing women and has raised over four hundred thousand dollars for one of the nation's largest domestic-violence shelters. She has more than two hundred hours of professional coach training and is a graduate of Coach University, the pioneer coach-training institution.

This is but a short list of Valorie's many accomplishments. This is a woman on purpose, a dynamo who can't be stopped. So with some fear and trepidation Lisa managed to flag her down for an e-mailed interview.

Lisa: Talk to us about the difference between potential and performance.
Valorie: Potential is about being. Performance is about doing. Potential is about what's possible for you. Your potential is maximized when you are living on purpose, because you will never be more successful doing anything other than what God created you to do. You perform best when you are focused on becoming more of who you are created to be. Then the things you do emerge from the essence of who you are—and you no longer need to perform.

Lisa: Is there a difference between meaning and purpose?

Valorie: These two words are interconnected. When you know your purpose, it gives clear meaning and direction to your life. You understand
why you do what you do—in your relationships, work, finances, and
personal and spiritual life. Knowing your purpose gives deeper meaning to your life.

Lisa: What does connection have to do with finding purpose in life?

Valorie: We connect in three ways—with God, ourselves, and others. It
is essential to hear from God, to know yourself, and to allow God to
connect you with others when they cross your path. All of these relationships play a role when you are discovering your purpose. Quiet
time with God as well as time for yourself help ground you and lead
you toward a purposeful life.

Lisa: You're good at helping people discover vision. What are three steps
that a woman could take to find her particular God-given vision?

Valorie: First, pray. Ask God what his vision is for your life. Then listen
for his answer. Next, write it down and make it clear and compelling.
Habakkuk 2:2 says, "Write the vision; make it plain on tablets"
[ESV]. While your purpose or mission statement is one simple sentence, your vision can be as long and specific as you want it to be.
The vision paints a picture that should pull you forward even when
you get tired on your journey. Third—dream big! What is it that you
really want? Don't be afraid to ask God for it. Ephesians 3:20 says,
"To Him who is able to do exceedingly abundantly above all that we
ask or think, according to the power that works in us" [NKJV]. Don't
limit God. Have faith that He wants more for you than you may
want for yourself!

Lisa: What's the most important question a friend could ask another in
helping her find her unique gifting?

Valorie: How is someone's life different because she or he crosses your
path? The answer to this simple question is your mission statement
for life.

Lisa: Anything else you'd like to tell women who are craving meaning
and purpose in their lives?

Valorie: Be sure to use your special gifts, talents, passion, and experiences that are unique to you in order to make a positive difference in the lives of others. Here are a few examples of what you can do:

- ⊙ Use the gift of music to inspire others toward praise and worship.
- ⊙ Be a catalyst for joy.
- ⊙ Be a beacon of light for healthy, harmonious living.
- ⊙ Encourage learning and growth.

Jesus's purpose, as He stated in John 10:10, was that he came "that they may have life, and that they may have it more abundantly" [NKJV]. Everything he did during his three years of public ministry was for the accomplishment of that mission.

Lisa: And if we follow him, learn to see him more and more each day, we get a little more of that abundant life.

A Well-Watered Garden

Growing in Your Relationship with God

> And so we're right back where we started, realizing that
> God is a Lover who created us for relationship with Him-
> self. That's what the Christian life is all about. It is not
> about all the things we do for God—it's about being loved
> by Him, loving Him in return, and walking in intimate
> union and communion with Him.
>
> NANCY LEIGH DEMOSS

I n chapter 2, we talked about God seeing us as an antique climbing rose bush, bearing many blossoms over our years. Rebecca and I are not gardeners (a vast understatement), but we do know that plants need tending, roses need pruning, and even beautiful spring bulbs sometimes have to be dug up, torn apart and replanted so they'll continue to spread and grow. Likewise, God can use some of our most excruciating circumstances to bring about the most growth. But it is our choice to welcome our trials as friends (see James 1:2, Phillips) or to resent or rebel against what sometimes feels like not-so-tender care.

Charlotte writes: Being in relationship with God means showing up, suiting up, being available for whatever he's got for me—even when it's way out of my comfort zone or it hurts. He can handle my being real. I just have to communicate with him every day, all day.

The hallmarks of a mature Christian faith are threefold: trust, love, and devoted obedience. We want to trust the Master Gardener enough to say, *Pull me on up, Lord, roots and all. Take me apart and put me back together again. You made me, I trust you, and I'm here to reflect your glory. So have at it!*

Survey Says

One of the sweetest things discovered in our survey was that 86 percent of the widows who responded said their relationship with God was the most important thing in their lives. Since most of these respondents were in the older age bracket (forties, fifties, and older), we concluded that with the wisdom of years well-lived, we all discover that ultimately only One person really matters.

Robert Benson writes in his excellent spiritual memoir,

When I was younger, I worried a good deal about whether or not I was going to make it home to God. I was never quite convinced that those who interpreted the Story in the [non-Grace-covered] way…were right, but I met enough of them to be more than a little afraid.

What I fear now is that I will somehow miss what it is that I am supposed to learn here, something important enough that the Dreamer dispatched me, and the rest of us, here to learn. What I fear now is that I will somehow miss the point of living here at all, living here between the dreaming and the coming true.[1]

For those of us who know we're heading to heaven when we breathe our last, the goal is to know our Savior so well that we recognize him everywhere and see our role in his plan. As we awake, as we watch the news, as we're on the road, in line at the store, in every interaction, God speaks to us if we are listening. But we are a deaf and blind people—our ears are filled with voices that do not build, enforce, and encourage. Our eyes are filled with fearful images that tear down, destroy, or hover in the shadows.

What do we crave in relationship with God? We crave to see the world as he does, with love, compassion, and hope. We crave the truth—to strip away the lies the world has taught us and to see ourselves as he sees us, brimming with potential, germinating greatness, grace, passion, and beauty. Do we begin to see him around us? Do we begin to see ourselves as he sees us? Do we begin to see others as he sees them? Do we begin to see him within us all? In the midst of every conversation, action, dream, hope, argument, and every silence? Of course, it all boils down to building a real and vital relationship with God. We set about to trust him in everything, love others as he loves, and love him with all our heart, mind, and strength.

TRUST IN THE RIPTIDES OF LIFE

Trusting the Lord in all things, at all times, and in all places is difficult. We've all had experiences in which trusting God was not easy. Sometimes it was a call for instantaneous trust; other times it was a call for trust over the long haul. The call to trust comes to us often in the midst of dangerous situations.

When I was thirteen, I was caught in a riptide and hauled so far out that I got exhausted. I fought wave after wave until it was taking more time with each wave to kick myself to the surface. With every stroke I seemed to get farther from the beach; the people, waving and shouting, became tiny in the distance. There were no lifeguards. I vaguely began to consider not coming up after the next wave, thinking I was not strong enough, that I should just give it up.

God whispered to me then. As I hovered underwater, the roar of waves above my head, God said, *Swim, Lisa. Swim!*

I rose to the surface, and after the next wave passed, I did swim. I finally swam at an angle, parallel to the beach as you're supposed to do (but didn't realize before). People on the beach were amazed. I was glad to be alive.

My second experience with trusting God in crisis came in the same year, when there was an armed robbery in our house. After dinner out with my family, a couple came to the door, asking for directions. My father was showing them the way on a map when they hit him over the head with a gun. By the time I reached the top of the stairs to see why the dog was barking like mad, the man was running upstairs, two at a time. He put a gun to my temple and said, "Lay down on the floor or I'll kill you." I'll never forget the cold steel, the perfect circular form of the gun's nozzle on my skin. He tied my little brother beside me. Mom was out of view. Dad was on the floor below me, shouting at me to do what they said.

Heaven is not here, it's There. If we were given all we wanted here, our hearts would settle for this world rather than the next. God is forever luring us up and away from this one, wooing us to Himself and His still invisible Kingdom, where we will certainly find what we so keenly long for. [2]
ELISABETH ELLIOT

I recognized the worst kind of evil in our house at that moment. The drug-addicted invaders' eyes were dilated, vacant, spooky. I braced myself, wondering if it would hurt when they shot me in the back. But there was light too. Our dog came and nestled by our heads, as if guarding us. I felt a deep peace in the midst of the madness, almost as if we were in a circle of light in a dark circus tent. There was a sense of protection, that it would be okay. Soon after, the robbers exited with valuables but, miraculously, left us alive.

Many of us have had near-death experiences, places and times when we've narrowly missed being in the next fatal car accident reported on the news. We breathe a quick "Thank God!" and move on with our lives, really not wishing to dwell on the fact that life could be over any second of any day of any week of any month of our lives. We prefer to not think about how temporary life is and that we really aren't in charge at all. But mark this as indicative of those who exude the fragrance of Christ: they recognize that life is temporary and scary, but they trust God in all things, in all places, even when life gets hard, even when their lives are at stake.

My mother's best friend for years was an amazing woman named Sue Bertell.

Pit Thoughts Versus His Thoughts

I'm just not good enough.
I will never be good enough on my own. I am saved by his grace (Ephesians 2:8–9).

Can I really trust God?
I can trust him completely (John 14:1).

I don't understand the Bible, so why try?
He will open my eyes so I can see amazing truth in his Word (Psalm 119:18).

He can't use me to lead others to him.
Many will see the new song in my heart and put their trust in God (Psalm 40:3).

Do I really belong to him?
God has lavished his love on me, and I am his child (1 John 3:1).

She was a devoted wife, involved mother of four, and Bible-study teacher. She ran the family household (sometimes for months at a stretch from her bedside) and endeavored to deepen her discipleship every day. Stricken with a severe form of lupus, she still found a way to push through, even on the most difficult days.

Those who trust in the LORD
are like Mount Zion, which cannot
be shaken but endures forever.
As the mountains surround Jerusalem,
so the LORD surrounds his people
both now and forevermore.
PSALM 125:1–2

Sixteen months before she died, her husband, a fabulous, devoted husband and father, died suddenly from complications of the flu. Those of us who knew God and this family railed against God: *How can you do this? Why are you not acting? Do you not see? How can you let this happen?* I don't know if Sue asked the same questions. But she always said that God did not fear our questions.

And I questioned God again when my niece, Madison, died at just six years of age. *Why, Lord? Why did you not act? Why did you not save her? Why did you have to take her?*

God welcomes our questions, because it means we're in relationship with him. God welcomes our questions even if we're hurt, angry, and confused (and maybe especially at those times). The only way I could come to terms with Sue's death, her husband's death, and Madison's death was to trust that someday I would understand. I trusted that someday I would heal. Someday the families who loved these people most would heal, because we all worshiped the Great Physician.

We worship a God who knew us at the beginning and will welcome us at the end, and in the meantime, wants us to learn to know, trust, and love him with everything in us. He wants us to trust him even when it makes no sense. Why? Because God is trustworthy.

Some of us haven't yet wrestled with the death of anyone close to us. Some of us wrestle with other issues that demand naked trust: the loss of a job or a retirement fund, a marriage, a friendship, a home, a dream, a hope. The best of us grope about in the dark but stay firmly footed upon our foundation of truth in God's Word. The weakest of us find that we stand on shifting sands, dissolving beneath us, sending us falling and reaching for our stronger sisters in faith to pull us back to safety, back to the foundation. That foundation is everlasting. If we stand upon it, we are like Mount Zion where God chooses to build his temple.

Trusting in all times, in all places, and in all things is a tall order. The secret? We only gain from his strength if we look to him and lean on him in the midst of the struggle. Proverbs 3:5–6 tells us, "Trust in the LORD with all your heart and lean not on your own understanding; in all your ways acknowledge him, and he will make your paths straight." As we get to know him better, we learn to believe that the mountains protecting us from our enemies still remain, even if they're shrouded in fog or the Enemy appears at our very gates. We learn to trust that he will see us through, he will see us through, he will see us through. He has made us strong enough to endure and strong enough to trust him through it all. We wait on him to show us how he will do so. We worship a huge God. When we are weak, he is strong.

Perhaps you're not facing the trial of losing a loved one, a job, or a marriage. Maybe your trial is the day-to-day drama of running a crazy household or the mind-numbing boredom of a mundane life. Whatever you're facing or are struggling over, God is present. He can see you through. He can renew your strength, your vision, your hope!

LOVE OTHERS

We covered how we might learn to love ourselves, and to see ourselves as God sees us in chapter 1, but how do we begin to truly love others?

Tanya writes: I spend every hour of every day doing the same things, saying the same things. I work as a checker in a grocery store, and people rarely look at me, I mean really look at me. I've begun to think I'm invisible. I've begun to think my life doesn't count.

Tanya makes a point we need to hear. We are all living lives at warp speed, rushing from one thing to the next, burdened by responsibilities at home, church, or school. But if we are following the God who sees, should we not stop to truly see everyone before us? Can we make ourselves stop and truly ask at least two people each day, "How are you?" and really mean it (rather than "Hi, how are you?" as a form of greeting and not bothering to wait for an answer)? Can we be prepared to hear? To look the other person in the eye and be like Jesus to them?

I am as guilty of this as anybody, but lately I've been trying to put five more minutes into each errand so that I'm not so rushed. That way I can spend a few minutes with someone God puts in my path. If he's ready to use me in this world, who am I to clench my teeth, suck in my breath, and say, *It's really not a good time, Lord; maybe tomorrow?*

Jesus himself reminded us of the greatest commandments—to love God with all our heart, soul, mind, and strength and to love others as we love ourselves (see Mark 12:30–31). Loving others as ourselves calls us to serve, to reach out, and to help. These are not things our culture supports. Our culture wants us to look out for number one, pay attention to self-care, get ahead, and make the most of our lives. Our Lord wants us to care for ourselves too. But if we were as focused on others as we are on ourselves, how drastically different would this world be?

Don't you smell it? It smells to me a bit like heaven.

BE DEVOTED TO THE LORD

To love the Lord your God with all your heart, soul, mind, and strength calls for a life of devoted discipleship. It means learning more about him everywhere you go and actively seeking him out. Like any task, this one demands some effort. God stands at our door and knocks, but we have to get up off the couch, turn off the television, and open it for him.

God knows we're all beginners at heart. Perhaps those of us who have been actively living our faith for decades know this the best. We never arrive and say, "Okay, good. I'm now the disciple Jesus called me to be." Some of us get pretty close, drawing accolades from others. Let us be the first ones to tell you: this is a

You Can Embody Love

Check off one or two things you can do today—and then follow through.

○ Call a friend you haven't talked to in several months.

○ Call (or e-mail) your pastor and tell him how grateful you are for his work.

○ Fill out a company comment card, not to complain but to praise a worker or a service.

○ Find out if someone at church or in your neighborhood needs a meal; make an extra portion of dinner tonight and take it to her.

○ Write a card to someone you know is struggling.

○ Offer to help with a friend's kids so she can go out with her husband.

○ Mow or rake an elderly person's lawn or shovel the sidewalk.

○ Plant a row of flowers in a neighbor's garden in the middle of the night.

○ Let someone go in front of you in line.

○ Smile at the clerk in the checkout line; call her by name.

○ Other: _____

blessing of circumstance and vocation, not of superior discipleship. Over the last years, Rebecca and I have learned so many things that we both thought we'd already figured out. We've both been called to trust before, but until this last year, we never knew how far, with how much, God could stretch us in that call. Over and over, we begin this road of discipleship again.

I've told study groups in the past that I feel I'm on a series of ladders. I get to the top of one and then climb to the next. I climb three-quarters of the way up that one and then slide all the way to the bottom. I get to the fifth and suddenly find myself back at step three again. The goal is this: Keep climbing even when you lose ground. Keep pushing forward, ever higher, trying to see God better. Or think of yourself as that heroine in an epic battle. You are fighting enemy forces who will do anything they can to push you back to your safe little foxhole. Don't you want to take the capital back and raise your flag, bearing the cross of Christ?

My great-grandmother awoke each morning on a dirt-poor North Dakota farm. They struggled during the Great Depression to feed their seven children, then sent all five of their daughters to college while their sons stayed on to work the farm. My grandmother told stories of getting on a train back to school with a nickel in her pocket. Through it all, my great-grandmother, Julia, would rise each morning, open the curtains, look out upon the windblown prairie, and repeat the scripture, "This is the day which the LORD hath made; we will rejoice and be glad in it" (Psalm 118:24, KJV).

This was the same woman who, on Good Friday, would always weep. Her daughter, (my grandmother), a thoroughly practical woman, asked her one year, "What on earth is the matter, Mother?" And Julia responded, tears sliding down her cheeks, "This is the day that my Jesus died." (My grandmother later repeated the story to me, tears running down her cheeks.) I share these stories in hopes that they will resonate with you as they have with me all these years. Life was hard for Julia. I doubt it was the life she had dreamed of or hoped for. But each and every day, she rose to praise her God in it, in spite of it, day in and day out. Julia carried a deep devotion for her Savior, an obvious understanding of her place in the world, and gratitude to the Messiah Jesus. She read her Bible, worshiped every Sunday, served others, and prayed. I'm pretty sure there was a fragrance of Christ about her, that she shined him through her bright blue eyes.

Rebecca found these lines, titled "A Last Wish," in her great-grandmother's memory book, a collection of prayers, poems, newspaper clippings, and other treasures. It was dated at the turn of the century. She wrote,

No funeral gloom for me when I am gone.
Think of me as having just passed through "The door into Eternity"—
Yours still, you mine.
Remember only the best of the past and forget the rest.
And to where I wait, come gently on.

—Mama

Isn't that lovely? We hope that you have a woman in your family who has gone before you on this wild walk of faith, someone you can look to for inspiration. But even if you don't, even if you're the pilgrim Christian in your clan, know that millions of women have walked this path before you. God has walked beside them, just as he will walk beside you. There is nothing you will go through that he hasn't seen before. The whole point of life is to walk hand in hand with God. And you are not alone. We are sisters. You are a part of our family. That means you can claim Rebecca's great-grandmother's poem as your own, or Julia's story from the North Dakota prairie. They are your Christian ancestors. They are yours. They are soul kin to you.

But God wants us to know him as kin too. He has outlined for us many ways in which we can know him better and serve him more fully. Richard Foster's classic *Celebration of Discipline: The Path to Spiritual Growth* outlines the inward disciplines of meditation, prayer, fasting, and study, and the outward disciplines of simplicity, solitude, submission, and service. These are followed by the corporate disciplines: confession, worship, guidance, and celebration.[3] We highly recommend you delve into Foster's book or some of the others we refer to in the back of this book under "Additional Resources."

ADD WATER AND MIX

We're not called to be instant disciples. We're called to place one foot in front of the other, diving into learning more about prayer, about serving, or about the disciplines listed in the previous paragraph. Which of the disciplines most interests you? Listen to your heart, listen to your mind. What you hear might be the Holy Spirit urging you on. Go after that discipline first. It doesn't all have to happen this month, this year, or even this decade. (I still haven't ventured into fasting…but I will someday!) Or find other ways to allow him near you, close enough to speak!

> Cyra writes: I want to get to know him better by spending time in his Word.

> Lynette writes: I want to allow him to reveal himself to me in unexpected ways…to accept his grace and forgiveness…to know him intimately.

> Shireen writes: I want to turn all aspects of my life into biblically based living. Not just some aspects. ALL aspects. I'm delving into Scripture more and more, asking him to give me insight.

You're on the right track, girlfriends! Wherever you are, whatever God has revealed to you during our time together in this study, remember that God loves you, adores you, and covers you in all the ways you fall short. You are a Phenomenal Creation of God. You are not invisible, you are seen. You are forgiven. No matter what you've done, no matter what you're doing now, he waits to hold you close. He will not leave you or forsake you—ever.

Only God can satisfy our deepest cravings. Of course, some of our cravings will not be fulfilled until heaven—by heavenly design. Martyred missionary Jim Elliot wrote, "Always seek peace between your heart and God, but in this world, always be careful to remain ever-restless, never satisfied, and always abounding in the work of the Lord."[4] Satan wishes for us to rest, not to pursue the Holy One. God himself has set in us this hunger, this unsettling, relentless search in life, drawing us toward him so he can feed us, filling us bit by bit. When we pair our hunger with his promises, we find peace, healing, health, wholeness, and true satisfaction. We find who we were truly meant to be: PCOGs.

May his glory be reflected in our lives. May we all go and serve him, sharing the good news with a starving world. Let it shine, sister, let it shine.

This is what the LORD says:
"Stand at the crossroads and look;
ask for the ancient paths,
ask where the good way is, and walk in it,
and you will find rest for your souls."
Jeremiah 6:16

In the Beginning Was Knowledge and Truth

A Chat with Kay Arthur
About Growing in Your Relationship with God

Kay Arthur's passion is that people would know God by knowing his Word and in the Bible discover the truth for themselves. That's why more than thirty years ago she started what would become Precept Ministries International by teaching a group of teenagers in her living room and then in an old barn on a Chattanooga, Tennessee, farm that's now the headquarters for the ministry. Today, Precept carries out the work of teaching adults, teens, and children to study the Bible inductively in 149 countries with Bible studies in seventy languages.

Well-known as a conference speaker and the author of more than 120 books and Bible studies, Kay's biggest thrill (and her husband Jack's) is still in teaching the Bible in an exciting, effective way—challenging people to change and equipping them to be used in the kingdom of God. Her authority comes from the Word of God, which she continues to study zealously, her compassion stems from a life touched by deep tragedy as well as great triumph, and her practicality springs from an openness of character. But how does this sought-after Bible teacher still grow in her relationship with God? Rebecca finds out in this exclusive chat.

Rebecca: Over our years of friendship, I've watched you on a public stage—and I've seen you live out what you speak in the privacy of your own home too. In each setting, I think of you as the kind of Christian Paul challenged the Corinthian believers to be "steadfast, immovable, always abounding in the work of the Lord" [1 Corinthians 15:58, NASB]. How have you developed that kind of faith?

Kay: There's a verse that answers that question. Psalm 119:102 says, "I have not turned aside from Your ordinances"—that's the steel—and the next part of the verse is the key, "for You Yourself have taught me" [NASB]. In that verse, the psalmist is talking to God and saying he's not turned aside from God's instruction, but "I've persevered, I've been steadfast, I've been immovable, and doing what you have called me to do, because You Yourself have taught me." In other words, I have done this because I know that what I know is true.

Rebecca: How can any of us know that what we know is true? Sometimes we just accept things because we've heard them so many times before. But how does it sink into our hearts and heads as our own?

Kay: We need to be able to say that we discovered a truth for ourselves; we know it, not just because some man or woman has taught us, but because God himself has shown and taught us these things through his Word.

Rebecca: You've been very influential in my life, teaching me many things, including how to discover those truths for myself. How important are teachers and pastors?

Kay: Oh, very important! We each need a teacher, someone to disciple us. But firsthand knowledge of the Lord and his Word is the absolute key. That's the way we can know it's God, not just another person's teaching. And as we grow more and more in our knowledge of him, we'll be able to discern truth from error in teaching. That's why I've devoted my life and this ministry to teaching others how to study the Bible for themselves.

Rebecca: How do we keep on growing in relationship with God, keep going over the long haul? I've been thinking about this a lot myself, but so many of the women in our survey say they wonder this too.

Kay: I often tell people that the Christian life is not a hundred-yard dash. It's a marathon. To make it over the long haul, the important thing is to seek him, consistently seek him and hear him as he speaks to us through the Word. God can speak to us through a single verse—

there's no limit to the way he can communicate with us—but the best way is to look at the whole counsel of God, in context. Think of Scripture as you would a conversation.

Rebecca: A conversation! Explain more what you mean by that.

Kay: I mean, not just picking out a verse here or there, but reading full passages of Scripture. God starts a conversation and finishes the conversation. He starts a story and finishes the story. He starts a teaching and finishes the teaching. We want to be listening all the way through the conversation.

Rebecca: Can you give me an example of what you mean?

Kay: Last week Jack came in late to a meeting, and so, of course, he didn't know what we were talking about. We had to stop the discussion and catch him up, because a couple of the questions he was asking had already been answered. Often, we do that sort of thing in listening for God. We open a book of the Bible and enter into the middle of what God is saying, missing a vital piece. If we would learn to go through the Bible, looking at a whole passage or, better yet, a book at a time, we'd learn a great deal more. We could really focus on these questions: What is God saying? What is his purpose in this book? What came before this passage? What's coming afterward?

Rebecca: We'd hear the whole conversation with someone, not just a fragment.

Kay: Yes. Otherwise, just picking out a verse is like those times we're with someone, and we catch ourselves not really listening, not paying attention to what they're saying, and we have to stop and admit it and ask them to repeat what they just said—or we try to bluff it because we don't want them to know that we haven't been hanging on their every word. It's the same with God and Scripture. We want to learn to linger, to hang on God's every word, so that we slow down and hear what he is saying and understand the truths that are there in the Bible.

Rebecca: To linger on his every word—I like that word picture.

Kay: When we linger or hang on his words, we begin to ask questions and then understand and apply the answers to our lives: What does

God say in this passage? What does he mean? How am I going to
think or live in the light of the truth of this passage?

Rebecca: This last year has been a hard one for you and your family,
particularly with health issues. (Not you, Kay!) How did you keep
going?

Kay: The trials that we've been through since last May…let's just say that
it's been a tough year. But it's not unique to our family. Everyone
goes through really tough years or even whole portions of their lives.

Rebecca: The comments from many of the struggling women we surveyed would often bring Lisa and me to tears. How do you keep persevering? How do you keep going in this world of hurt?

Kay: If we understand that God is sovereign but don't couple that with
his true character, then our perception of him is flawed. The more
we know him and understand his ways, the more we will trust him,
even when life is difficult.

Rebecca: This is one of the reasons that I love the study on the names
of God. I learned so much about God's character by studying his
names in your book *Lord, I Want to Know You,* and I felt like I truly
did know him better. During tough times, I often call out to him in
prayer as El Roi or Jehovah Nissi. Can you talk a bit about those
two names?

Kay: Ah, yes. To know that he is El Roi, the God who sees, is to know
that he is completely aware of our circumstances and how we got
there. He also sees us exactly as we are and knows what we need.

As Jehovah Nissi, he gives us our deliverance. He is, as the name
translates, "The Lord, our Banner." You know, in ancient times a
banner was a standard carried at the head of an army headed into
battle. The soldiers would look across the chaos of the battlefield for
a glimpse of the king's banner; as long as the banner was flying high,
they would fight with courage. We can do the same knowing that
our confidence is in the Lord himself.

Rebecca: And we are in a battle, aren't we? Especially since we women
tend to take on all battles—not just in our own lives, but the burdens of our friends, family, city, the world!

Kay: You can wear yourself out worrying about it all. But it's not going to change anything. What can change is the way we respond, remembering that "His sovereignty rules over all" [Psalm 103:19, NASB]. And that's the truth we cling to, each and every day: God has not left his throne.

Rebecca: What would you say to a woman who says I just can't find the time to be with God?

Kay: Frankly, I'd tell her that she doesn't have time *not* to—if she doesn't, she's not going to walk in the confidence, calm security, and serenity that only an intimacy with God brings. The thing that keeps me from looking at earth and being overwhelmed with my circumstances is that time of total quiet, reading the Word and bringing everything into perspective.

Rebecca: Having God's perspective on our lives and our unique purpose is another need that we heard over and over. How can we know our part in God's plan?

Kay: It's so easy to start comparing our lives with the life of a friend or someone we might know or even a hero. We're such admirers of individual people today. But God knows our hearts and that we each have our own part to play in his kingdom work. We just have to get to know him well enough to discover what that part is—and my role is no more important than yours, and yours is no more important than Lisa's. In Colossians 1:16 we learn that we were created by him and for him, and each one of us is vital to God.

Part 2

How God
Satisfies

How God Satisfies

Your Guide to Reflection, Bible Study, and Discussion

"Nothing has transformed my life like the study of God's Word." So shares our friend Joanna Weaver in the introduction to the Bible-study section of her best-selling book *Having a Mary Heart in a Martha World.*

In Romans 12, Paul exhorts his flock to "take your everyday, ordinary life—your sleeping, eating, going-to-work, and walking-around life—and place it before God as an offering. Embracing what God does for you is the best thing you can do for him. Don't become so well-adjusted to your culture that you fit into it without even thinking. Instead, fix your attention on God. You'll be changed from the inside out" (Romans 12:1–2, MSG).

That's what we want: to be transformed, changed from the inside out, and we've both learned that transformation occurs only when we discover the truth for ourselves in the Word and allow God to work his work in us.

FOR PERSONAL STUDY

Grab a notebook or journal and use this section of *What Women Want* as your guide to delving deeper into God's Word and following where he leads you. You don't have to be in a church or a group to do this study—you really can start on your own. We celebrate that you're taking the time to meet with God and reflect on his Word too! It's the *most* important part of your day.

FOR GROUP DISCUSSION

Since any one of us can benefit from the wisdom and insight another sister brings, *What Women Want* is specially designed for group discussions as well as personal study. We encourage you to gather with a group of friends from work, church, or even your neighborhood, to go through this study together. You'll each need a book, and you may want to get a separate notebook or journal for additional writing space. (Lisa and I—Rebecca speaking here—tend to ramble, so if you're like us, you may want a *big* notebook!)

Group discussion always benefits when every person reads the lesson and answers the questions ahead of time. However, we know that sometimes life gets crazy, so the first few questions in each chapter are intended to get the discussion going, regardless of the time you've spent in preparation (or if you didn't get to prepare at all). No one needs to feel left out!

In addition, we've included ways to take steps to live out the truth in your ordinary "walking-around life." That's why in this section you'll also find:

- ◉ A "Think/Talk About It" section with initial questions that you (or anyone) can answer, whether you've read through the chapters in part 1 or not.

- ◉ A "Go Deeper" section with additional questions or suggestions to help you really cement God's thoughts on the subject in your mind.

- ◉ A "Make It Real" question or suggestion to push you to a greater understanding of your faith (but don't worry—that push isn't as hard as it sounds).

- ◉ A "Live It Out" suggestion and prayer that will help make the process even more personal—one of the best ways to remember what's been learned.

For additional info on how to use *What Women Want* for a twelve-week group study or weekend retreat, visit our Web site at WhatWomenWantBook.com. You'll find resources ranging from icebreakers to get your group going to leader's guides for each chapter. Plus more survey responses and interviews with women just like you—on how they're learning to let God satisfy their deepest needs.

So, dear friends, our hope is that you'll get with a group of like-minded women—of all ages—and dive in. Share your hopes and dreams, needs and wants, fears and failures. Dig into the Word on your own, then learn from one another— and watch the transformation begin.

The Word on What You Want Most

How God Satisfies Your Craving to Be Whole and His

We've been asking a lot of questions, haven't we? And this is just the beginning! We hope you'll read this book and work through the Bible study with a group of women who will encourage and challenge you—and that you'll do the same for them. Since you're a unique PCOG, your answers and insights will be unlike anyone else's. However, even if you're on your own, please take the time to think through the following section and perhaps share your thoughts with a friend you trust.

Here are some questions to get you started this week—you can use these for personal reflection or as discussion starters for your small group. We hope you'll dig deep into his Word as you learn how God satisfies!

Think/Talk About It

1. How does God remain your strength when things go sour?

_____

_____

_____

2. When you hear the word *crave,* what's the first thing that comes to your mind?

3. The *Random House Webster's Dictionary* defines *crave* as "to long for, desire eagerly; to require, need; to ask earnestly for; to beg or plead." How does this compare to your answer to question 2?

4. Share your number one priority or craving from "Your Five-Minute Survey" at the opening of this book. Which definition of *crave* (from the four meanings noted in question 3) would you attach to your first priority? Why?

Go Deeper

5. As you read through Psalm 73:25–26, think about what you desire more than anything on earth. What do you learn from this verse about your craving and how God satisfies?

6. How does Psalm 107:8–9 tell you about God's provision for you?

Make It Real

Get two pieces of paper, different colors if possible (you might want the most terrible color and happiest color you can find). Write *Pit Thoughts* at the top of the terrible-colored one and *His Thoughts* at the top of the happy-colored one. On the Pit Thoughts sheet, write down the thoughts that keep you from believing you are a PCOG, a Phenomenal Creation of God. Nothing is off limits! On the His Thoughts sheet, write down scriptures, quotes, or thoughts that help you believe you are a PCOG.

Live It Out

Take your sheets of paper and lay your hands on both, in your lap. Pray over both: *God on High, I need your help. The Enemy whispers to my heart in the worst way. I want to believe that I am phenomenal, special, your sacred creation. Help me to identify the whispers from the pit for what they are, and learn to trust in the promises you have given me on my His Thoughts sheet. Work in my mind, Jesus. Work in my heart. Amen.*

The Word on Your Relationship with God

How God Satisfies Your Craving for Him

I n our survey, most women said that their relationship with God was either their highest priority or that they wanted it to become number one. As you go through this study, we encourage you to answer honestly—not just write down what you think you should. Ask God to open the eyes of your heart to the truth in your heart...and to make himself real to you in new and vibrant ways.

Think/Talk About It

1. What do you think women long for most in their relationship with God? Why do we let other things crowd out this most important relationship?

2. What do you think when you hear the word *shame*? What's the difference between shame and sin? How do these affect your relationship with God?

3. Think for a moment about your own relationship with God. Would you describe it as warm and intimate or cold and distant? Is your relationship with God like a relationship between strangers or a relationship between friends? How so? How and when do you connect with God every day?

_____

_____

_____

Go Deeper

Pick a version of the Bible that you're comfortable with for study. An actual translation like the New International Version or the New American Standard Bible is best to start with for in-depth Bible study. Reading a contemporary paraphrase, such as The Message, can help you see things in a new light, however. We encourage you to have one translation and one paraphrase as you do your study.

4. Read Ephesians 2:4–8. If this is a familiar passage to you, try looking at it as though you are reading it for the first time. What do you learn in this passage about God? What do you learn about Christ Jesus? What do you learn about you?

_____

_____

_____

5. What do these verses from Ephesians teach about grace? about faith? about shame?

_____

_____

_____

6. Look back at your answers to question 3 in the "Think/Talk About It" section. What do you desire in your relationship with God? How can you grow in this relationship?

_____

_____

_____

7. In Psalm 63, David cries out to God from the wilderness of Judah. Read through this Psalm at least two, if not three or four, times. In verse 1, how does David describe himself?

_____

_____

_____

8. Per Psalm 63, what prompted David to seek God? How does the psalmist say we find him? What are the results?

_____

_____

_____

9. List aspects of God's character and provision recounted in Psalm 63.

_____

_____

_____

10. Has there ever been a situation or period of time in your life when you felt like David? How would knowing the truths of Psalm 63 have helped you through that time?

_____

_____

_____

Make It Real

Write Ephesians 2:8 in the space below (or in your notebook), making it personal by substituting your name every time you see the word *you*. Now write the verse on a three-by-five card and take it with you this week, memorizing the verse and celebrating the truth that it is by grace you have been saved. Thank God for his rich mercy!

Live It Out

Take a piece of paper and write a note to God as if you could stick a stamp on it and mail it tomorrow. Tell him what's kept you away, and what you plan to do to help build on your relationship with him. Read it in a whisper to him, in a silent place, as if you were making a solemn, heartfelt promise to a mate. Sign and date it, and place it in your Bible. Refer to it as needed.

Pray: *Father, I am sorry for walking away from you, ignoring your persistent call. Thank you for being my God, a reachable God, a God who wants to be called Daddy. I hear the tenderness, the love in that, Abba. Help me to find ways to know you better, more and more each day. Amen.*

The Word on Love in Your Life

How God Satisfies Your Craving for Your Heart's Desire

W|hen we talk about love, it's usually in the context of relationships, whether it's between a parent and child, spouses, friends, or God's love for us and ours for him. In this study, we'll focus on the characteristics of love in the relationships we all enjoy. As you answer the questions, ask God to help you apply these truths to your closest relationships—and him.

Think/Talk About It

1. How does our culture define love? How is this different from the way Scripture defines love?

    _____

    _____

2. Look back over this chapter. What are the three types of love? Discuss how these are different from each other. How do these three definitions affect your understanding of love?

    _____

    _____

3. Think about a time in your life when you knew you were loved unconditionally. Who loved you? What was the reason you knew this love was unconditional?

_____

_____

_____

4. Describe some of the aspects of God's unconditional love for you.

_____

_____

_____

Go Deeper

Start your study by reading 1 Corinthians 13, one of the most well-known passages in Scripture about love.

5. To understand the context of 1 Corinthians 13, now read chapters 12 and 14. How do these two chapters bookend the familiar love passage of 1 Corinthians 13?

_____

_____

_____

6. What is the topic of 1 Corinthians 12 and 14? How does this help you understand 1 Corinthians 13:1–3? How do these verses apply to sex?

_____

_____

_____

7. How does Paul compare love to other desirable gifts?

_____

_____

_____

8. Reread 1 Corinthians 13. List the characteristics of love in the chart below (and continuing on the next page), and write the definition of each. Use a dictionary or simply write your own definition. Now think of ways each particular aspect of love is demonstrated or played out in your daily life. You may want to write out all the characteristics first, then come back to the chart and fill it in as you think of things. We've done the first one for you.

Characteristic	Definition	Opposite	How Demonstrated?
patient	willing to wait for outcome, persevering	impatient, intolerant, irritated	time allowed for things to happen: allow small child time to tie her shoes

Characteristic	Definition	Opposite	How Demonstrated?

9. Which of these characteristics do you find the easiest to emulate in your relationships? Which do you find the most difficult? Why?

_____

_____

_____

10. Which one of these aspects of love hurts you most when absent, or when the opposite characteristic is present in a relationship?

_____

_____

_____

11. What conclusion does Paul draw in verse 13? How would you write out this verse in your own words?

_____

_____

_____

12. Read 1 John 4:7–13. What do you learn from these verses about love?

_____

_____

_____

13. Where does love originate? How do we know this?

_____

_____

_____

14. How does God show his love? What is your response?

_____

_____

_____

15. What is the result of God's love?

_____

_____

_____

Make It Real

Write out 1 Corinthians 13:4–7 on a three-by-five card, substituting your name for the word _love_ (for example: _Rebecca is patient. Rebecca is kind…_). Now read through your card aloud. Do you think, _Wow, that's me!_ or do you wince as I (Rebecca) did? Think about what your friends or family would say if asked how this passage describes you. You may want to take this card with you, or place it in your Bible as a bookmark. Ask God to help you demonstrate this kind of love to one particular person this week.

Live It Out

Scripture is God's love letter to us. Look back over this study and some of the verses you've studied. Write your own love letter back to God, thanking him for his demonstrated love for you, and expressing your love for him.

Pray before you begin: _Lord God, thank you for how you love me in such an outrageous manner I do not deserve. I crave your love and long to show your love to others. Begin to show me how I can see more of your love in my life, day by day, and show others your love as well. Flow into me, Lover of my soul. Flow out of me. I am yours. Amen._

The Word on Friendship

How God Satisfies Your Craving for Soul Sisters

A lthough friendship may not be our number one longing, we all want and need good friends. Where does friendship fall on your list?

Think/Talk About It

1. Why do you think friendship is so important to women? What do you look for in a friendship?

_____

_____

_____

2. The section on Class V friendship describes a friendship where you would each go through fire and flood for the other. Have you ever had such a friendship? How did you develop that deep level of friendship? Identify the defining moments of that friendship's development.

_____

_____

_____

3. Have you ever had a friendship that's died or where you just grew apart from a friend? How did you respond? Is there anything you'd do differently, given another chance?

_____

_____

_____

4. Refer to the "Strengthen Your Friendship Score" sidebar on the next page. What do you think you bring to some of your closest relationships? Write about one or more here.

_____

_____

_____

Go Deeper

In the book of Proverbs you will find a wealth of wisdom about friends and friendship.

5. What do you learn about friendship from the following verses?

Proverbs 17:17 _____

Proverbs 18:24 _____

Proverbs 27:6 _____

Proverbs 27:9–10 _____

Proverbs 27:17 _____

Strengthen Your Friendship Score

To gain the best of friendships, we must first be a good friend. Ask yourself the following questions:

- ☉ *Am I a good friend?*

- ☉ *Do I want what is best for her? Do I keep jealousy out of the mix?*

- ☉ *Do I sympathize with her?*

- ☉ *Do I empathize with her?*

- ☉ *Do I recognize the difference between sympathy and empathy? Do I employ both?*

- ☉ *Do I encourage her? cheer her on?*

- ☉ *Do I accept her unconditionally?*

- ☉ *Can I bear an honest word from her, even if it makes me accountable for something I wish no one would comment on?*

- ☉ *Do I pray for her?*

- ☉ *Am I gutsy enough to address things that bother me about our relationship?*

- ☉ *Am I courageous enough to speak the truth, softly, gently, lovingly to her?*

- ☉ *Do I strive to help her find God's best path in everything she does?*

- ☉ *Are we growing together in mutual understanding by seeking out new ways to grow together—experience, knowledge, day-to-day life?*

6. Referring again to Proverbs 18:24, list one or two friends who are (or have been) closer than a sister. Identify what aspect of the friendship is (or was) the most important to you and why.

_____

_____

7. How do you think your friend would respond to question 6 about you?

_____

_____

8. What do you believe you have brought to the relationship?

_____

_____

9. The Bible warns us about choosing the right friends. Read the following passages from Scripture and consider each one or discuss them with friends.

Proverbs 12:26 _____

Proverbs 16:28 _____

Proverbs 17:9 _____

10. Describe a friendship where you wish you had known and followed the warnings from Proverbs 22:24–25? What was the outcome?

_____

_____

11. Have you had a time in your life when you felt abandoned by your closest friends? Describe.

_____

_____

_____

_____

12. What do you learn in the following verses about our most important relationship?

    James 2:23 _____

    Exodus 33:11 _____

    John 15:9–17 _____

    1 Corinthians 1:8–9 _____

13. How can you develop and strengthen your relationship with your Friend of friends, Jesus?

_____

_____

_____

_____

Make It Real

Pick out one or two of your favorite verses from question 12 and write them out on a note card. Tuck the card into your purse, and take advantage of the snatches of time you have during this week to read them again. Ask God to show you what it means to be a friend of God. Record the ways he has proved himself to be your most faithful friend. And ask him how to be a faithful friend to the women in your life.

Live It Out

Some friendships happen instantly. Others take time and intention. Try one or more of the following ways to intentionally develop more friendships.

- ◉ Begin praying for a friend or multiple friends—women who can become heart-level, Class V friends in time.
- ◉ If you don't often have the opportunity to meet anyone, find a community or church group to attend during the week. Smile often, and be open to the women you meet there.
- ◉ If you go to church but never venture to say hello to anyone, do so this Sunday. Sit near someone you think looks friendly. Introduce yourself afterward and ask a few leading questions: "How long have you attended here?" "I love it here. Do you? What do you like best?" "Do you have children? Where do they go to school?" "Do you attend a small group or Bible study here?" Then look for her the next time you go, and remember her name!
- ◉ Take the leap! If you've met someone who interests you, make a coffee date before the inspiration passes.
- ◉ Keep praying for good friends to enter your life, and look for them with a hopeful, expectant heart. You can begin with: *Father, thank you for being my Friend of friends. But I need some girlfriends, Lord. You know that. Help me to see them as they enter my life. Help me to spot them and venture out there, say something, begin a conversation. Help them to be open and interested in me too. Make me courageous here, Father. This isn't easy. I need you. Amen.*

The Word on Peace

How God Satisfies Your Craving for Contentment

J ust finding time to do a Bible study on peace can be overwhelming! This isn't meant to be another item on your to-do list or another exercise in perfection. So grab a cup of tea and sit down as God uses this time to speak to your heart about the peace only he can provide.

Along with freedom from war, dictionaries define peace as freedom from anxiety, or a state of tranquillity. The biblical concept of peace is much larger, though, conveying the New Testament meaning "to be complete or whole" or "to live well."

Think/Talk About It

1. How would you define peace from a personal perspective?

    _____

    _____

    _____

2. Reread the section "Peace in the What-Is" on pages 91–92 in chapter 5. What are some of your personal might-have-beens? How do your thoughts about them affect your attitude toward daily life?

    _____

    _____

    _____

3. What is the difference between reaching for excellence and striving for perfection? How does this relate to finding spiritual peace?

_____

_____

_____

Go Deeper

Sometimes comparing the same passage in various Bible versions and translations helps us understand the context of the message more clearly. Try this in this chapter's study.

4. Read Isaiah 26:3 in your Bible. Now take a look at the same verse in these different translations: the New International Version and the New Living Translation.

> You will keep in perfect peace him whose mind is steadfast, because he trusts in you. (NIV)

> You will keep in perfect peace all who trust in you, all whose thoughts are fixed on you! (NLT)

Now write Isaiah 26:3 in your own words. You may want to call this the "New [write your name here] _____ Version!"

_____

_____

_____

Who will keep us in perfect peace? How?

_____

_____

_____

What does "perfect peace" mean?

_____

_____

_____

5. What do you learn in these passages about becoming a woman character-
    ized by peace?

    Psalm 119:165 _____

    Galatians 5:22–23 _____

6. Read about the Prince of Peace in Isaiah 9:6. Have you heard this name
    before? Who does this describe? What does "Prince of Peace" mean?

    _____

    _____

    _____

7. What do you learn about the Prince of Peace from the following verses?

    John 16:33 _____

    Romans 5:1–2_____

    Colossians 1:20 _____

8. Reread Romans 5:1–2. Can you say that you have peace with God as de-
    scribed in this passage? Describe when this took place and how. Do you
    recall the defining moments? If you have questions about this, ask your
    leader or a group member how you can know you have peace with God.

    _____

    _____

    _____

Make It Real

Write several of your favorite verses from this week's study on sticky notes. Place one on your refrigerator and one on your bathroom mirror, perhaps another on your car dashboard or your computer screen. Use these as reminders to thank God for the *what-is* in your life!

Live It Out

Fold a sheet of paper in half. On one side, write out something you've experienced that was hard to thank God for—a situation or circumstance, relationship, event or incident, crossroad. Now on the other half of the paper, write what you learned through the experience and what you think God taught you through it. How do you view your circumstance now that you have the perspective of time?

If thoughts of it still rile you up, or if you have a new situation/event you're trying to get through, pray: *Father, I need to find peace over this event in my life. I need healing, and I need to let it go. Move within my heart and mind, now, Great Physician. Wash this clean. Help me to see it with new eyes. Help me to move on from this and find it in my heart to even give thanks over it—for what it has taught me, shown me, for how it has grown me. I pray this with all the fervent desire in me, Lord. Heal me! Heal me! Heal me! And let this be at peace in my mind. Amen.*

The Word on Your Financial Health

How God Satisfies Your Craving for Security

A s a wise sage once said, if money weren't important, then the Bible wouldn't have so much to say about it. But just *thinking* about talking of finances can make many of us nervous, especially in a small-group setting.

Think/Talk About It

1. For many of the women surveyed, financial health equals security. Is this true for you? How does money (or lack thereof) relate to security for you?

_____

_____

2. How would you describe your own attitude toward money and financial health? How do your underlying beliefs impact the way you make decisions and live day to day?

_____

_____

3. Review the section "Do You Really Believe That God Owns It All?" on pages 116–17 in chapter 6. Randy Alcorn's *Treasure Principle* states: "You can't take it with you—but you *can* send it on ahead." What do you think this means? Do you agree?

_____

_____

_____

_____

Go Deeper

4. Read the following passages. How does each passage shape your view of money and financial security?

Psalm 24:1 _____

_____

Matthew 6:19 _____

_____

Luke 12:22–29 _____

_____

Ephesians 5:15–17 _____

_____

5. Using the chart on the next page, read each of the passages listed in column one. Come up with a title or phrase that captures the general theme of the passage, and write it in column two. Elaborate a bit on the theme in column three, and list its key principles in column four. Don't let these empty boxes scare you! Just jot down your thoughts and remember this is just for you, not for a presentation.

Passage	Title	Theme	Principle
Luke 12:13–21 (the parable of the rich fool)			
Matthew 25:14–30 (the parable of the talents)			
Mark 12:41–44 (the story of the widow's mite)			

6. Read 2 Corinthians 8:1–12 several times in both a trusted translation, such as the New International Version, and in a contemporary version, such as The Message. Now go back, and in your Bible underline the words, *giving*, *gift*, and *grace*. How does Paul pair the concepts of giving and grace?

_____

_____

7. List three to five basic principles you learn from this section of Scripture. Challenge yourself to use principles from each verse. Draw your conclusions from the passage, not just because you know them to be true.

_____

_____

8. Do you sense God is bringing any one of these truths to your immediate attention? If so, how can you begin to put this principle into action?

_____

_____

_____

Make It Real

Review your answers to the questions, and look at any notes you made as you read this chapter. What are three key principles you want to remember? Share these with a close friend you trust. Ask her to check in with you once a week for the next six weeks to talk about your progress toward an attitude change on finances. Remember: a change of life always follows a change of heart.

_____

_____

_____

Live It Out

Log on to www.crown.org and see if there are resources that apply to you. Do you need a budget? the right heart for giving? the means to come out of debt? Begin today by taking a step, any step, forward. You can do it!

Pray this with us: *Father, I want to serve you with everything I am and have. Rule over my finances. Help me to keep a proper perspective and to know that money never affects who I am in your eyes. Help me to see it that way too. Amen.*

The Word on Joy

How God Satisfies Your Craving for Happiness

A s children in Vacation Bible School, we sang the old chorus, "I've got the joy, joy, joy, joy down in my heart," shouting, "Where?" just as loudly as we could. Well, we want to be women whose lives shout *joy* loudly enough so those around us are drawn to the Savior. As we delve into what Scripture has to say about joy, ask God to help you shout a little louder by your actions, responses to life, and even everyday conversation with those around you.

Think/Talk About It

1. Take a minute to jot down the first things that come to mind in answering each of the following questions: What makes you happy? What brings you joy?

_____

_____

2. Many levels of joy are described in the Bible, including gladness, contentment, cheerfulness, and delight. How would you distinguish true joy? Do you think that joy and happiness are different? How?

_____

_____

3. Read the section "The Fragrance of Joy" on pages 125–27 in chapter 7. Have you ever known someone you would describe this way? Describe some of her character traits and how being around her made you feel.

_____

_____

_____

4. Was there one woman's story in this chapter that mirrors your own experience? In what ways (or not)?

_____

_____

_____

Go Deeper

5. What do you learn about the source of joy and its result from the following scriptures?

    Psalm 119:14 _____

    Isaiah 61:10 _____

    Jeremiah 15:16 _____

    Acts 8:5–8 _____

    3 John 4 _____

6. What do we learn from Psalm 51:8, 12 about what can rob us of our joy? What restores that joy?

_____

_____

_____

7. Read James 1:2–4. What are we to do when facing trials? Why can we do this? What is the end result?

Bible Study Tip

Reviewing the context of a verse (meaning reading through the verses around it for a broader perspective of the setting, time, and overall story) can help us understand the teaching more fully. You may find that some of the individual verses are familiar, but then the context helps you see the complete thought.

8. Have you been through a trial recently? Describe your trial and how you handled it. (If you haven't, you will! So make a game plan here on how you'd like to handle it when it comes.) How does James 1:2–4 alter the way you think (or will think) about this experience?

---

9. Read John 15:1–17 to get the full context of the passage. Now look more closely at verses 4 and 9–11. What does it mean to abide (NASB) or remain (NIV)? What kind of word picture does verse 4 bring to mind?

---

10. Based on the scriptures you've read, how do we abide/remain in Christ?

11. What are the benefits of abiding/remaining in Christ?

12. How will we know that we are abiding/remaining in him?

13. What have you learned during experiences of true joy? How can this make a difference in your daily life?

Make It Real

To talk about abiding in Christ may sound overwhelming. Break down the concept this way: What's one step you can take this week to help you get to know Jesus better? Try memorizing a verse of Scripture that's captured you in this study, or turn off the radio in the car and use those snatches of time to pray. Share your thoughts with a friend. Next week report back to each other what you've learned from this experience: Has it changed your outlook, the way you respond to situations or people, and the way they respond to you? In what ways?

Live It Out

Close your eyes and think for a moment about Jesus's joy alive and complete within you.

- ☉ What would that look like? What would it feel like?
- ☉ How would it change the way you hold your shoulders, your chin? the way you breathe?
- ☉ How would you look at the world differently?

Are you smiling? We hope so. Because in that smile, you begin to resemble one of those fragrance-of-joy people we all want to become.

Pray with us: *Lord, I want to be a sweet aroma in your nostrils. I want to breathe in you and you in me. I want to feel your joy. Take away the barriers. Remove the obstacles. Free me to be joyful, this day and forever. Amen.*

The Word on Your Emotional Health

How God Satisfies Your Craving for Hope

Emotional health. *Boundaries. Self-control. Balance.* These are loaded words, and because of that, your study this week may bring up issues that you would just as soon push aside. Take this time to ask God to give you new insights into the areas he wants to change or heal. Also, ask him to help you be sensitive to the deep needs of those around you.

Think/Talk About It

1. When you hear the phrase *emotional health*, what do you think of? Would you say your perspective is healthy? How do emotional health and balance relate to each other?

_____

_____

_____

_____

2. Review the section "The Beauty of Self-Control" on pages 143–44 in chapter 8, and read Proverbs 25:28. What's the relationship between strong boundary walls and self-control?

_____

_____

_____

3. On a scale of 1 (balanced) to 10 (out of control), what number characterizes your life right now? In what ways? List at least two reasons or examples and a specific "for instance."

_____

_____

_____

4. Identify why you're in control or out of balance. What are your major stressors? What are some small steps you can take that can help put your life in balance?

_____

_____

_____

Go Deeper

Sometimes the first step in becoming emotionally healthy is to face the truth about your current situation—or your past.

5. Read Psalm 25:4–6 several times. What do these verses teach you about truth and hope? Take some extra time this week to think about this passage, then write your thoughts next to each phrase.

Show me your ways, O LORD, _____

teach me your paths; _____

guide me in your truth and teach me, _____

for you are God my Savior, _____

and my hope is in you all day long. _____

Remember, O LORD, your great mercy and love, _____

for they are from of old. _____

6. Read Psalm 119:28–32 several times. What do these verses teach you about truth and hope? Take some extra time this week to think about this passage, then write your thoughts next to each phrase.

My soul is weary with sorrow; _____

strengthen me according to your word. _____

Keep me from deceitful ways; _____

be gracious to me through your law. _____

I have chosen the way of truth; _____

I have set my heart on your laws. _____

I hold fast to your statutes, O LORD; _____

do not let me be put to shame. _____

I run in the path of your commands, _____

for you have set my heart free. _____

7. Is there an area in your life where you need to face the truth squarely? This could be a relationship, a situation, a sin, or even a character trait that you know isn't healthy and is something you want to change.

_____

_____

_____

8. Spend a few minutes meditating on the following verses and consider God's faithful love for you and provision for your future: Proverbs 24:14; Jeremiah 29:11–13; Philippians 3:12–14.

_____

_____

_____

9. Choose one of the scripture phrases from questions 5, 6, and 8, and write it in your own words, making it personal to your situation. If you don't feel this way now, ask God to do these things in your life.

_____

_____

_____

10. Do you believe things can be different in your life? Why or why not? Review the verses in this study, asking God to reveal his truth to you in ways you may not have seen before.

_____

_____

_____

Make It Real

Write out Jeremiah 29:11–13 on a card you can carry in a pocket, purse, or your day planner. Use the card throughout the week to help you memorize this verse: "'For I know the plans I have for you,' declares the LORD, 'plans to prosper you and not to harm you, plans to give you hope and a future. Then you will call upon me and come and pray to me, and I will listen to you. You will seek me and find me when you seek me with all your heart.'"

Live It Out

Take a moment to think through the following:

Three things I can say no to or resign responsibility from:

_____

_____

_____

Three things I can say yes to:

_____

_____

_____

Three things I need to change my perspective on:

_____

_____

_____

Now sit for a moment, visualizing yourself somewhere utterly still and quiet, perhaps sitting across from Jesus, his hands covering yours.

Pray: *Prince of Peace, come and abide with me. Help me to repair my castle walls and find healing within. Help me to make choices that keep me and mine healthy and at peace. Keep evil at bay. Bring calm to my chaos. Help me to stop and listen, truly listen for you. Help me to live out each day, with this sense of peace I gather from you now. Amen.*

The Word on Your Marriage and Home

How God Satisfies Your Craving for Connection

W hether married or single, divorced or widowed, we all want to have relationships that work. As you go through the study this week, look at how you can apply the principles we discuss to your personal home life and relationships. Your group may include women from a variety of situations and seasons of life. Have a wonderful time encouraging and learning from one another!

Think/Talk About It

1. How would you describe your home life and family relationships? Is your home one of honor? Why or why not?

2. What does it mean to be vulnerable? How does this affect intimacy in your relationships?

3. Review the section "The Power of Time" on pages 159–62 in chapter 9. What are some ways that you fall into the time trap with your family? What practical steps can you take to make the most of the time you do have with your loved ones? Think beyond just your immediate family.

Go Deeper

4. Now list right here your closest family relationships. Include your husband and kids, siblings, and parents. Even list an ex-husband, if you share parenting with him. How would you characterize your relationship with each person?

5. The Bible has much to say about how we treat those in our family and those closest to us, so we're going to look at some of the "one another" passages in Scripture (as in "love one another"), using the chart on the next page. You may want to take a few days with it so that you're able to think about what each passage means and how it applies in your own relationships. Don't be overwhelmed by the long list! Just look up as many as you have time for. Once you are finished, you could continue the exercise, if you like, with many more passages, including Romans 12:16–21; Ephesians 5:19, 21; Colossians 3:16; Hebrews 10:25; and 1 Peter 1:22 and 3:8.

Reference	The One Another	What Does This Mean?	Practical Application
John 13:34–35			
Romans 12:10			
Romans 14:13			
Romans 15:7			
Galatians 5:13			
Ephesians 4:2			
Ephesians 4:32			
Colossians 3:13			
1 Thessalonians 5:11			
James 4:11			

Make It Real

Look back at the list of people you created in question 4. Try this thirty-day experiment: Write each person's name at the top of a page in a small spiral-bound notebook or in your journal. Pray for your relationship with each person every day. Ask God to show you how to honor each one. Record your thoughts, insights, and answers to prayer. At the end of thirty days, review your notebook, noting any patterns that have emerged. Thank God for what he has done!

Live It Out

Dare to discuss how to honor the "one another" commandments with each person that comes to mind, whether a parent, spouse, ex-spouse, child, or friend. Are you brave enough to begin discussions about this with one, two, or three people? Or would it be better to begin with some other action? Pray about this, and intentionally write out for yourself how you will begin. You might start this as a letter to each person that you don't mail but pray over: What will you say to start a discussion? What will you do to demonstrate care for each person? Note at least one idea for each.

_____

_____

_____

Now pray: *Lord God, I want to be happy in my home, happy in my heart. I want to know intimacy with my loved ones and be at peace with everyone in my life. Help me to be more than I can be on my own. Shine through me, Father. Help me to learn the true meaning of love, devotion, acceptance, service, and encouragement and to fully embody all those things for others. Feed my soul by bringing me people who give me the same. In your holy name I pray. Amen.*

The Word on Your Health and Appearance

How God Satisfies Your Craving for Acceptance

Being healthy physically means different things to each of us. Some of you will be in prime shape physically, while others may be facing a serious illness. However, at some point all of us will either go through a tough time ourselves or with a friend or family member. As you read through this chapter and study, why not look for ways to encourage someone you know who needs help in a struggle with a chronic illness?

Think/Talk About It

1. When you ranked your "wants" on pages 6–7 of this book, where did physical health rank for you? Now rate your physical health on a scale of one to ten below, with ten being excellent.

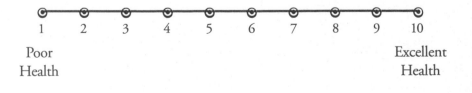

| 1 | 2 | 3 | 4 | 5 | 6 | 7 | 8 | 9 | 10 |

Poor
Health

Excellent
Health

2. How do you think your ranking relates to your assessment of your health?

3. Discuss what it means to you to have a body by God. How does your answer relate to our culture's obsession with physical appearance?

4. What things or circumstances affect your physical health? Do you have control over any of these things? Why or why not?

Go Deeper

5. Read 1 Corinthians 6. What do verses 18–20 mean to you, particularly the reference to your body as "a temple of the Holy Spirit"?

6. In 1 Corinthians 6, considering the verses before and after verse 19, how does your understanding change about what Paul is teaching in this passage? What is the broader application of verse 19?

7. Read Psalm 139 several times. Ask God to give you insight into how he has created you and cares for you. Pay special attention to verses 13–16 listed below, and write out your insights beside each verse.

For you created my inmost being; _____

you knit me together in my mother's womb. _____

I praise you because I am fearfully and wonderfully made; _____

your works are wonderful, _____

I know that full well. _____

My frame was not hidden from you _____

when I was made in the secret place. _____

When I was woven together in the depths of the earth, _____

your eyes saw my unformed body. _____

All the days ordained for me _____

were written in your book _____

before one of them came to be. _____

8. Do you consider yourself "fearfully and wonderfully made"? What do you appreciate about the way God has made you? What is hard for you to accept?

_____

_____

_____

9. What are your most urgent needs with regard to your physical health?

stress _____

lack of sleep _____

lack of exercise _____

fatigue _____

eating right _____

weight (over or under) _____

eating disorders _____

living with or managing chronic illness _____

dealing with a serious or life-threatening disease _____

other (you name it!) _____

10. When it comes to overall health, whatever your unique physical needs, what do these verses teach you about God's direction and provision?

Jeremiah 32:17 _____

Romans 12:1–2 _____

2 Corinthians 1:3–4 _____

Hebrews 4:14–16 _____

1 Peter 1:13 _____

11. What is the one thing you would like to work on in your physical life over the next month or two? Identify what you need from God to make real changes in this area. Can you think of three steps to help you begin?

Make It Real

Review Psalm 139:13–16. Write out your own prayer to God, thanking him that you are fearfully and wonderfully made, and asking him to show you the truth of this verse.

Live It Out

Review your answers to question 11. Dare to tell your friend or spouse about your thoughts. Pray about the steps you need to take, and ask for the encouragement you need to move forward. Are you willing to let your spouse or friend hold you accountable for each step, checking in with you each week? Remind your spouse or friend that you need encouragement to begin again whenever you falter.

Now pray: *Father, you knit me together in my mother's womb. Me. Thank you for creating me this way. I am your phenomenal creation, but I don't take care of myself the way you intend. Help me to follow the principles for healthy living that I know but tend to avoid. Keep illness at bay. Walk with me each day, helping me to make strong decisions, right decisions, when I want to give in to weakness. In your name I pray. Amen.*

The Word on Your Purpose

How God Satisfies Your Craving for Meaning

P urpose, meaning, call, gifting—these are big words, right? Not multi-syllable words, but words big with *meaning*. (There's *that* word again.) If your head is spinning on the Circle of Purpose (page 200), simply ask God to give you insight into how *he* has made *you*, what he's created you for, as you reflect upon the following.

Think/Talk About It

1. What gives meaning to your life? How would you define your purpose? If this is a struggle to answer, just jot down your thoughts and share with others only if you're comfortable with that.

_____

_____

_____

2. Do you think God has a purpose for you? Why or why not? What hinders you from discovering this purpose?

_____

_____

_____

3. Read the section "What's Holding You Back?" on pages 206–8 in chapter
    11. How would living in light of the fifth dimension or the unseen world
    of the spiritual realm change your priorities and the way you think about
    your life?

_____

_____

_____

Go Deeper

Read Ephesians 1:11–12 in The Message: "It's in Christ that we find out who we
are and what we are living for. Long before we first heard of Christ and got our
hopes up, he had his eye on us, had designs on us for glorious living."

4. Look at that verse closely. Write it out, substituting _I, my,_ and _me_ in
    place of the words _we, our,_ and _us._ Also write down if you think this
    is true—and why or why not. Note a "for instance" or reason for your
    thinking.

_____

_____

_____

5. Now look at the following Scripture passages. Next to each verse, note at
    least one thing you learn about God's purposes for your life.

    Matthew 6:33 _____

    Acts 20:24 _____

    Philippians 3:13–14 _____

    2 Thessalonians 1:11–12 _____

6. Romans 8:28 is a familiar verse to many of us. Take a few minutes to read the context of the verse by reading Romans 8:26–39. How does this larger passage help you better understand the meaning of verse 28? List any new thoughts or insights about what it means to be "called according to his purpose" that you gained from studying this passage.

7. The great theologian Frederick Buechner talks about finding that place of God's call: "the place where your deep gladness and the world's deep hunger meet." Where do you see this intersection of "your deep gladness" and "the world's deep hunger" in your own life?

8. Is mission and serving the same as discovering God's purpose for you? How can well-meaning people and good ministry programs affect you as you seek to develop your relationship with God and to fulfill his purpose for your life?

9. Review the Scripture passages in this discussion and study section of this chapter. What's been the most important discovery for you in this lesson?

10. What's holding you back from finding out who you are and what you are living for (see Ephesisans 1:11, MSG)?

_____

_____

_____

11. Read and reflect upon Ephesians 1:11. What is one step you can take this week to move forward on the journey of discovery?

_____

_____

_____

Make It Real

Meditate this week on Ephesians 1:11–12, asking God to give you new insight into what you're living for and what his purposes for you are. Take a small notebook or pad with you and record thoughts as they come—don't censor them! At the end of the week, review your notes, asking God to show you another step on your path to purpose.

Live It Out

Ask for help: Tell your three best friends, and a couple of trusted family members, that you're trying to figure out how God has gifted you—and you're having a hard time seeing it. Ask them to list times they've noticed when you excel or shine and seem to enjoy a moment, task, or circumstance.

You may want to do this as a circle of friends, all for each other, so it doesn't seem like you're asking for praise. But in essence, you are. Sometimes others, especially others who love us, can see things within us that we can't. Reach out! Your sisters are there to support you and encourage you.

Another idea is to go to the pros: to better understand who you are and how you see the world, take an aptitude or personality profile. One we've found helpful is the personalized profile report from Servants by Design, which identifies your motivators, abilities, strengths, viewpoints, and how these affect relationships. For the profile tools, go online to this Web page: www.youruniquedesign.com

And through all these things, pray: *Father, I'm beginning to understand. I do have a purpose. I can see meaning in my life. Help me to better understand my gifting so that I might answer your call, when you call. And please do call me, Lord. Lead me forward into roles that bring me fulfillment and satisfaction—and teach me how to find those here, where I am now too. Amen.*

The Word on Growing with God

How God Satisfies Your Craving for More

How does God satisfy our deepest needs? With himself! As we finish our study and you ponder the following questions, our prayer is that "Christ will make his home in your hearts as you trust in him. Your roots will grow down into God's love and keep you strong" (Ephesians 3:17, NLT).

Think/Talk About It

1. Are you, or do you know, an avid gardener? Describe how someone committed to her garden goes about tending the plants so that the outcome is lush and hardy. How does this relate to the Divine Gardener and you?

_____

_____

_____

_____

2. Review the section "Trust in the Riptides of Life" on pages 215–20 in chapter 12. Do you find it easier to trust God in the big stuff more than in the day-to-day drama of life? How have you grown in this area? What has helped you do so?

_____

_____

_____

3. Reread the quote from Elisabeth Elliot on page 216. Do you agree or disagree with her assertion that "God is forever luring us up and away from this [world]"? Why or why not?

_____

_____

_____

4. In chapter 2, question 3, we asked you to think for a moment about your own relationship with God. Would you describe it as warm and intimate or distant? How has your view of God changed over the past few months? In what ways have you discovered that he is the One who satisfies?

_____

_____

_____

Go Deeper

5. Look up the word _satisfy_ in the dictionary. One definition is "to fulfill the desires, expectations, needs, or demands of; make content." What are some of your desires, expectations, needs, or demands? What are some things you truly hunger for? How can you pair your hunger with God's promises?

_____

_____

_____

The Word on Growing with God

6. Read Matthew 5:6. How does this verse help you understand your hunger? When Jesus says, "they will be filled," what does he mean?

_____

_____

_____

7. How does it feel to be really thirsty? Think of this as you read the following verses and jot down what you learn or observe in each verse.

Psalm 42:1–2 _____

_____

Psalm 63:1 _____

_____

Psalm 107:9 _____

_____

Isaiah 41:17_____

_____

Matthew 5:6 _____

_____

John 4:14 _____

_____

8. Oswald Chambers said, "Thirsting for God is more important than understanding all of His ways." What does it mean to thirst for God? How does he satisfy that thirst?

_____

_____

_____

9. How do the following verses in Psalms help you understand the God who satisfies?

Psalm 81:16 _____

_____

Psalm 90:14 _____

_____

Psalm 91:16 _____

_____

Psalm 145:16 _____

_____

Make It Real

Read and meditate on Isaiah 58:10–11. Write out your prayer to God. Pour out your heart before him, asking him to satisfy your hunger and thirst, and to make you like a well-watered garden and like a spring whose waters never fail.

Live It Out

Practice discipleship today with any of the following six exercises. You might try a different exercise for each day this week.

- ◉ Get a Scripture-a-Day calendar (with pages for each day that you can tear off). Position this next to your bed. Each morning rise, read the day's scripture, drink your coffee, read it again, and commit the verse to memory. Meditate on this verse throughout the day. What does this scripture mean to you? How can you apply it now?
- ◉ Start your morning routine ten minutes early each day. Spend two minutes of that time writing out to-dos for the day, and two minutes writing out things you're worried about. Spend the other six minutes in the steam of your shower or in a quiet spot talking to him about those things.

- ◉ Go to bed fifteen minutes early. Read a devotional and make notes in the margin about what God may want you to learn from that reading: underline, highlight, draw arrows, add asterisks, circle to your heart's content! You'll be amazed at how many daily devotionals seem to be speaking directly to you. Coincidence? We think not.
- ◉ Find one way every day to be the fragrance of Jesus—giving a whiff of him—to someone else.
- ◉ Sign up for a Bible study and schedule everything around it. Read what the teacher assigns and show up consistently.
- ◉ Read the Bible as a love letter that was written to you.

Now pray: *Lord Jesus, I want to know what it is to truly be your disciple. I want to walk so closely behind you, that dust covers me from your sandals before me. Show me what it means to find peace and satisfaction in you, first and foremost, and everything will follow. Amen.*

Meeting the Invisible

The Authors on a Great Mystery
That Will Change Your Life

We call him Invisible. But he's everywhere. All around us. Surrounding you. Surrounding us too. He's with you, right now, right where you are. Even in the midst of whatever's happening (or not) in your home. Yes, we mean *you*!

Both of us were raised in Christian homes, taught the books of the Bible, the basic principles…but it was later, as young adults, that we placed our stake in the ground and said to God: *Here I stand. I am yours.*

It's as if you just have to put on a special set of glasses, and then you see—you truly see in the manner in which the man from the Bible screams with delirious joy, "I was blind, but now I see!"

Wash the mud from your eyes, friend, and see anew. Imagine that he holds you in his arms, right there, where you are. The Holy Spirit—the supernatural, mystery itself, drawing near to you.

And you are invited into relationship with him. Into relationship with the Divine. Right now. Right here.

You may have done this before. Today may merely be a time for recommitment. Or it may be the first commitment you've ever made in your life. To anyone.

But he calls. Hungering for a relationship with you, just as you hunger for a relationship with the Holy. There is so much, sweet friend. So much ahead of you!

We smile as we write this… Come join us! It's as if we're in an unexplored lake, yelling, "Come on in! The water's fine!" And it is. We understand the hesitation before the Unknown. But he will envelop you, surround you, invigorate you, guide you with his currents.

Need the words?

I'm weak, Lord. So weak.
I've failed you in so many ways.
I am not deserving of you.
And yet you love me!

Take a moment to think about that, fully counting the cost. See Jesus on the cross, eyes gazing down in love—sheer, unmitigated, no-strings-attached love—for you.

I'm a sinner.
I need you.
You died as a gift to me. A gift I cannot repay.
You have died to make me free!
Wash me clean. Forgive me.
I want a relationship with you.
I crave intimacy, dialogue, awareness of your presence, direction for my steps.
Come into my life.
Come into my heart.
Come, Jesus.
You are my Savior.
I am your servant.
Thank you! Praise you!

You have just made the finest, smartest move you could ever make. In comparison, nothing else matters. This relationship with God—this is what your soul craves. Take the time to know him, to study his Word, worship him, and enter into fellowship with other sisters and brothers.

Sister—and you are our sister in every sense of the word—welcome. Here you stand, Beloved:

- glorious
- amazing
- gifted
- beautiful
- phenomenal
- God's own
- family

We love you already,

Lija & Rebecca

Still Want More?

Get *What Women Want* Online

Do you want a *What Women Want* (WWW) retreat schedule for a private day away? a one-night or three-night group retreat? song downloads to match WWW content? devotionals? inspiration to stay on the path to satisfy your soul's hunger? insightful interviews from today's Christian leaders and women just like you?

Go to WhatWomenWantBook.com and SatisfiedHeart.com. Both addresses will get you to the same site. We want you to come and see it. Please check it out!

Notes

CHAPTER 1: YOU, FABULOUS YOU

The epigraph for this chapter is taken from Ruth Myers, *The Satisfied Heart: 31 Days of Experiencing God's Love* (Colorado Springs, CO: WaterBrook, 1999), back cover.

1. Reese Witherspoon, acceptance speech for the Oscar for Best Actress, for portraying June Carter Cash in *Walk the Line,* Kodak Theater, Hollywood, California, 5 March 2006; quoted in Simran Khurana, "Thank You Speeches From Oscars 2006 Winners," http://quotations.about.com/od/movieandtvquote/a/oscar0602.htm.
2. Lee Strobel, untitled speech given at the Christian Booksellers Association's International Convention (Anaheim, California, 15 July 2002).

CHAPTER 2: HOLDING HANDS WITH THE INVISIBLE

The epigraph for this chapter is taken from Thomas Merton, *Contemplative Prayer* (Garden City, NY: Doubleday, 1969), 31, quoted in Richard J. Foster, *Celebration of Discipline: The Path to Spiritual Growth* (New York: HarperSanFrancisco, 1978), 2.

1. Dr. Gary D. Chapman, endorsement of Alan D. Wright, *Shame Off You: Overthrowing the Tyrant Within* (Sisters, OR: Multnomah, 2005), i.
2. Wright, *Shame Off You,* 56–57.
3. Foster, *Celebration of Discipline,* 6–7.
4. John Eldredge, *The Journey of Desire* (Nashville: Nelson, 2005), 203–4.
5. Jan Winebrenner, *Intimate Faith* (New York: Warner, 2003), 2–3.

CHAPTER 3: HEART'S DESIRE

The epigraph for this chapter is taken from Max Lucado, *A Love Worth Giving* (Nashville: W Publishing, 2002), 2.

1. Holly Miller, letter to the editor, *Kalispell (MT) Daily Inter Lake,* 22 December 2004. Used by permission.
2. Rob Bell, NOOMA *Flame* DVD (Grand Rapids: Zondervan, 2005), www.nooma.com/Shopping/ProductDetails.aspx?ProductID=271&Mode=WMV&PMID=123.
3. Victor Hugo, *Les Misérables* (New York: Random House, 1992), 145.
4. Beth Moore, *Living Beyond Yourself: Exploring the Fruit of the Spirit* (Nashville: LifeWay, 2004), 49–50.
5. Moore, *Living Beyond Yourself,* 51.

CHAPTER 4: SOUL SISTERS

The epigraph for this chapter is taken from Brenda Hunter, *In the Company of Women* (Sisters, OR: Multnomah, 1994), 21.
1. The Free Library by Farlex, Samuel Taylor Coleridge (1772–1834), http://coleridge.thefreelibrary.com or www.worldofquotes.com/author/Samuel-Taylor-Coleridge/1/index.html.

CHAPTER 5: THE MIND AT REST

The epigraph for this chapter is taken from Becky Harling, *Finding Calm in Life's Chaos* (Colorado Springs: NavPress, 2005), 20.
1. Jan Silvious, *Look at It This Way* (Colorado Springs: WaterBrook, 2003), 33.
2. Silvious, *Look at It This Way,* 33, 24.
3. Foster, *Celebration of Discipline,* 7.
4. Cynthia Heald, *Becoming a Woman of Excellence* (Colorado Springs: NavPress, 1986), 24.
5. Kawrie Mifflin, "Cosbys Want to Grieve with Dignity," San Diego *Union-Tribune,* 28 January 1997, A-4, quoted in Karen O'Connor, *Basket of Blessings: 40 Days to a More Grateful Heart* (Chattanooga, TN: Living Ink/AMG, 2005), 16–17.
6. Harling, *Finding Calm,* 20.

CHAPTER 6: THE PATH TO FREEDOM

The epigraph for this chapter is taken from Randy Alcorn, *The Treasure Principle: Discovering the Secret of Joyful Giving* (Sisters, OR: Multnomah, 2001), 17.

1. "Principles of Financial Success," Kingdom Advisors, http://cfpn.org/principles.html.
2. Adapted from page 93, in Randy Alcorn, *The Treasure Principle* © 2001 by Eternal Perspective Ministries. Used by permission of WaterBrook Multnomah Publishing Group, a division of Random House Inc.
3. Mary Hunt, *Debt-Proof Your Marriage* (Grand Rapids: Revell, 2003), 174–76. Used by permission.

CHAPTER 7: THE SMILE WITHIN

The epigraph for this chapter is taken from Myers, *Satisfied Heart*, 180.

1. Carole Mayhall, *Lord of My Rocking Boat* (Colorado Springs: NavPress, 1981), quoted in *Today's Christian Woman*, March/April 1998, 46.
2. Moore, *Living Beyond Yourself*, 70.
3. C. S. Lewis, *Surprised by Joy* (New York: Harcourt Brace, 1955), 78.
4. Mayhall, *Rocking Boat*, in *Today's Christian Woman*, 46.
5. Moore, *Living Beyond Yourself*, 75.
6. Adapted from Moore, *Living Beyond Yourself*, 82–83.
7. Henry F. Lyte, "Abide With Me," *Lutheran Book of Worship* (Lutheran Church in America, 1978), hymn 272.

CHAPTER 8: A LIFE IN BALANCE

The epigraph for this chapter is taken from *Life Under Control*, First Place Bible Study (Ventura, CA: Gospel Light, 2002), 28.

1. Moore, *Living Beyond Yourself*, 189, 191.
2. Henry Cloud, quoted in, "The Simple Scoop on Boundaries," www.cloud townsend.com/Articles/7articles6.htm; see Henry Cloud and John Townsend, *Boundaries* (Grand Rapids: Zondervan, 1992).

3. Cloud, "Simple Scoop."

4. Kay Arthur, *Lord, Heal My Hurts* (Colorado Springs: WaterBrook, 2000), 26.

5. Richard A. Swenson, *A Minute of Margin* (Colorado Springs: NavPress, 2003), reflection #11.

CHAPTER 9: REALLY, TRULY HAPPY AT HOME

The epigraph for this chapter is taken from Gary L. Thomas, *Devotions for Sacred Parenting* (Grand Rapids: Zondervan, 2005), 9.

1. Tim Kimmel, *Grace-Based Parenting* (Nashville: W Publishing, 2004), 62.

2. Tracy Klehn, "A Morning Prayer," in *Prayer Starters for Busy Moms* (Bloomington, MN: Bethany, 2006), 78. Used by permission of Bethany House, a division of Baker Publishing Group, © 2006.

3. Klehn, *Prayer Starters,* 164.

4. Gary D. Chapman, *The Five Love Languages* (Chicago: Northfield, 1995), 123.

5. Angela Thomas Guffey, *Tender Mercy for a Mother's Soul* (Wheaton, IL: Tyndale, 2001), 31–32.

CHAPTER 10: BODY BY GOD

The epigraph for this chapter is taken from Charles R. Swindoll, *Getting Through the Tough Stuff* (Nashville: W Publishing, 2004), 135.

1. Stephen Arterburn and Linda Mintle, *Lose It for Life: The Total Solution—Spiritual, Emotional, Physical—for Permanent Weight Loss* (Brentwood, TN: Integrity, 2004), 18–19.

2. Arterburn and Mintle, *Lose It for Life,* xiv.

3. Mehmet Oz, and Michael Roizen, "How to Save Your Own Heart," *Oprah* magazine, October 2006, 220.

4. Oz and Roizen, "Save Your Own Heart," 220.

5. Joni Eareckson Tada, *Heaven* (Grand Rapids: Zondervan, 1995), 183.

6. Adapted from Lisa Copen, *Beyond Casseroles* (San Diego: Rest Ministries, 2005), 7–11, www.restministries.org. Used by permission.

CHAPTER 11: ON GOD'S ROAD

The epigraph for this chapter is taken from Jan Johnson, *Living a Purpose-Full Life* (Colorado Springs: WaterBrook, 1999), 16.

1. Johnson, *Purpose-Full Life,* 31.
2. Johnson, *Purpose-Full Life,* 19.
3. Adapted from Rick Warren, *The Purpose-Driven Life* (Grand Rapids: Zondervan, 2002), 320–22, quoted in www.purposedrivenlife.com/thebook.aspx.
4. Rick Warren, foreword to Erik Rees, *S.H.A.P.E.* (Grand Rapids, Zondervan, 2006), 8, quoted in www.purposedrivenlife.com/s.h.a.p.e.htm.
5. John Eldredge, *Waking the Dead* (Nashville: Thomas Nelson, 2006), 30.
6. Eldredge, *Waking the Dead,* 30.
7. Katie Brazelton, *Pathway to Purpose For Women: Connecting Your To-Do List, Your Passions, and God's Purposes for Your Life* (Grand Rapids: Zondervan, 2005), 173.
8. Eldredge, *Waking the Dead,* 34.
9. Charles W. Colson, *Against the Night* (Ann Arbor: Servant, 1989), 165–68.
10. Brazelton, *Pathway to Purpose,* 30.

CHAPTER 12: A WELL-WATERED GARDEN

The epigraph for this chapter is taken from Nancy Leigh DeMoss, *A Place of Quiet Rest* (Chicago: Moody, 2000), 43.

1. Robert Benson, *Between the Dreaming and the Coming True: The Road Home to God* (New York: HarperCollins, 1996), 8–9.
2. Elisabeth Elliot, *Keep a Quiet Heart* (Grand Rapids: Revell, 1995), 28.
3. Foster, *Celebration of Discipline.*
4. Jim Elliot, quoted in www.christianquotes.org.

Additional Resources

What Women Want, in addressing big issues, really only begins a woman's deep exploration. This book was written in an attempt to help you discern where God might want you to grow and learn. Each chapter could be a full-length book, and many are, written by the experts we interviewed throughout part 1. So if you'd like to delve deeper into any of the topics covered in this book, we highly encourage you to do so—and we offer the following books and Web sites we've found helpful and believe could help you too.

Believing You're a PCOG

Bad Girls of the Bible: And What We Can Learn From Them. Liz Curtis Higgs. Colorado Springs: WaterBrook, 1999.

Believing God. Beth Moore. Nashville: Broadman & Holman, 2004.

Captivating: Unveiling the Mystery of a Woman's Soul. John and Stasi Eldredge. Nashville: Nelson, 2005.

A Day with a Perfect Stranger. David Gregory. Colorado Springs: WaterBrook, 2005.

Embrace Grace: Welcome to the Forgiven Life. Liz Curtis Higgs. Colorado Springs: WaterBrook, 2006.

Shame Off You: Overthrowing the Tyrant Within. Alan D. Wright. Sisters, OR: Multnomah, 2005.

Relationship with God

Believing God. Beth Moore. Nashville: Broadman & Holman, 2004. www.life way.com/bethmoore.

Celebration of Discipline: The Path to Spiritual Growth. Richard J. Foster. New York: HarperCollins, 1998.

Having a Mary Heart in a Martha World: Finding Intimacy with God in the Busyness of Life. Joanna Weaver. Colorado Springs: WaterBrook, 2000.

Heaven. Randy Alcorn. Carol Stream, IL: Tyndale, 2004.

Living Beyond Yourself: Exploring the Fruit of the Spirit. Beth Moore. Nashville: Lifeway, 2004.

Lord, I Want to Know You: A Devotional Study on the Names of God. Kay Arthur. Colorado Springs: WaterBrook, 2000.

LOVE

The Five Love Languages: How to Express Heartfelt Commitment to Your Mate. Gary Chapman. Chicago: Northfield, 2004.

The Four Loves. C. S. Lewis. New York: Harcourt Brace, 1960

NOOMA *Flame,* DVD. Rob Bell. Grand Rapids: Zondervan, 2005.

The Sacred Romance: Drawing Closer to the Heart of God. John Eldredge and Brent Curtis. Nashville: Nelson, 1997.

FRIENDSHIP

In the Company of Women. Brenda Hunter. Sisters, OR: Multnomah, 1994.

Sisterchicks series. Robin Jones Gunn. Sisters, OR: Multnomah, 2003–2006. This series of novels features characters dealing with many issues of faith and friendship.

A Song I Knew by Heart: A Novel. Bret Lott. New York: Random House, 2004. (This contemporary novel, based on Ruth and Naomi's friendship in the Old Testament, says much to us today.)

Take Flight! A Sisterchicks' Devotional. Robin Jones Gunn and Cindy Hannan. Sisters, OR: Multnomah, 2006.

PEACE

Basket of Blessings: 40 Days to a More Grateful Heart. Karen O'Connor. Chattanooga, TN: Living Ink /AMG, 2005.

Calm My Anxious Heart: A Woman's Guide to Contentment. Linda Dillow.
  Colorado Springs: NavPress, 1998.

A Little Pot of Oil: A Life Overflowing. Jill Briscoe. Sisters, OR: Multnomah,
  2003.

*Strong Women, Soft Hearts: A Woman's Guide to Cultivating a Wise Heart and a
  Passionate Life.* Paula Rinehart. Nashville: W Publishing, 2001.

When I Lay My Isaac Down: Unshakeable Faith in Unthinkable Circumstances.
  Carol Kent. Colorado Springs: NavPress, 2004.

FINANCIAL HEALTH

The Total Money Makeover: A Proven Plan for Financial Fitness. Dave Ramsey.
  Nashville: Nelson, 2003. (You might also tune into *The Dave Ramsey Show,*
  which the author hosts, on radio. Check for local listings on Ramsey's Web
  site at www.daveramsey.com.)

The Treasure Principle: Discovering the Secret of Joyful Giving. Randy Alcorn.
  Sisters, OR: Multnomah, 2001.

www.crown.org

EllieKay.com (and all her books)

Mary Hunt's organization Debt-Free Living, found online at www.cheapskate
  monthly.com, offers newsletters, books, tips from women for women, and
  more.

JOY

Calm My Anxious Heart: A Woman's Guide to Contentment. Linda Dillow.
  Colorado Springs: NavPress, 1998.

A Heart That Dances: Satisfy Your Desire for Intimacy with God. Catherine Martin.
  Colorado Springs: NavPress, 2003.

*Secret Longings of the Heart: Overcoming Deep Disappointment and Unfulfilled
  Expectations.* Carol Kent. Colorado Springs: NavPress, 2003.

31 Days of Praise: Enjoying God Anew. Ruth Myers. Sisters, OR: Multnomah,
  2000.

BALANCE

Boundaries: When to Say YES, When to Say NO To Take Control of Your Life. Dr. Henry Cloud and Dr. John Townsend. Grand Rapids: Zondervan, 1992, www.cloudtownsend.com.

Having a Mary Heart in a Martha World: Finding Intimacy with God in the Busyness of Life. Joanna Weaver. Colorado Springs: WaterBrook, 2000.

Tender Mercy for a Mother's Soul. Angela Thomas Guffey. Wheaton, IL: Tyndale Publishers, 2001.

Working Families: Navigating the Demands and Delights of Marriage, Parenting, and Career. Joy Jordan-Lake. Colorado Springs: WaterBrook, 2007.

The Worn Out Woman: When Life Is Full and Your Spirit Is Empty. Dr. Steve Stephens and Alice Gray. Sisters, OR: Multnomah, 2004.

EMOTIONAL HEALTH

Boundaries: When to Say YES, When to Say NO To Take Control of Your Life. Dr. Henry Cloud and Dr. John Townsend. Grand Rapids: Zondervan, 1992. www.cloudtownsend.com.

Look at It This Way: Straightforward Wisdom to Put Life in Perspective. Jan Silvious. Colorado Springs: WaterBrook, 2003.

Margin: Restoring Emotional, Physical, Financial, and Time Reserves to Overloaded Lives. Richard A. Swenson, M.D. Colorado Springs: NavPress, 1992.

MARRIAGE

For Women Only: What You Need to Know About the Inner Lives of Men. Shaunti Feldhahn. Sisters, OR: Multnomah, 2004.

40 Unforgettable Dates with Your Mate. Gary and Barbara Rosberg. Carol Stream, IL: Tyndale, 2002.

Love & Respect: The Love She Most Desires, the Respect He Desperately Needs. Dr. Emerson Eggerichs. Brentwood, TN: Integrity, 2004.

Sacred Marriage: What if God Designed Marriage to Make Us Holy More Than to Make Us Happy? Gary L. Thomas. Grand Rapids: Zondervan, 2000.

10 Great Dates for Empty Nesters. David and Claudia Arp. Grand Rapids: Zondervan, 2004.

When He Doesn't Believe: Help and Encouragement for Women Who Feel Alone in Their Faith. Nancy Kennedy. Colorado Springs: WaterBrook, 2001. (An encouraging and helpful book for women married to husbands who aren't believers.)

PARENTING

Devotions for Sacred Parenting: A Year of Weekly Devotions for Parents. Gary L. Thomas. Grand Rapids: Zondervan, 2005.

The Five Love Languages of Children. Gary Chapman and Ross Campbell. Chicago: Moody, 1997.

Grace-Based Parenting: Set Your Family Free. Tim Kimmel. Nashville: W Publishing, 2004.

Sacred Parenting: How Raising Children Shapes Our Souls. Gary L. Thomas. Grand Rapids: Zondervan, 2004.

Taking Care of the Me in Mommy: Becoming a Better Mom—Spirit, Body & Soul. Lisa Whelchel. Brentwood, TN: Integrity, 2006.

SEX

Every Man's Battle: Winning the War of Sexual Temptation One Victory at a Time. Stephen Arterburn and Fred Stoeker. Colorado Springs: WaterBrook, 2000. (This is a great resource for you and for your husband!)

Every Woman's Battle: Discovering God's Plan for Sexual and Emotional Fulfillment. Shannon Ethridge and Stephen Arterburn. Colorado Springs: WaterBrook, 2003.

Intimacy Ignited: Conversations Couple to Couple: Fire Up Your Sex Life with the Song of Solomon. Dr. Joseph and Linda Dillow and Dr. Peter and Lorraine Pintus. Colorado Springs: NavPress, 2004.

Intimate Issues: 21 Issues Christian Women Ask About Sex. Linda Dillow and Lorraine Pintus. Colorado Springs: WaterBrook, 1999.

Real Sex: The Naked Truth About Chastity. Lauren Winner. Grand Rapids: Brazos, 2005.

PHYSICAL HEALTH

Giving Christ First Place and other studies on overall health from First Place Bible Study. Ventura, CA: Gospel Light, 2001.

Lose It for Life: The Total Solution—Spiritual, Emotional, Physical—for Permanent Weight Loss. Stephen Arterburn, M.Ed. and Dr. Linda Mintle. Brentwood, TN: Integrity, 2004.

Staying Alive: Life-Changing Strategies for Surviving Cancer. Brenda Hunter. Colorado Springs: WaterBrook, 2004.

www.firstplace.org (weight and overall health—emotional and spiritual application to the physical)

www.yourbestlife.com (a Web-based accountability and mentoring program on weight and healthy eating from Oprah's trainer).

PURPOSE

Becoming a Woman of Influence: Making a Lasting Impact on Others Through Mentoring. Carol Kent. Colorado Springs: NavPress, 2006.

Conversations on Purpose for Women: 10 Appointments That Will Help You Discover God's Plan for Your Life. Katie Brazelton. Grand Rapids: Zondervan, 2005.

In Light of Eternity: Perspectives on Heaven. Randy Alcorn. Colorado Springs: WaterBrook, 1999.

Pathway to Purpose for Women: Connecting Your To-Do List, Your Passions, and God's Purposes for Your Life. Katie Brazelton. Grand Rapids: Zondervan, 2005.

Praying for Purpose for Women: A Prayer Experience That Will Change Your Life Forever. Katie Brazelton. Grand Rapids: Zondervan, 2005.

The Purpose-Driven Life: What on Earth Am I Here For? Rick Warren. Grand
    Rapids: Zondervan, 2002.
*What's Really Holding You Back? Closing the Gap Between Where You Are and
    Where You Want to Be.* Valorie Burton. Colorado Springs: WaterBrook,
    2005.
Prayer: Finding the Heart's True Home. Richard Foster. San Francisco: HarperSan-
    Francisco, 1992.
Praying the Names of God: A Daily Guide. Ann Spangler. Grand Rapids: Zonder-
    van, 2004.
Sisterchicks Down Under. Robin Jones Gunn. Sisters, OR: Multnomah, 2005.

Interviewed Authors'
Ministry Web Sites

Liz Curtis Higgs: LizCurtisHiggs.com

Shaunti Feldhahn: Shaunti.com

Robin Jones Gunn: RobinGunn.com, Sisterchicks.com

Carol Kent: CarolKent.org, SpeakUpForHope.org, SpeakUp
    SpeakerServices.com

Ellie Kay: EllieKay.com

Jan Silvious: JanSilvious.com

Joanna Weaver: WaterBrookPress.com (some information)

Barbara Rainey: FamilyLife.com

Dr. Linda Mintle: DrLindaHelps.com

Valorie Burton: ValorieBurton.com

Kay Arthur: www.precept.org

Acknowledgments

This book could not have been completed without many friends, known and unknown, who answered our initial and secondary surveys with heartfelt stories. We deeply appreciate your investment and trust. Eighty-five percent of the quotes are verbatim (with a little cleanup for clarity and grammar) and 15 percent are combined stories from surveys, personal interviews, conversations, and thoughts from friends who gave us permission to share.

In addition, these writers and speakers took time out of their own busy schedules to thoughtfully respond to our interview questions: Kay Arthur, Valorie Burton, Shaunti Feldhahn, Robin Jones Gunn, Liz Curtis Higgs, Ellie Kay, Carol Kent, Dr. Linda Mintle, Barbara Rainey, Jan Silvious, and Joanna Weaver. Their thoughts added a depth and dimension to our book we could not replicate—thank you. Friends and family members bravely let us share their stories (beware if you have a writer in your life!): Jim and Karen Grosswiler, Lynn Hood and Susan Drake, the McKay family, the Bertell family, Kathy Boyles, Melissa Bonser, Sarah Shonts, Kathy Searcy, Leslie Kilgo and many, many others.

Our "Pit Thoughts Versus His Thoughts" were inspired by Amy Carmichael's classic *His Thoughts Said... His Father Said...* We are indebted to her fine book in spurring us on our own track of creativity.

Our publishing home, WaterBrook Press, did a phenomenal job in pulling this book together. Special thanks to Jeanette Thomason, Marlee LeDai, Laura Wright, as well as the acquisitions team led by Steve Cobb and Ginia Hairston. Last but not least, thanks to our agent, Steve Laube, who believed in this project from the start.

About the Authors

Lisa T. Bergren is the author of twenty-eight books that have sold many more than she ever believed. She writes a lot from the heart and in whatever category that currently interests her—from gift and children's books to medieval fiction and Bible studies. She is a wife to Tim, an artist, and mother to their three phenomenal children—Olivia, Emma, and Jack. The Bergrens live in Colorado Springs, Colorado, and worship at Trinity Lutheran Church in Monument. For more specifics on Lisa, see her Web site at www.LisaTawnBergren.com.

Rebecca Price credits a long career ("Twenty-five years—yikes!") in the Christian publishing industry as providing opportunities to meet and learn from many gifted teachers and authors. She has worked in marketing and executive positions at NavPress, Word, Multnomah, and WaterBrook Press. After moving around the country (and to London and back), she returned to her home state, embarked on a business venture with Lisa, and is now a publishing and marketing consultant. Rebecca lives in Little Rock, Arkansas, and is actively involved at Fellowship Bible Church.

To learn more about WaterBrook Press and view
our catalog of products, log on to our Web site:
www.waterbrookpress.com

WATERBROOK
PRESS